THE LIFE AND LETTERS
OF JOHN HAY

IN TWO VOLUMES
VOLUME I

Lincoln and his Secretaries
Nicolay and Hay

THE LIFE
AND LETTERS OF
JOHN HAY

BY

WILLIAM ROSCOE THAYER

VOLUME I

BOSTON AND NEW YORK
HOUGHTON MIFFLIN COMPANY

SIXTEENTH IMPRESSION, JUNE, 1916

TO

HELEN HAY WHITNEY

ALICE HAY WADSWORTH

AND

CLARENCE LEONARD HAY

CHILDREN OF

JOHN HAY

THE AUTHOR DEDICATES

THIS BIOGRAPHY

PREFACE

IN order that readers may not be disappointed in their expectations, let me say at the outset that this is a personal biography and not a political history. The time has not yet come when it would be proper to give the names of all witnesses and to cite by direct reference the official documents, as is required in a formal history. There is also much material in the State Archives of England, France, Germany, and Russia, which may not be available for publication for a long time to come, if ever. So I have endeavored to let John Hay tell his own story, wherever this was possible. Being in many respects an ideal letter-writer, he recorded his impressions so freshly and so vividly that he never leaves us in doubt as to what he thought of persons, political affairs, or life's experiences. My part has been to sketch in a sufficient background to render intelligible each episode or situation, so that Hay's relation to it would be clear almost at a glance.

Shortly after Mr. Hay's death, Mrs. Hay assembled a considerable mass of his letters to his more intimate correspondents, which she edited with selections from his Diaries. She had a few copies of these memorials printed privately for distribution among friends. Her volumes form the basis of the present biography; but I have drawn from a still larger store of material, including Mr. Hay's letter-books, documents in the Department of State, and files, not only of his own letters, but also of those of his official colleagues and friends. In addition, many persons who knew him in his middle and later life have kindly given me their recollections of him.

Wherever the actual form of word or phrase seemed to require exact reproduction, I have printed it as he wrote it; but in many cases he used abbreviations, and in his Journals even short-hand symbols, which I have not hesitated to expand, always taking care, however, not to change his meaning. For the convenience of the reader should be kept in view, when it does not involve the sacrifice of essentials. In those volumes which Mrs. Hay edited she scrupulously substituted capital letters or dashes for all the proper names. I have been unable in several cases to recover the original letters which she used and so I have been obliged to rely upon the version which she printed. This will explain the appearance here of capital letters and dashes where I could not identify the original names; but occasionally I too have suppressed names where it seemed advisable to do so.

It is not possible for me to mention here, as I should like to do, all those persons who have assisted me in the preparation of this work, but I cannot close without making grateful acknowledgment to Mr. Hay's daughters, Mrs. Whitney and Mrs. Wadsworth; to the Honorable and Mrs. Charles E. Hay; to Mr. Samuel Mather; to President Theodore Roosevelt; to President William H. Taft; to Senators Henry Cabot Lodge and Elihu Root; to the Honorable Henry White, late Ambassador to Italy and to France; to the Honorable Joseph H. Choate, late Ambassador to Great Britain; to General John W. Foster, former Secretary of State; to the Honorable Charlemagne Tower, late Ambassador to Germany and to Russia; to the Honorable Alvey A. Adee, Francis B. Loomis, and William Phillips, Assistant Secretaries of State; to the Honorable Herbert W. Bowen, former Minister to Venezuela; to Professor Harry L. Koopman, Librarian of the John Hay Library at Brown University; to Professor Brander Matthews; to Admiral and Mrs. F. E. Chadwick; to the Honorable Wayne MacVeagh; to Mr. William D. Howells; to Mr. James Ford Rhodes; to Dr. W. W. Keen; and to Miss Helen Nicolay.

Needless to say, the responsibility for all statements and opinions rests with me, except in cases where my informants have authorized me to give their names.

As I have been prevented from revising the final proofs, I shall be grateful to readers who will notify to me any errors they may find.

The index has been made by Mr. George B. Ives, to whom I am also indebted for many suggestions.

CAMBRIDGE, MASSACHUSETTS,
    August 1, 1915.

CONTENTS

ABBREVIATIONS

Addresses = *Addresses of John Hay.* New York, 1907.
N. & H. = *Abraham Lincoln: A History.* By John G. Nicolay
  and John Hay. 10 vols. New York, 1890.
Poems = *Poems.* By John Hay. Revised Edition. Boston, 1890.
Poet in Exile = *A Poet in Exile. Early Letters of John Hay.* Edited
  by Caroline Ticknor. Boston, 1910.

ILLUSTRATIONS

THE LIFE AND LETTERS OF JOHN HAY

CHAPTER I

BEGINNINGS

DURING the second half of the nineteenth century, the vicissitudes in the personal fortunes of Americans were so swift, and yet so common, that contemporaries took them almost as matters of course. In truth, however, not since the Elizabethan age, and then on a much smaller scale, had anything similar been seen. It was as if, in the animal kingdom, not merely individuals but whole varieties should change their nature so rapidly as to become scarcely recognizable after the lapse of a single generation. The children of privation grew up to be masters of untold wealth. An obscure railsplitter became President of the United States, wielding a power surpassing that of Europe's absolute monarchs. And as if the natural expansion over a vast continent did not offer sufficient opportunities for individual development, there intervened a Civil War which served as a ladder for talents which lie dormant in peace.

Among the many who were a part of this process of transformation was John Hay. Born the son of a frontier doctor, in a small dwelling on the edge of the Western wilderness, he lived, as Secretary of State, in a palace at Washington, in the midst of a world crisis which his counsel helped to direct.

Hay himself, at a dinner of the Ohio Society of New York, on January 17, 1903, summed up in pleasant fashion the contrasts in his career. "When I look back on the shifting scenes of my life," he said, "if I am not that altogether deplorable creature, a man without a country, I am, when it comes to pull and prestige, almost equally bereft, as I am a man without a State. I was born in Indiana, I grew up in Illinois, I was educated in Rhode Island, and it is no blame to that scholarly community that I know so little. I learned my law in Springfield and my politics in Washington, my diplomacy in Europe, Asia, and Africa. I have a farm in New Hampshire and desk-room in the District of Columbia. When I look to the springs from which my blood descends, the first ancestors I ever heard of were a Scotchman, who was half English, and a German woman, who was half French. Of my immediate progenitors, my mother was from New England and my father was from the South. In this bewilderment of origin and experience, I can only put on an aspect of deep humility in any gathering of favorite sons, and confess that I am nothing but an American." [1]

An American he was, on both sides of his house, but with an heirloom to which theorists in heredity might attribute his cosmopolitan affinities. For although the Hays had their roots in Scotland, one of them, in the early part of the eighteenth century, took service under the Elector Palatine. What rank he held in the Elector's army I do not know, nor whether he himself emigrated with the swarm of Germans who came over from the Palatinate to Pennsylvania about 1750. Certain it is, however, that of his four sons John, the eldest, settled at York, Pennsylvania, while Adam went on to Berkeley County, Virginia, and made his home at the bottom of the Shenandoah Valley. Adam probably did his share of Indian fighting; possibly he enlisted in the Revolution; at any rate, his son John remembered being patted on the head by General Washington. This John, born February 13, 1775, growing restive under his father's severe treatment, struck out for himself at the age of eighteen, joined a party of Virginians who tramped across the mountains into Kentucky, and found an abode at Lexington. There he married Jemima Coulter, who bore him fourteen children. For thirty-five years he helped to upbuild

[1] *Addresses*, 219–20.

that town, which boasted of its refinements and intellectual interests; and he had for a neighbor, Henry Clay, another Virginian, who also sought his fortune in Kentucky soon after John Hay's arrival. Hay became one of Clay's followers, hated Andrew Jackson and detested slavery.

The latter antipathy led him in 1830 to cross the Ohio River into the free State of Illinois, where he established himself at Springfield. That same year Abraham Lincoln moved into Sangamon County, and as time went on he and the elder Hay were friends. Old John Hay died May 20, 1865, having lived "to watch Lincoln's funeral pass his windows."

Among his many children, Charles, born February 7, 1801, in Fayette County, Kentucky, was educated at Lexington, where he received the diploma of doctor of medicine, and being, like his father, a hater of slavery, he crossed into Indiana in 1830, and began to practice his profession in the village of Salem, a few miles north of the Ohio River. The following year, on October 13, 1831, he married there Helen Leonard,[1] three years his junior, a young woman of pure New England stock, come into the west from Middleboro, Massachusetts, to live with her sister. The husband of this sister, John Hay

[1] Born at Assonet, near New Bedford, Massachusetts, February 7, 1804.

Farnham, was the leading lawyer of Salem and its neighborhood.

Thus, after four generations of wanderings out of Scotland to the Rhenish Palatinate, and thence to Pennsylvania, Virginia, Kentucky, and Indiana, the Hay line met that of the Leonards, who had emigrated from England to Massachusetts in the days of the Stuarts.

At Salem, John Milton Hay, the third child [1] of Dr. Charles and Helen Hay, was born October 8, 1838, in a small one-storied brick house, symbolical of the straitness of pioneer existence. But out of those border cabins, like oaks out of acorns, sprang many a man whose life became a part of the nation's history.

In 1834, Dr. Hay, in partnership with Royal B. Child, issued the *Salem Monitor*, a newspaper of approved Whig views, to which he contributed articles. During the Harrison campaign of 1840 he wrote the

---

[1] The other children were: *Edward Leonard*, b. Nov. 9, 1832; d. Oct. 8, 1840. *Augustus Leonard*, b. Dec. 2, 1834; served in the Civil War, and became captain of the Ninth U.S. Infantry; d. Nov. 12, 1904. *Mary Pierce*, born Dec. 17, 1836, married Captain A. C. Woolfolk, U.S.A., in 1863; he was later a circuit judge, and died at Denver, Colorado, in 1880; she died March 21, 1914. *Charles Edward*, b. March 23, 1841; served during the Civil War in the Third U.S. Cavalry and on General Hunter's staff; was subsequently Mayor of Springfield, Illinois; married Mary Ridgely, May 10, 1865. *Helen Jemima*, b. at Warsaw, Illinois, Sept. 13, 1844; married Harwood O. Whitney in 1870; died June 19, 1873. Dr. Charles Hay died at Warsaw, Sept. 18, 1884; his wife died there Feb. 18, 1893.

political leaders, which show, according to a local writer, that he had a thorough knowledge of the issues of his time and "handled them in a masterly manner."

Either because Salem offered too narrow a field for an energetic young doctor, or because Charles Hay was impelled by the desire, common to the Western settlers of his time, to move on in search of better conditions, he took his family in 1841 to Warsaw, Illinois. This frontier settlement, perched on the banks of the Mississippi, at the head of the navigation of the great river, and opposite the mouth of the Des Moines, counted then only a few hundred inhabitants; but the surrounding country was fertile, its climate was healthful, and its outlook on Missouri and the boundless possibilities of the Far West seemed to promise that it would become an important distributing center.

Many years later Hay wrote to a friend: "Towns are sometimes absurdly named. I lived at Spunky Point on the Mississippi! This is a graphic, classic, characteristic designation of a geographical and ethnological significance. But some idiots, just before I was born, who had read Miss Porter,[1] thought Warsaw would be much more genteel, and so we are

---

[1] Jane Porter (1776–1850) published, in 1803, *Thaddeus of Warsaw*, a romance which had a great vogue for half a century.

Nicodemussed into nothing for the rest of time. I hope every man who was engaged in the outrage is called Smith in Heaven." [1]

At Warsaw, the young Hays passed their childhood. Their father's practice, which he pursued on horseback, led him far up and down the river and inland through the neighboring counties. Life was undeniably hard. It provided the material necessaries, but few luxuries; it called for enterprise, courage, resourcefulness, versatility. The husband must be a jack-of-all-trades; the wife must not only perform the duties of cook and maid and housekeeper, but nurse and rear the children, and, outside of the small towns, she must spin and make the family clothing. During the forties of the last century, the cruelest hardships of the pioneer days had been outgrown in the Western Illinois settlements, but the railroads had not yet brought the conveniences of civilization, or opened the way to Eastern markets, or quite dispelled the brooding sense of isolation which, no matter how bravely self-reliance may face it, prevents a well-rounded life.

John Hay himself, in writing of Lincoln, traversed the notion, spread by a few survivors, that the pioneers enjoyed a glorious existence. "They see it," he says, "through a rosy mist of memory, transfigured

[1] Hay to Miss H. K. Loring, June 30, 1870.

by the eternal magic of youth. The sober fact is that the life was a hard one, with few rational pleasures, few wholesome appliances. The strong ones lived, and some even attained great length of years; but to the many age came early and was full of infirmity and pain. If we could go back to what our fore-fathers endured in clearing the Western wilderness, we could then better appreciate our obligations to them." [1] And he cites a letter from Lincoln who, at the age of thirty-nine, calls himself an old man.

We must not, however, confuse the pioneers who blazed their way into Indiana, Illinois, and the North-west Territory with the successive waves of immi-grants from Ireland, Southern Italy, Hungary, Po-land, Greece, and Western Asia which latterly have at times threatened to submerge our institutions. The Irish bog-trotter was as illiterate and bigoted as the Calabrian peasant or the Russian serf; while the pitiable offscourings of the European capitals surely planted the slums in our own cities and rendered honest and efficient municipal government an almost insuperable task. The pioneers of Indiana and Illinois, on the other hand, whether they came from Virginia through Kentucky, or from Pennsyl-vania down the Ohio, or from New England direct, had been nourished on certain common principles.

[1] N. & H., I, 68–69.

Whether they traced their descent from Covenanter, Roundhead, or Cavalier, they believed in political and religious liberty. They respected trial by jury and those other safeguards of the individual, which were the cornerstone of Anglo-Saxon justice. Their fathers, North and South, had fought in the Revolutionary War to uphold the proposition that there should be no taxation without representation, and they themselves placed passionate trust in popular government. The New Englanders brought with them the town meeting and the country school. Whoever would might read the Bible unforbidden by priest and unprevented by illiteracy. Even among the 'poor white trash' from the South there lingered, however dimly, traces of the Anglo-Saxon tradition. Young Abraham Lincoln, as bereft of opportunity for culture as any lad in the country, had access to the Bible and "The Pilgrim's Progress," Æsop's "Fables," and "Robinson Crusoe," and, a little later, to Shakespeare, Burns, and Blackstone's "Commentaries." With the English Bible and Shakespeare one may inherit not only the Anglo-Saxon tradition, but also the world's supreme achievements in prose literature, in poetry, and in religion.

No doubt the settlers, men of energy and initiative, were too busy developing the new country to

pay much heed to books; but they recognized the
need of education in technical concerns, and they
had not wholly lost the respect for learning as an
ideal which had come down to them from their British forebears. To them the spoken word was the living word. Lawyers, politicians, preachers, lecturers
flourished among them. Politics, which involved the
interpretation of the Constitution and fundamental
conceptions of morals and humanity, became their
vital interest. Should Slavery be allowed in the new
communities? If not, where draw the line of restriction? If the South persisted in slaveholding, how
long could the nation survive, half bond, half free?
Was not the preservation of the Union more important than the welfare of the negro?

However unequipped with the refinements of civilization, a people which, besides conquering for itself
a home in the wilderness, was earnestly confronting
such questions, could not be charged with stagnation.

These were the general conditions, material and
intellectual, which formed the background of John
Hay's boyhood; and as his father, grandfather, and
uncle made their homes in towns which New Englanders had settled, he grew up in an anti-slavery
atmosphere.

Among the Hay papers the earliest I find are two

letters from Charles Hay at Salem to his parents at Springfield. They are yellow, time-stained documents, folded and wafered as was the custom before the days of envelopes, without postmark, and with the postage, 18¾ cents each, written in ink on the cover. Letter-writing was a costly pleasure then.

The first letter reads as follows: —

SALEM, Nov. 25th, 1832.

DEAR FATHER AND MOTHER —

I presume before this time that you have received my former letter and although I have not received an answer to it I deem it proper to write you another. I hope before this time that you are comfortably settled and perhaps nearly or quite ready for business. I shall be gratified to hear from you soon, and to hear as much as possible in regard to every particular. My chief motive in writing this letter is not to inform you that I have received a legacy or a fortune in any other way, but to receive that which poor people are much more certain of. On the 9th of the present month we had a son born which is of course your first grandson; he weighed 7½ pounds the day after he was born and is a very thrifty fellow. Now I suppose you would like to know what your first grandson looks like and I must endeavor to tell you. When Helen asked me first whom he looked like

I said he looked like John; when Cornelia was asked whom he looked like she answered like the Dr.'s brother John without knowing what had been my opinion; his eyes are quite black and his head is covered with more hair than I have usually seen [on] children at 3 or 6 months old, both he and his mother are doing well. His name is Edward Leonard after Helen's deceased brother. It would have been John had it not been for the circumstance [of] her brother's death who was a great favourite in the family. I hope you are all enjoying health and contentment; you may all expect to have the blues more or less for a while but courage will overcome all difficulties. I will close my letter and wait till I hear from you again.

Your affectionate son

CHARLES HAY.

JOHN HAY
JEMIMA HAY

How much a single letter like that brings with it!

The only other letter in this earliest packet is dated, "Salem Indiana Dec 4th 1834" and addressed to "Dear Father and Mother."

"I have of course something to write, you will think; true. Well, what is it; nothing dreadful of course or I would not write it; well what is it you will say. Why it is simply this that on the morning of the

2nd inst a stranger came to visit us; and who was it? Why he could not tell his name although he was neither deaf blind nor dumb; but he has tarried with us and for convenience we have agreed to call him John Augustus Hay. What, another boy you will say. Well, be it so. His weight with the little trappings about was nine pounds and three quarters full 2 pounds more than the first born. Well done, say you. And both mother and son are doing well in every way. . . .

"I am still in hopes that you can let one of the boys come to live with us. I am not sanguine in promises to myself or others but I think I could get one of them into tolerable good business here before long if he would come. Clerks in stores are often wanted and there are few native hoosiers who are fitted either by education manners or habits for the business. Of course merchants are often disappointed or compelled to take these entirely unfit for the business. Even a good overseer in a factory, should their feelings incline that way, is often wanted, and good wages given. But I will wait till your next letter before I say more on the subject. Mr. Farnham's children are still with us and will stay till spring; perhaps then they may go to Boston. Our town is healthy and business prosperous generally.

"Yours affectionately."

The firstborn son, Edward, lived only a few years: the second — who was named Augustus Leonard, and not John Augustus, as the parents first intended — was the hero, in youth, and through life, of John Hay, the statesman. When he died, on November 12, 1904, the younger John, then Secretary of State, and nearing the end himself, told his grief in a noble letter to President Roosevelt. It can best be placed here, because it gives what, after half a century, he remembered as the brightest aspects of his boyhood.

Nov. 16, 1904.

DEAR THEODORE —

I cannot talk about it — so I will write you a word. My brother was my first friend and my best. I owe him everything. He was only four years older than me, but he had a sense of right and of conduct which made him seem much older. He was always my standard. He was not so quick at his books as I was, but far more sure. He taught me my Latin and Greek so that I made better recitations than he did, and got higher marks — which was a gross injustice. But he took more interest in my success than in his own. He made many sacrifices for me, which, with the selfishness of a boy, I accepted as a matter of course. He fought my battles. It was ill for the big boy whom he caught bullying me. Once I dreamed we were Christians thrown to the beasts in the Coliseum. He stepped between me and a lion and whipped the great cat with his fists, then seized me and dragged me through a subterranean passage till we came out on the Appian Way. Years afterwards when I went to Rome, I looked about to see where all that had taken place. It was as clear and vivid as any real action of my life.

He was my superior in every way but one — the gift of expression. His scholarship was more exact than mine. He had wonderful skill with his hands; could make better balls, bats, kites, fishing-rods, etc., than could be bought in the shops. Once he gathered up all the pamphlets in the house, and bound them neatly though he had never seen a book-bindery. He was — as I have been told by those who served with him — the best company officer and the best adjutant in the army. Yet he had no luck in promotion. His rigid sense of duty forbade him to seek advancement, and he sternly forbade me ever to mention his name at headquarters. I obeyed him because I knew he would have refused a promotion which came through the solicitation of his friends.

He was the chief of my tribe, in birth as well as in mind and in character. We were not a handsome family, the rest of us — but he was unusually good-looking, tall and straight and brave.

Now he has left us, and I never had a chance to get even with him for all he did for me when we were boys. My uncertain health, the weather, and other futilities have even kept me away from his funeral. I feel remorsefully unworthy of him.

Yours affectionately.

Happy the older brother who could inspire such memories! happier still the younger, with such a capacity for hero-worship!

Of Hay's childhood and youth at Warsaw there is little to record. He attended the public school, taught by a Mr. Holmes, and joined in the play of his companions. Great affection bound the family together. Dr. Hay prospered, according to the measure of prosperity of country doctors in the West. Above all, both he and his wife saw to it that their children should enjoy every procurable means of improvement, and the Doctor himself helped John in his Latin.

From our earliest glimpses of him, John Hay appears as an imaginative child. His oldest sister remembers that, when he was still a little boy, he had "the habit of stringing words together into rhymes." His brother Charles tells this incident, which dates back to John's sixth or seventh year. One morning John came and sat down beside him on a log in front of the new brick house their father was building, and

JOHN HAY'S BIRTHPLACE, SALEM, INDIANA

presently John said: "'I have seen the end of the world.' I asked him: 'What did you see there?' He replied: 'Nothing, only trees and flowers and some birds.' Later on he mentioned this himself, and we then understood that it was only the wild forest land beyond the reservation, on which had been built, in 1814, Fort Edwards on the bank of the Mississippi River."

Other anecdotes furnished by his brother Charles help us to a further acquaintance.

"When he was a small boy, a German of education called on my father to ask assistance in forming a class for the study of German. John listened with a great deal of interest and whispered to his father, 'I would like very much to study German.' This pleased both my father and the German professor, and John became a student with the others, who were all men grown. John was so small that he would occasionally fall asleep during the evening, but he surprised them all by showing he had learned his lesson and could recite equally well with the best of them when awakened."

The following recollection, like a flash of lightning in the night, reveals one of the tragic possibilities of life on the borderland of slavery.

"When we were both quite young," Mr. Charles Hay writes, "he [John] told me he was in the basement of our house, and he heard a ghost, which spoke to him and said: 'Little Master, for the love of God bring me a drink of water.' John said he was so frightened he hurried upstairs and went to his room. The next day my father told at the table that three runaway slaves had been overtaken by a party of officers from Missouri and the slaves had resisted arrest, and one was captured and taken back, one of the other two was fired upon and killed, and the third had been badly wounded, but escaped, leaving blood tracks in the wood. I saw my brother John staring at me across the supper table, but saying nothing. After the meal, he told his father about the voice he heard in the basement. My father, John, and I went down to investigate, and on a pile of kindling wood was the appearance of some one having used this for a bed; but there was a stain of blood nearly eighteen inches in diameter. This was probably the blood shed by the runaway slave who had escaped capture. What became of the slave afterward, I never heard. Fully forty years afterward I asked John if he remembered this occurrence, and he replied: 'I will never forget it, and that incident has given me a greater horror than anything I ever heard or read about slavery.'"

From the primary school, John, with his older brother Leonard, was placed under an Episcopal clergyman, the Reverend Stephen Childs, who conducted a private school at Warsaw. There he began Latin and Greek; and perhaps it was Mr. Childs who referred to him as "honest and efficient," — praise which greatly pleased the boy. "I feel my character has been established — 'honest and efficient,' — " he confided to Charles: "this is my pride for my after life." "I am glad to hear that John is progressing so well in his study of Latin," his brother Augustus writes from St. Louis, on July 17, 1851, to Mr. N. W. Bliss, at Warsaw; "but as regards Greek, I expect he *is* somewhat 'lazy'; however, I hope he will soon get over that and go ahead."[1] In 1851, John was sent to a private academy at Pittsfield, the county seat of Pike County, a town which emigrants from Pittsfield, Massachusetts, had settled and stamped with genuine Yankee ideals. In that seminary, kept by Mr. and Mrs. John D. Thomson, he met John George Nicolay, a Bavarian by birth, his elder by six years, who was destined to have a decisive influence on his career. "We all remember John Hay at that time," one of his boyhood companions wrote in 1898, "as a red-cheeked, black-eyed, sun-

[1] For this letter, I am indebted to Mr. Nelson Thomasson, of Chicago. He says that Mr. Bliss tutored John for Brown University, and subsequently became eminent at the Chicago bar. Augustus Hay seems in 1851 to have been employed in an apothecary's shop in St. Louis.

shiny boy, chock-full of fun and devilment that hurt
nobody. . . . He spoke German like a native, having
picked it up, just as he gathered an inexhaustible
repertoire of 'river slang' from the Mississippi River
steamboatmen, which served its turn later on in the
'Pike County Ballads.'" [1] In 1852, Hay went on to
the college at Springfield — a promotion which might
well seem to the lad as the introduction to a larger
world. For Springfield was the capital of Illinois,
and when the legislature sat, the town bustled with
politicians, attorneys, lobbyists, and business men.
The boom in railroad-building had begun. At all
times visitors were coming and going on legal or
judicial errands. In the streets you might meet men
of more than local reputation: Senator Stephen A.
Douglas, the "Little Giant," who was trying, with
apparent success, to serve the God of Freedom and
the Mammon of Slavery; or gaunt, lanky Abraham
Lincoln, with his backwoods manner, and strange,
sad eyes, and the gifts of humor and direct speech
which already made him a prominent figure throughout the State; or Lyman Trumbull and David Davis,
leaders in Illinois, whose eyes were turned to the
national stage in Washington.

For such a quick-witted youth as John Hay, a

[1] W. E. Norris, in the *Pike County Democrat;* quoted in the *Century Magazine*, N.S., vol. LVI, p. 449. Norris's recollection of the color of Hay's eyes is inaccurate.

small capital like the Springfield of those days was more educative than a great city could be. A young community, where individuals stand on their own merits, and society is not yet stratified into classes, comes very soon to form an accurate estimate of character; and Springfield also laid open before him the machinery of a republic in operation. Presumably, he listened occasionally to debates in the legislature, or went to the court-house when some sensational trial was up, or applauded the anti-slavery stump speakers during the political campaigns; for he had a healthy curiosity to see how the world was run, and to watch those who ran it. He must have known the celebrities, at least by sight, and he must have heard his uncle and grandfather utter candid opinions about natives and strangers alike.

In the college at Springfield, which was really no more than a preparatory school, Hay studied so well that, by the spring of 1855, he began to think of going to a university. His schoolmates envied his capacity for "getting his lessons without apparently any study." An unusual memory enhanced his innate brightness. He was "bookish," in that he devoured books for pleasure, but he was no grind. Full of life and spirits, he entered eagerly into the modest gayeties — the "sociables, picnics, and dances" — of Springfield.

So Hay went back to Warsaw, his schooling over, to discuss with his parents his future career. As the "scholar" of the family, all agreed that he must continue his education at a university. The New England tradition imposed that, even if Dr. and Mrs. Hay had had other intentions for him. They decided that he should go to Brown University, at Providence, Rhode Island, where Mrs. Hay's father, David Augustus Leonard, had graduated as Class Orator in 1792. His uncle, Milton Hay, who had paid for his education during the past four years, promised to support him through college, and accordingly, towards the end of the summer, John journeyed eastward in order to matriculate at Brown when the first term of the academic year began, on Friday, September 7, 1855. He still lacked a month of being seventeen years old.

CHAPTER II

LIFE AT BROWN UNIVERSITY

THERE is a story that John Hay planned to enter Harvard, as being the oldest, most distinguished, and best equipped of American universities; but that when he stopped over at Providence to visit Brown, the attractions of that institution, and the recollection of his grandfather Leonard's career there, so impressed him that he went no farther. From a letter he wrote at the time, however, we can separate fact from legend.

BROWN UNIVERSITY, September 30, 1855.

DEAR FRIENDS: —

As I am now all completely settled and arranged for the term, I proceed to give you notice of this important fact and to let you know I still am an inhabitant of earth. I had a whirling, hustling time on the way here, but at last arrived without any accident on Tuesday evening, safe and sound in everything, except my eyes, mouth and ears were full of cinders and dust. Saw nothing on the way so remarkable as the miserable soil of Michigan and a part of Canada and Massachusetts. To one foot of soil there were about three feet of cobblestones and in the clacks weakly, consumptive-looking corn was struggling for life. Such corn as a sucker farmer would cut down and hide for fear it would hurt the reputation of his farm. In Canada I noticed a great profusion of bull-headed Englishmen, free negroes, and Indian turnips.

I came into Boston about four o'clock in the afternoon Tuesday. Bought a mince pie for three cents and a cake for two, and feasted royally. Taking the cars for Providence, arrived there in a couple of hours. Went to a hotel, and after supper walked up to the college, found Billy Norris and moved my traps up forthwith. The next morning was examined, admitted and commenced my studies, which are Chemistry, Rhetoric, and Trigonometry. The first two are by lectures which we are required to take down as they are delivered and recite the next day. We also have exercises in speaking and writing essays.

My room is a comfortable and conveniently furnished one on the second floor of the college, costing about 50 dollars. My chum is a young man from the State of New York, steady, studious, and good scholar, so I stand a chance of doing a good deal of hard study this winter. It is not here as in Springfield. Here I am acquainted with no one in the city and have no inducements to leave the college, while in Springfield my circle of acquaintance was far from limited, and entirely too agreeable for my own good.

I shall wish often this winter, that I could light in Springfield for a few hours and then evaporate, but so mote it *not* be, and I do not know whether I will come back to Illinois next summer or not. That is too far ahead to look at present.

My best love to all, Grandpa, aunts, uncles, cousins, and cats and all inquiring friends.

J. M. HAY.

Tell Aunt Deniza that while I was passing through Canada I looked for the handsome features of Josiah Condell at every station, but, to my great regret saw them not.

Somebody write soon — soon — do you hear? SOON.

To an imaginative youth, come from the mushroom communities of the West, Brown University, founded nearly a century before, seemed venerable; and Providence, with about fifty thousand inhabitants and a past stretching back to 1636, was both ancient and robust.

The city ranked second in size among those of New England. It possessed thriving industries, railways, and steamboats, and a general high level of material well-being. The defects of industrialism had not yet pushed menacingly to the front; nor had immigrant labor swarmed in, bringing its indigestible alien survivals. How uniformly American the population was, appears from the fact that out of the fifty-three churches in the city only six were Roman Catholic. Providence alternated with Newport as the seat of the capital of Rhode Island — an honor which added political importance to her commercial prestige.

But not on the material side only was Providence fortunate. The place itself, which Roger Williams had chosen to be the home of the first settlement in America dedicated to toleration, was by nature very beautiful. Narragansett Bay, freshened by the breezes of the Atlantic, ended there in a partly enclosed harbor which divided the city; and several small rivers flowed seaward through the hills which, ranged in an irregular semicircle, formed the background. The residences of the well-to-do and rich rose amid luxuriant foliage along the slopes or on the crests. There was evidently great prosperity, but little display. No amount of wealth could dim the luster of the old families, many of which were themselves rich; and the presence of the college teachers served as an intellectual leaven for society and possibly as a rebuke to vulgar extravagance. The well-stocked Athenæum Library, supported by private subscription, was a favorite resort; while here and there some person had begun to collect rare books, or paintings, or prints, or to regard it as his duty to contribute to the expansion of the University.

In a word, Providence was at that happy stage when it still preserved its individuality, and had not become for travelers merely a railroad junction between New York and Boston. It displayed a lively civic consciousness, and it felt both the buoyancy which belonged to communities then in the heyday of industrial development, and the sense of satisfaction which comes when material prosperity has not yet dulled respect for spiritual and intellectual ideals. Providence was large enough to put forth and sustain the organs through which a community enjoys in some measure a varied civilization; but not so large as to lose its social solidarity, much less its identity. Like Portsmouth, Worcester, and two or three other provincial centers of old New England, it seemed a microcosm of many of the New England characteristics.

Although a Baptist institution by origin and direction, Brown University adhered to that provision of its charter which forbade religious tests and declared that all its members should "forever enjoy

full, free, absolute, and uninterrupted liberty of conscience." In 1855 the students numbered only two
hundred and twenty-five, and the faculty only nine,
but smallness did not mean lack of vitality. The
students came from all parts of the country, and some
of the professors ranked among the best of their
generation. With classes of from thirty-five to sixty-
five members, a student must have been a hopeless
mollusk who did not know all his classmates, and,
indeed, most of the men in the University. The conditions favored wide acquaintanceship, close common interests, and intimate friendships: and between the students and some of their teachers
friendly relations sprang up outside the classroom.

The curriculum provided by Brown aimed at
what used to be called a liberal education. It laid
stress on Latin and Greek and mathematics, but it
recognized the French and German classics and the
modern sciences — chemistry, physiology, geology,
and political economy — which were crowding their
way to the front in spite of their treatment as par-
venus by the classicists. The term for Master of
Arts was five years, for Bachelor four years, and for
Bachelor of Philosophy three years. The last course,
designed for those students "who are intended for
the pursuits of active life," hoped to "confer a high
degree of intellectual culture, without the necessity

of studying the Ancient Languages." [1] Clearly, Brown University, like the other American colleges of that period, wished to make "scholars and gentle· men," not specialists in any narrow field of research, or engineers, doctors, or lawyers. It accepted as its task the furnishing of those essentials without which the specialist is doomed to remain an unculti- vated man.

John Hay took up his quarters in Number 19, University Hall, with Wallace W. Corbett [2] as room- mate. Being admitted to advanced standing, he escaped most of the usual trials of a Freshman. At his arrival, he attracted attention by being out of style in his clothes and appearance: the fellows dubbed it "Western." He wore his thick shock of brown hair long, cut horizontally like a Roundhead's, and coiled about his ears. His features had not taken on their mature definiteness: the slightly turned- up nose, the pouting lips, still suggested the lad; but his forehead was already large and deep, and his hazel eyes at once arrested attention. "They were eyes," one of his intimates of those years tells me, "which you could look into for a mile, and they looked through and through yours." They were the eyes of the young man who sees visions, of the bud-

---

[1] Brown University Catalogue, 1855–56.
[2] From Bridgewater, New York.

ding poet rapt by the beauty his imagination unfolds to him.

One other letter pertaining to Hay's first year in college deserves to be quoted entire.

BROWN UNIVERSITY, November 28th [1855]

MY DEAR FRIENDS: —

To-morrow is Thanksgiving. We have no lessons this week and many of the students have gone home. I thought that when this time came I would have plenty of time to catch up with my correspondence and make some excursions to the surrounding country. But here half the week is gone and I have done nothing at all. The fact is, I am so much occupied with my studies that when a few days of release come I cannot make a rational use of my liberty. You know I entered the Junior Class behind the rest, and consequently have several studies to make up before I can be even with them. And as the prescribed studies are about as much as I can attend to, I do not know whether I can finish the course, with justice, in two years. I think I can *graduate* in that time, but will not stand high, or know as much about the studies as if I had been more leisurely about it. Again, if I go through so hurriedly, I will have little or no time to avail myself of the literary treasures of the libraries. This is one of the greatest advantages of an Eastern College over a Western one.

This matter, however, I leave for you and Pa to decide; but you may be assured that whatever time I remain here I am determined to show you that your generous kindness has not been misapplied or ungratefully received. I am at present getting along well in my class. The Register tells me that I stand in the first class of honor, my average standing being 18 in 20. The life here suits me exactly. The professors are all men of the greatest ability, and what is more, perfect gentlemen. They pursue a kind and friendly course toward the students as long as they act in a manner to deserve it, but any violations of the rules of the institution are strictly punished. There have been several expulsions and suspensions since I came here.

I have no acquaintances out of the college, consequently know very little of the city. There is not much excitement here on any occasion, except Thanksgiving and Training-Day, and then it is a quiet Yankee excitement as much as possible unlike the rough, hearty manner of the West.

I heard Oliver W. Holmes deliver a poem here last week, which [was] a splendid thing; also a lecture by Professor Huntingdon. Thackeray will be here before long and I expect to hear him lecture.

It is getting very late and I close this excuse for a letter with my best regards for all the family and all my friends in Springfield.

P.S. *Thursday morning.* — I have just received and read with pleasure Aunt D.'s and Cousin S.'s letter. Augustus has only written once to me since I have been here. I am anxious to hear from him.

P.P.S. Please remit at your earliest convenience some of "the root of all evil," alias, "tin," alias, pewter.

P.P.P.S. Some one write soon and I will answer likewise.

P.P.P.P.S. I will return good for evil and answer Cousin Sarah on a whole sheet, instead of a few lines at the end of this.

P.P.P.P.P.S. I received a letter from Dad lately.

P.P.P.P.P.P.S. That is all.
Yours truly,
J. M. HAY.

Hay's family saw the wisdom of not forcing him to rush through his college education in two years; and as the generous uncle pledged the necessary

UNIVERSITY HALL, BROWN UNIVERSITY (BUILT IN 1770)

The cross indicates the room occupied by Hay

support, he soon settled into the Class of 1858 as a Sophomore, with leisure to read and also to play, as fancy dictated.

If some of the "intellectual bullies" were inclined at first — as a contemporary reports — to heckle the awkward Westerner, they soon learned that they could neither intimidate him nor rouse his anger, and that he was quite their match in wit. Good-natured by temperament, he held himself somewhat reserved except with those whom he knew well. His intimates remembered his flashes of fun, his cozy friendliness, his brilliance as a talker, his moments of exhilaration followed by fits of depression, which recurred throughout his life. That he had little money to spend, did not shut him out from comradeship; nor did his studiousness, which was that of the dilettante and not that of the pedant. Without any ambition to head the rank list, he stood well in his classes. The person who knew him best in those days says that he was "very humble." Perhaps he was already contrasting his unfledged talents with the soaring achievements of the masters whom he worshiped. The college library, where he browsed at will, "meant more to him as an undergraduate than all the rest of the college." And no wonder, for the college instruction, even in the elective courses, was conducted wholly by recitation, and what that was can be inferred from this reminiscence furnished me by Hay's classmate, the Reverend J. H. Gilmore: —

"The method of studying English literature which existed at Brown fifty-odd years ago was not one which tended to stimulate literary enthusiasm. We had six pages of advance, six pages of immediate review, and six pages of back review in Spalding's 'English Literature,' to be recited every Friday afternoon throughout the Junior year; and there you were. Why, one of my classmates, who graduated *summa cum laude*, told me that he had never read one of Shakespeare's plays, and that he had 'never consciously read a line of Tennyson's,' although 'In Memoriam' was published in 1850."

To a youth who was feeding his imagination on Shelley, those weekly exercises in Spalding's treadmill could not have been inspiring. At least one of his teachers, however, Professor James B. Angell, — subsequently, President of the University of Michigan, — both stirred Hay's enthusiasm and recognized his ability. They read together several of the great French and German masterpieces, and Hay proved the best translator Dr. Angell ever had in his classes. Marks give only an uncertain indication of capacity, especially when we do not know the interaction of teacher and pupil which determines

marks; but it is odd to discover that Hay stood
highest in political economy (under Professor William Gammell), which he elected during his last
half-year in college. As his standing improved year
by year, we infer that his growing zeal in interests
outside the classroom did not cause him to scamp
his studies.[1]

But from first to last Hay was evidently one of
those youths whose college career cannot be summed
up by marks. His fellows quickly discovered his unusual qualities of wit and good-nature and thought-
fulness. At the first Freshman dinner, the toast-
master, after calling on everybody who wished to
speak, summoned Hay to his feet. "We don't want
anything dry," a youth shouted. "Hay that is green
can never be dry," the unfashionable stranger from
Illinois retorted; and then he poured out a sparkling
speech, which delighted his enthusiastic hearers and
made his reputation. How suddenly those college

[1] I am indebted to the Registrar of Brown University for the following record of Hay's standing. — 1855–56. *First semester.* Chemistry,
19.50; mathematics, 17.01; rhetoric, 18.65. *Second semester.* 3 Latin,
19.37; physics, 19.21; rhetoric, 18.79; 3 Greek, 18.90. — 1856–57.
First semester. French, 19.00; German, 19.32; moral philosophy,
14.93; declamations, 19.00. *Second semester.* Moral philosophy, 17.25;
French, 19.12; German, 19.83. — 1857–58. *First semester.* History,
19.83; intellectual philosophy, 19.45. *Second semester.* History,
19.64; moral philosophy, 19.35, political economy, 19.95. These are
half-yearly averages, based on a possible total of 20 for each study.
Hay's rank for the three years admitted him to the Phi Beta Kappa
Fraternity.

reputations shoot up under the influence of song and wine and comradeship!

That was the era when Greek letter fraternities ran riot in American colleges. Among undergraduates the rage for secret societies seems to be as incurable as is falling in love. Who does not remember the preliminary suspense, the weeks or months in which you wondered whether you would be chosen, and, if chosen, by which fraternity? You heard that Brown "was sure" of the A.B.C., that Green had been approached by the D.E.F., that Gray's grandfather had been president of the X.Y.Z., that White had a cousin in the Tiger's Claw or the Shark's Skull. Although you lacked any similar favoring connection, yet you could not help feeling that you were quite as desirable as Brown or Green or Gray. At last an emissary came to sound you for the X.Y.Z. Genuinely surprised, you accepted with fervor, while protesting that you knew you were not worthy of so great an honor.

Then followed the preparations for your initiation and your dread lest you might flinch during the terrible ordeal; until you comforted yourself by the reflection that if Timkins, notoriously puny of body and feeble of will, had gone through, you might hope to do likewise. Of the initiation itself, — the frightful tortures, the harrowing tests of endurance, the oaths more awful than those uttered in the court-room or at the altar, and the sense of omniscience which permeated you when you heard the meaning of the mystic Greek letters, — these are matters never to be revealed to the profane. How joyfully you called each fellow member "Brother," and how suddenly you discovered all sorts of attractions in even the most commonplace of them! What a thrill passed through you when you tried the grip on an upper classman, and he responded, and you fell to exchanging confidences as if you had been babies together! However modest you were, you could not doubt that the whole college must see at a glance that a great change had been wrought in you over-night, and that, although you wore no visible halo, you were indubitably one of the elect.

Looking backward, after many years, you smile at the exaggerations of that experience; but your smile is wistful and tender, rather than satirical, for you recognize that the secret society was but one of the forms of glamour by which you were led from adolescence into manhood. The glamour passes; the sweetness of the memory of youth itself abides. And you reserve your sarcasm for those silly dotards who in after life hold their society pins more sacred than wife and children, or leave the room if any out-sider whispers the name of their society. The best of

fraternities have serious drawbacks, but they have
also compensating positive benefits, the chief being
opportunity for friendship.

Coming to Brown as a stranger, John Hay had not
been pledged to any of the competing fraternities.
But we learn that "his sterling worth" soon gave
the "intellectual bullies" pause. "Nor had he been
long matriculated," says his fraternal biographer,
"before Brothers Burdge and Simons, looking deeper
into character, saw in him the future development
of a strong nature." Accordingly, those discerning
brothers "made it their study to place before Hay
the great advantages over all other societies which
were to be found under the protecting ægis of the
Theta Delta Chi Fraternity."

Hay was persuaded, and was initiated at a ceremony of extraordinary solemnity, which Brothers
French and Taylor attended from Tufts College,
and Brother Alexander L. Holley ("who had already
become famous"!) from New York. A right royal
Theta Delta supper followed at the "What-Cheer,"
where Pond and French made their happiest
speeches, — Depew "never equaled them," — and
Brother Hay responded to everybody's satisfaction.

"The next morning," continues Brother Stone,
the chronicler, "imagine the horror (yes, that word
exactly expresses it) of the members of the rival

fraternities when they saw Hay come into chapel,
escorted by Burdge and myself, wearing the *Shield*
with the emblematical letters $\Theta\Delta X$, emblazoned on
its sable field! Notwithstanding the awful presence
of President Wayland and the august professors,
an universal and audible howl went up from the opposition, which evoked a corresponding cheer from
our side. The triumph was complete; and Dr. Wayland, pushing his spectacles up from his nose onto
his brow, was constrained to stand some moments
till the commotion had subsided, before offering up
his interrupted orisons." [1]

So vividly, after the lapse of half a century, did the
recollection of John Hay's capture by Theta Delta
Chi lie in the memory of Brother Stone — an indication of the importance attached by undergraduates to their societies and clubs! Hay proved
himself a loyal Theta Delt. His wit enlivened the
meetings and suppers; he wrote verses abundantly,
— one of his poems being sung at every reunion; [2]

[1] W. L. Stone in *The Shield*, XXI, 319-20 (September, 1905); organ
of the Theta Delta Chi Fraternity.

[2] The final stanza of this is: —

> " And if, perchance, one sadder line
>   May mingle with the strain,
> For those, the lost, whose loving voice
>   We ne'er shall hear again;
> Let this rejoice the heavy heart,
>   And light the dimming eye;
> The Gates of Eden are not closed
>   To Theta Delta Chi!"

and he formed lifelong associations with many of the brothers. A few years later, while serving as Secretary to President Lincoln, he saved from undeserved execution two Theta Delts; and afterwards, when he had risen to a position of great influence, he never forgot the claims of members of his fraternity.

But Johnny Hay — as his intimates called him — was too healthy-minded to be puffed up or spoiled even by the honor of election to Theta Delta Chi. During his first winter vacation, he writes his mother: "I am enjoying myself very well here, reading the newspapers, etc., writing a batch of letters, and loafing around in the city reading-rooms, varying these amusements with a quiet game of dominoes with Ed Morris.[1] . . . Certainly one of the greatest advantages of an Eastern college is the society into which a student is thrown. We live in a perfectly independent way, choose our own associates and our own mode of life, and if we belong to a secret society we have never any need of friends. Our society embraces many whom I shall be proud to know in after life, and whose friendship I now consider a 'feather in my cap.'"[2]

[1] Edgar R. Morris, of Quincy, Illinois.
[2] Hay to his mother, February 6, 1856. This seems to be one of the few early letters of Hay to his family that have not been destroyed. Not long before his death he burned all his home letters that he could find.

The more we see of him at Brown, the more we find him normally sensible, — if, indeed, to be sensible be normal. Possessing a good mind, with a natural hunger for literature, and especially for poetry, he read with zest; having also the desire to write, he used his pen freely, joyously, and with such success that he earned the reputation of being the best undergraduate writer in college. Over his admiring intimates his conversation cast a spell. With uncritical but pardonable enthusiasm they hailed him as "a young Dr. Johnson without his boorishness, or a Dr. Goldsmith without his frivolity." But while he inclined to intellectual pursuits, and perhaps got his keenest pleasure from them, he took part gladly, as has been hinted here, in undergraduate fun.

"'In those days, all text was memorized,' Mr. Norris relates; 'and it was the general opinion that Hay put his book under his pillow and had the contents thereof absorbed and digested by morning, for he was never seen "digging," or doing any other act or thing that could be construed into hard study. His quick perception, ready grasp of an idea and wonderfully retentive memory, made a mere pastime of study. His enthusiasm was boundless, and his love for and appreciation of the beautiful in nature and in art was acutely developed. If he was smitten with

(over)

the charms of a pretty girl, he raved and walked the
room pouring out his sentiment in a flood of furious
eloquence. He would apostrophize a beautiful sunset till the last glow had expired. I remember being
called out of bed by him one night to witness a
beautiful display of Northern Lights. The display
was gorgeous, but the night was cold, and after
stating my view of the situation, I retired to my
room leaving him with chattering teeth and eloquent
language addressing Aurora B.'" [1]

His college life meant more, however, than could
be reckoned by marks in the classroom, or by his
chats and frolics with his companions. Even his admission to the fraternity, which may have seemed,
at the time, to be the turning-point in his career, was
unimportant compared with some of the deeper
stirrings within him — signs not merely of growth,
but of capacities in himself which he had hardly suspected. Residence in an old community was quietly
transforming him. If he could have analyzed the
process he would have found that those traits of the
Westerner, which his comrades supposed to be of his
very essence, were, on the contrary, mere accidents.
Like the noble's child who, stolen by gypsies and
forced to lead their squalid life, on being restored

[1] A. S. Chapman, "The Boyhood of John Hay," *Century Magazine*, LVI, 450.

in manhood to his own people, quickly falls into their ways, so John Hay returned in Providence to the culture which he had vaguely craved all his days. Civilization in the making, as he saw it in Illinois, did not satisfy his instinctive longing for the finished product. Providence, though no Edinburgh or Florence or Athens, spoke to him of culture. Providence looked toward Europe and the East, the cradle and home of the ideals of the white man's race. Warsaw, Illinois, faced westward, upon the wilderness, which the imaginative little boy had mistaken for the end of the world.

In Providence there were some men and more women who not only understood what you meant by learning and literature and arts and the things of the spirit, but who actually had time to cherish them, and believed that neither making money nor any other material concern could equal them in importance. Outside of the academic circle, Providence boasted of a literary set, which encouraged lectures, welcomed passing authors, discussed the latest and read the standard books, and created that intangible thing which artists of all kinds hanker after — an atmosphere.

"In the summer of 1845, while passing through Providence, Poe had seen a lady among the roses of her garden in the moonlight. He had learned that she was a poetess — Mrs. Sarah Helen Whitman "; [1] and ten years later, when Hay went to Brown, this poetess held a place apart, both on account of her own productions and of her brief engagement to Poe. Although Mrs. Whitman, well on toward the middle fifties, might seem rather a dowager-like muse, she still kept alive the embers of passion, and she had the art of impressing those who knew her as an unusual person. It certainly was not genius, it might well be talent, that distinguished her. Handsome in youth, she kept her good looks into old age, and she let slip no means which might heighten the indefinable quality that attracted even strangers to her. She dressed always in white, and she appears to have sprinkled her garments with ether, instead of cologne or other perfume, which shed a fragrance suggestive of a neurotic condition in the wearer.

Toward the end of his college days, Hay was privileged to know Mrs. Whitman. She evidently appreciated his winning nature and lively wit, and looked very kindly upon his verses: but she was not an injudicious flatterer. She criticized frankly, and he accepted the criticism gratefully; for he was "very humble" in the presence of those whom he regarded as his superiors; and Mrs. Whitman's interest seemed to him an almost incredible favor. In his

[1] G. E. Woodberry, *Edgar Allan Poe* (Boston, 1909), II, 265.

letters to her after quitting Brown, he addressed her simply, "Mrs. Whitman," as if he dreaded to appear familiar or presuming. His reverence for her was unfeigned. "If I had had the honor of knowing you earlier," he writes, "I would have had less to regret in my collegiate course." [1]

The so-called romance of Mrs. Whitman's middle life — her bizarre relation with poor Poe, already ruined by drink and laudanum — added to her impressiveness; but Hay had probably read Poe's poems and tales before he met her. Among his undergraduate pieces several show Poe's influence. The following stanzas, unpublished so far as I know, might easily pass for one of Poe's pot-boilers: —

> "In a glimmering Kingdom of woe
>   On a plain demon-haunted I lie,
> And the specters that glide to and fro
>   With their wings blot the joy of the sky.

> "Let thy spirit shed o'er me the light
>   That it gained from the Father above,
> And my soul shall come out of the night
>   To the sunshine of Infinite Love." [2]

His acquaintance with Mrs. Whitman, the "priestess" at whose feet he sat, came at the end of Hay's Senior year. Almost at the same time he knew Nora

[1] From an unpublished letter in Brown University Library.
[2] MS. in Brown University Library.

Perry, a young poetess who had achieved local fame when the recently established *Atlantic Monthly* printed two or three of her poems. She, too, was drawn to the sympathetic youth, with his sparkling gifts. Although she was only five or six years his elder, he treated her with almost pathetic deference.

"The very fact of your writing to me," he says, in reply to a letter from her, "proved that you had an opinion of my powers which I might vainly strive to justify; and when I read the poems which you added, I was still more embarrassed in view of my situation. I despair of ever carrying on a correspondence on terms in any degree approaching equality with one whose mental plane is so far above my own." [1]

We hear of a Dr. Helme and other congenial members of the literary coterie, and of that erratic Celt, and future eulogist of Walt Whitman, William Douglas O'Connor, with whom Hay had cordial relations. Among his teachers, he found a hospitable welcome from Professor Angell, and when the students presented a cradle to the professor's first-born child, Hay wrote some lively verses, loaded with puns, which they sang to the tune of "Cocachelunk" and to the satisfaction of the Angells. Brown had two literary societies, of which the Philermenian elected

[1] *Poet in Exile*, p. 17; October 12, 1858.

Hay its vice-president. He was an editor of the *Brown Paper*, an undergraduate journal, and to its first number (November, 1857) he contributed "Sa! Sa!" a parody on Emerson's "Brahma," beginning: —

> "If the hazed Freshman thinks he's hazed,
>   And that he's passed his hazing pain;
>   He's sold — too high his hopes are raised,
>   The Soph'more goes but comes again."

Hay's parody, like many another, tickled brains that had never quite understood the original.

His classmate, Gilmore, relates an incident which illustrates Hay's inquiring disposition: —

"On one occasion, at least, his enthusiasm for literature was carried to excess. 'The Hasheesh-Eater' had recently appeared (1857); and Johnny must needs experiment with hasheesh a little, and see if it was such a marvelous stimulant to the imagination as Fitzhugh Ludlow affirmed. 'The night when Johnny Hay took hasheesh' marked an epoch for the dwellers in Hope College. It's fifty-six years ago; but I remember it well."

During his Junior and Senior years, Hay roomed at 44 Hope College. His life with his cronies grew more delightful term by term. His class recognized his ability by electing him Class Poet. Every one thought of him as of a fellow who would neither do a mean act nor tolerate it. As an indication of the happy memory his college contemporaries had of his chivalry, the story went the rounds, not long before he died, that at Brown he had rescued a Freshman named Gordon who was being smoked out by Sophomores. On being appealed to for the facts, Hay, then Secretary of State, replied that he did n't remember. "But," he added playfully, "my recollections of everything in those far-off days is dim, and heroism was my daily habit. I could n't sleep nights if I had n't saved somebody's life. Now I only save a nation now and then." [1]

So the last months of his college life glided happily by. Secure in his classmates' good-will and esteem, he enjoyed also the deeper satisfaction of being admitted to the group of literary men and women who lisped the language of his ideals. The only cloud that hung over him was the realization that he must soon renounce all this and go back to the West, which he had learned to loathe. There are also hints of a love-affair which made parting still harder.

On Class Day, June 10, 1858, he read his poem at Manning Hall to an audience which was enchanted by it. "His theme," says one reporter, "was 'The Power of Song,' [and] was marked by a fertility of conception, a depth of sensibility, and a power of

[1] *Brown Monthly*, February, 1906; pp. 141–42.

JOHN HAY WHEN A STUDENT AT BROWN UNIVERSITY

poetic expression, which we have rarely heard
equaled, and never surpassed, at any of our literary
anniversaries. It was agreeably enlivened by passages of keen wit and of pleasing humor, and was,
in every respect, a most scholarly and brilliant performance." According to another hearer, "the effort
caused tears and deafening applause to succeed each
other during its delivery." The recollection of Hay's
triumph lived on, and to-day it has become a tradition at Brown that no class poem ever matched his.
Old men can still recite for you its concluding lines,
which he cast in a stately and sonorous metre: —

> "Where'er afar the beck of fate shall call us,
>   'Mid winter's boreal chill or summer's blaze,
> Fond memory's chain of flowers shall still enthrall us,
>   Wreathed by the spirits of these vanished days:
> Our hearts shall bear them safe through life's commotion;
>   Their fading gleam shall light us to our graves;
> As in the shell the memories of ocean
>   Murmur forever of the sounding waves."

That evening there was a Class Supper at Hum-
phrey's; then, packing and good-byes. Hay always
kept a loyal and even affectionate regard for his
classmates, but he came back only once to their re-
unions, and many years elapsed before he revisited
Brown. He received the degree of Doctor of Laws
in 1897.[1] For the centennial of the University in

[1] His degree at graduation was Master of Arts.

1864 he wrote the ode, but his duties in Washington prevented him from reading it in person. He never ceased to be grateful to his *alma mater* for the windows on life she had opened to him; and his friendship for his classmates, although he saw them very seldom, did not die out. Toward the end of his life, he wrote to Mr. Henry Adams: "Why don't you go to your class anniversaries and get lionized and handshook and interviewed? I know why *I* don't — because I am an ass and a *dégénéré*, whose initiative is dead."

A few months later, looking back upon the three years he spent there, he wrote Miss Nora Perry: —

"If you loved Providence as I do, you would congratulate yourself hourly upon your lot. I turn my eyes Eastward, like an Islamite, when I feel prayerful. The city of Wayland and Williams, that smiles upon its beauty glassed in the still mirror of the Narragansett waves, is shrined in my memory as a far-off, mystical Eden, where the women were lovely and spirituelle, and the men were jolly and brave; where I used to haunt the rooms of the Athenæum, made holy by the presence of the royal dead; where I used to pay furtive visits to Forbes' forbidden mysteries (peace to its ashes!); where I used to eat Hasheesh and dream dreams. My life will not be utterly desolate while memory is left me, and while

I may recall the free pleasures of the student-time; pleasures in which there was no taint of selfishness commingled, and which lost half their sin in losing all their grossness. Day is not more different from night than they were from the wild excesses of the youth of this barbarous West." [1]

[1] *Poet in Exile*, pp. 22–23.

CHAPTER III

THE POET IN EXILE

JOHN HAY did not linger in Providence to receive his diploma at the Brown Commencement, which came in September, but he journeyed home by slow stages, stopping here and there to pay visits. That he had made an unusual impression on his college mates and teachers cannot be questioned, although a biographer must be on his guard against the natural tendency to magnification which the contemporaries of an illustrious man fall into when they look back. Hay's Class Poem and enough of his other verses remain to show that he fairly earned his distinction at Brown; and, although we cannot fail to regret that he destroyed his youthful letters home, we can surmise from other fragments and hints how his inner life was unfolding. He returned to Warsaw transformed from an expectant lad into a young man who believed that he had discovered his mission. Unfortunately for his peace of mind, that mission was as unadapted to his surroundings as a "rainbow to Wall Street."

Wanting to be a poet and a man of letters, Hay felt within himself the capacity therefor; and he dreamed that laurels awaited him. Whether they did or not, he knew that any other achievement would be empty compared with the satisfaction of serving the Muse. But although Illinois was pouring millions into the lap of many a business man or "railroad magnate," it would not then have furnished a daily mess of porridge to either a Milton or a Byron.

Hay's family welcomed him with joyful pride; yet even their affection could not supply what his enkindled nature now craved. His thoughts were fixed continually on the "good-bye lande" he had left. The change was too sudden, the contrast too bitter. He felt that he had been transplanted from a congenial soil and climate, to a land where winds were bleak and the earth was poor. He saw no hope for the future. To the youth capable of lively emotions, it seems inevitable that to day must be always.

As a foil to these introspective shadows of the young poet himself, we have the following letter, written by his father to his uncle, Milton Hay, to whom the youth owed his college education.

WARSAW, ILL., Sept. 6th, '58.

MY DEAR BROTHER, —

. . . John is now at home, and I am somewhat undecided as to what course I will advise him to pursue. Augustus and his mother both protested

against his becoming a schoolmaster in Warsaw —
at least ere entering upon the study of a profession.
So I did not put in his claims before our board of
education at the reëlection of teachers which took
place before John's return. I am not certain that
a berth of that kind would be a pleasant one for him
in Warsaw, and at all events the vacancies were so
far filled before his return that I suppose his position now would have to be one so subordinate, perhaps, that it would neither suit his self-esteem nor
his pecuniary wants. I have some reasons too for
not wishing to place him in a law office in Warsaw,
which it is unnecessary to name here now, and some
further reasons for not wishing him to remain at all
in Warsaw through the winter.

In the meantime some of his friends urge him to
turn his attention immediately to the law, while
others, especially some valued ones at the East, advise him to turn his attention at once and wholly to
literature. I wish him, of course, to have some profession upon which he can fall back, or rather rise
upon, while he is rising, *higher*. Upon what terms
can he enter your office and spend twelve months
as a student? His board bill I would endeavor to
render account for with the girls and sisters. He is
restless and wishes to know his destiny, although he
expects me to decide for him entirely. Augustus,

with his native ambitious aspirations, would have him set out on a splendid career at once. That is, if his purse were long enough he would have [him] return as a resident graduate to Brown, read extensively, and write for Eastern periodicals until a time and opening offered for taking a high position *somewhere*. But the purse is not full and will not be shortly at all events. I feel that I would do wrong not to encourage him to acquire a profession at once, and then do the best afterwards in that profession until a surer and better opening was apparent in some other direction. He thinks now that he cannot make a speaker, but I believe in the maxim of old Horace, "*Poeta nascitur, orator fit.*" The Poet is born, but the orator is made by cultivation. I will wait your answer before I make up my final decision as to what course he will be advised to this winter.

Hay passed through a long period of melancholy. How fully his family were aware of it, I have not learned. Outwardly, he meant to keep up a smiling front, so that perhaps they attributed any gloom they detected to his constitutional fits of depression. He had scarcely reached Warsaw before he referred to his life at Providence as a "happier state of existence," and he looked forward to "the solitude of a Western winter" with foreboding. His letters, few in number, to Miss Perry and to Mrs. Whitman, are truly representative. To those sympathetic ladies he revealed what he hid from others. Poets themselves, they would understand a poet.

On October 12, 1858, he writes to Miss Perry: —

"I shall never cease to congratulate myself upon the acquaintances I formed during the last few months of my stay in Providence. I found among them the objects for which my mind had always longed, true appreciation and sympathy. It is to their own goodness and generosity that I render all the kindness which I met with, and not to any qualities of my own; for it is the highest glory of genius to be quick in sympathy and prodigal of praise. But now when I am removed to a colder mental atmosphere, and the hopes and aspirations that gilded the gliding hours of my last year at college are fading away, I still can console myself with a dream of the possibilities that once were mine, and soothe my soul with the shadowy Might-have-been.

"In spite of the praise which you continually lavish upon the West, I must respectfully assert that I find only a dreary waste of heartless materialism, where great and heroic qualities may indeed bully their way up into the glare, but the flowers of existence inevitably droop and wither. So in time I shall change. I shall turn from 'the rose and the rainbow' to corner-lots and tax-titles, and a few years will find my eye not rolling in a fine frenzy, but steadily fixed on the pole-star of humanity, $!

"But I am not yet so far degraded that I cannot love poetry and worship a poet. So let me implore you to ask a favor of me as often as you possibly can — whatever it is, it is granted as soon as asked, if you will only acknowledge it as you did the last. If you will so far favor me, your letters will be a thread of gold woven into the dusky texture of a Western life.

"With unalloyed pleasure I copy that delicious 'La Papillon,' but are you not ashamed of your unnatural neglect? I would take the bright wanderer and claim it for my own if I dared. But it would look in my household like the last hope of Persia in the hovel of a cobbler of Bagdad." [1]

The highly literary quality of this letter need not lead us to suspect the sincerity of Hay's feelings. Addressing a poetess, he naturally indulged in the Parnassian dialect.

To Mrs. Whitman he wrote less exuberantly, but in the same vein: —

"I very much fear that if I remain in the West, I will entirely lose all the aspirations I formerly cherished, and see them fading with effortless apathy.

[1] *Poet in Exile*, pp. 17–19.

Under the influence of the Bœotian atmosphere around me, my spirit will be 'subdued to what it works in,' and my residence in the East will remain in memory, an oasis in the desolate stretch of a material life. So before the evil days come on I cling more and more eagerly to the ties which connect me with Providence and civilization, and only hope that those whose genius I have long admired and whose characters I lately learned to love, may not utterly cast me off, but sometimes reach me a hand in the darkness to raise and console."

Whatever tragedies of dashed hopes, thwarted ambitions, and mordant regrets were being enacted in John's distempered heart, he seemed fairly normal to those around him. From the next letter, which he wrote to his Uncle Milton, we infer that the young man was not only willing but eager to have the decision made which should put an end to his perplexity and self-searchings.

WARSAW, ILLINOIS, Jan. 28th, 1859.

MY DEAR UNCLE, —

Although I have very little to say, I write according to your request to let you know how I am getting along. I am not making the most rapid progress in the law. I have, as you advised, read all of Hume consecutively, and, to speak with moderation,

remember *some* of it. I would then immediately
have made an attack upon Blackstone, had I not
been prevented for a while by the general worth-
lessness induced by the distemper that has troubled
me more or less all the season. During the last few
weeks I have been occupied in making preparations
for a lecture before the "Literary Institute" in this
town. I delivered it last Saturday evening to the
best house I have ever seen in Warsaw. I think it
was well received. People did not expect much from
a boy, and so were more than satisfied. I have been
asked to write again but shall not. It is too great
an expenditure of time for no pay but nine days'
glory.

It has had one effect, at least. It has convinced
my very pious friends in this place that there is no
sphere of life, for me, but the pulpit. I have been
repeatedly told by lawyers here that I will never
make my living by pettifogging. This is, of course,
very encouraging, but I think, if my manifest destiny is to starve, I prefer to do it in a position where
I will have only myself to blame for it. I would not
do for a Methodist preacher, for I am a poor horse-
man. I would not suit the Baptists, for I dislike
water. I would fail as an Episcopalian, for I am no
ladies' man. In spite of my remonstrance, however,
I am button-holed in the street daily, and exhorted

to enter into orders. Our minister here has loaded
me with books which he innocently expects me to
read — as if my life was long enough. I find it the
easiest way to agree with everything they say and
to follow the example of the shrewd youth in the
parable, who "said, 'I go,' and went not."

I have a quiet room here to myself in which I can
do as much as I could anywhere, alone. I suppose
that I miss the personal superintendence of a precep-
tor, but hope that I can make up for that loss hereafter. If you think, at any time, that I can engage
in anything profitable, either to myself or others,
by coming to Springfield, I am ready to come. You
spoke of a possibility of my succeeding, in case of a vacancy, to a berth in the Auditor's office. That would
be especially pleasant, as I suppose it would give
me free access to the libraries in the State House.
However, I am very easily contented, in whatever
sphere I may be placed, and can always wait for the
tide of circumstances without any inconvenience.
Meanwhile, I will go on and read Blackstone at
home. It is as pleasant as possible in Warsaw now.
. . . I send you what our paper has to say about my
lecture.

Please remember me to all the family, especially
to Grandfather.

JOHN M. HAY.

The newspaper clipping says that Mr. J. M. Hay's lecture, upon the "History of the Jesuits," was "a very able and eloquent effort, indeed, considering the age of the speaker — being not yet twenty years of age. . . . The church was crowded with listeners, many of whom were unable to get seats. . . . His voice was strong and clear, and his manner of delivery excellent — far surpassing that of any person we have before heard in our city. . . . Being raised in this city, of course many turned out to hear him, and not one have we heard who was not well pleased with his effort, and who does not accord to him all praise for historical research, and for the fine flights of eloquence of which he delivered himself at intervals throughout the lecture. The parents of this young man may justly feel proud of him, as do the citizens of our city, for his intelligence and manly bearing. He has the talents, and if he does not make his mark in the world as a bright and shining light, the fault is with himself."

John Hay lived to read many eulogies on his writings, but perhaps he rarely felt a more genuine thrill than when he saw this first certificate to local fame. His letter to his uncle reveals his inner nature not less certainly than do his dithyrambic effusions to Miss Perry and Mrs. Whitman. Especially noticeable is the trait, which clung to him through life, of reluctance to push himself forward. This was due not to self-distrust, but to a shy fastidiousness.

On December 15, 1858, Hay writes again to Mrs. Whitman: ". . . It may seem little to you to give a few words of generous praise to a moody boy or to send an exile in the West stray glimpses of the pleasant world he has left forever." He then refers to her description of Niagara Falls, which reminded him "of thoughts that came dimly to me as I stood in the spray of that infinite torrent, and which seemed to me unutterable. And is not this the office of Genius? to set in clear and intelligible forms of beauty the vague and chaotic fancies that flit across the minds of the multitude? Is not the poet rather an Interpreter than a Creator? It is almost the same in effect. All the Greeks thought Olympus majestic till some shepherd-poet peopled it with gods. Those fancies which in the common mind are the wild and restless float of the waves, become embodied in the mind of the poet, in the perfect beauty of Aphrodite hanging forever in god-like loveliness above the tumultuous waste of the unresting seas." He excuses his silence of several months. "I have been very near the Valley of the Shadow. I felt the deprivation keenly in the fall, when the woods were blazing with the autumnal transfiguration, and the night slept tranced in the love of the harvest moon.

I am now as well as ever." But he despairs of going East to live. "A few months of exile has worn the luster from my dreams and well-nigh quenched all liberal aspirations. I do not see how I could gain either honor or profit by writing, so I suppose the sooner I turn my attention to those practical studies which are to minister to the material wants in the West, the better it will be. . . . It is dangerous for me to write the names of Eastern friends. It makes me discontented with my surroundings." [1]

On January 2, 1859, Hay writes to Miss Perry, whom he ventures to address as "Nora," and congratulates her on her ideal position. "The world must be very fair as seen through the rosy atmosphere of luxuriant youth and maidenhood." He, on the contrary, is called to the "barbarous West," yet he accepts "calmly, if not joyfully, the challenge of fate. From present indications my sojourn in this 'wale of tears,' as the elder Weller pathetically styles it, will not be very protracted. I can stand it for a few years, I suppose. My father, with more ambition and higher ideals than I, has dwelt and labored here a lifetime, and even this winter does not despair of creating an interest in things intellectual among the great unshorn of the prairies. I am not suited for a reformer. I do not like to meddle with

[1] From an unpublished letter in Brown University Library.

moral ills. I love comfortable people. In the words of the poet Pigwiggen . . . 'I know I'm a genus, 'cause I hate work worse'n thunder, and would like to cut my throat — only it hurts. . . .' There is, as yet, no room in the West for a genius. . . . Impudence and rascality are the talismans that open the gates of preferment. I am a Westerner. The influences of civilization galvanized me for a time into a feverish life, but they will vanish before this death-in-life of solitude. I chose it, however, and my blood is on my own head." In conclusion, he encloses as an offering to Mrs. Whitman, two poems, "Parted" and "In the Mist." [1]

Throughout the autumn and winter, Hay experienced that disenchantment with the world which often overshadows alike the artistic and the devout in their first serious encounter with life. Common though the disillusion is, each of its victims supposes that he is the first to suffer under it. In Hay's case, it coincided with one of his periodic fits of melancholia. He desired to be a poet. His recent happy years in the East had not only developed his poetic talents, but they had also brought the confirmation of the persons whose judgment he trusted. If Nora Perry, if Mrs. Whitman encouraged him in his ambition, how could he doubt?

[1] *Poet in Exile*, pp. 22–25.

But "being a poet" is such a different matter from what the young aspirant imagines! Primarily, because the world, with its hard common sense, cares in the long run for only good poetry; and since it often requires a generation to sift the bad from the good, the poet may be dead before his work is accepted. By what seems a sardonic decree, poets — privileged beholders and describers of the ideal — are locked up in human bodies, which must be fed, clothed, and housed: and the unrecognized bard, if he have only his poems to pay for the necessaries, will go hungry and naked. Instead of charging Fate with cruelty, however, we ought to perceive that this provision automatically saves the world from being overrun by third-rate poetasters: and we may even argue that Fate is on the side of the good poets. The Muse is as jealous a mistress now as ever she was; and when any of her young devotees dreams that he could worship her best if he had a sufficient bank account, he reveals that he is either unworthy or callow.

Through those bitter months Hay ruminated on these things. Having set his heart on the brightest, he learned that the cosmic laws would not be changed for his benefit. When a youth discovers that special favors are not accorded to the virtuous, he feels as Job, the just man, felt, that he has been betrayed by the moral scheme in which he confided, and he asks himself whether it is worth while to go on living in a world capable of such treachery. Hay drank his cup of wormwood to the bottom. How deeply he suffered appears in the following letter.

"I have wandered this winter in the valley of the shadow of death," Hay wrote Miss Perry in the spring. "All the universe, God, earth, and heaven have been to me but vague and gloomy phantasms. I have conversed with wild imaginings in the gloom of the forests. I have sat long hours by the sandy marge of my magnificent river, and felt the awful mystery of its unending flow, and heard an infinite lament breathed in the unquiet murmur of its whispering ripples. Never before have I been so much in society. Yet into every parlor my Dæmon has pursued me. When the air has been fainting with poisoned perfumes, when every spirit thrilled to the delicate touch of airy harmonies, when perfect forms moved in unison with perfect music, and mocked with their voluptuous grace the tortured aspirations of poetry, I have felt, coming over my soul, colder than a northern wind, a conviction of the hideous unreality of all that moved and swayed and throbbed before me. It was not with the eye of a bigot, or the diseased perceptions of a penitent, that

I looked upon such scenes; it was with what seemed
to me —

"Thus far I wrote, and turned over the page and
wrote no more for an hour. You have had enough
of that kind of agonized confession, have n't you?
An open human heart is not a pleasant thing. I only
wanted to tell you why I had not written. It would
have been easier to say it was simply impossible." [1]

Again we note the premeditated, literary quality
of his personal confession, and we wonder whether
the suffering could be genuine which he described in
such nicely balanced, rhetorical sentences. But we
must remember that he was consciously trying to
write up to what he assumed to be Nora Perry's
ethereal plane; that he had been feeding on the works
of the Romanticists then in fashion; and that, as is
the way with young authors absorbed in their own
emotions, he dramatized himself.

Poet he wished to be, and if his wit had had the
compulsion of genius, neither poverty, nor hardships,
nor the world's neglect would have restrained him.
He would have managed somehow to sing in Warsaw, Illinois, as validly as Robert Burns did in Moss-
giel, Scotland. He gave up his career reluctantly,
with poignant regret, but without any after effects of
cynicism. First love may be sweetest, but it is not

[1] *Poet in Exile*, pp. 41–42: Springfield, Illinois, May 15, 1859.

the deepest; and although Hay could not forsake all
else to follow the Muse, still he never lost his enthusiasm for her; and up to the end of his life, when any
emotion stirred him greatly, he sought a vent for it
in verse.

Hay's family recognized his literary achievement
at Brown, and were proud of it, and they allowed
him ample time to choose his life-work. When he
had convinced himself that his poet dream could not
be realized, and had canvassed and discarded various
suggestions, — including the ministry, — he finally
settled upon the law. "They would spoil a first-
class preacher to make a third-class lawyer of me,"
he is reported to have said. His father would have
been glad to have one son follow his own profession:
but John and his brothers had seen too much of the
laboriousness of the life of a country doctor to care
to undertake it. The law, on the other hand, held
out special inducements: for John was to enter the
office at Springfield of his Uncle Milton, who stood
among the leaders of the Illinois Bar. Might not the
law be regarded almost as a literary profession?
Had not the ranks of men of letters been recruited
from the lawyers? At that very moment did not
James Russell Lowell's case prove that, given the
right endowment, one might mount from apprenticeship in the law to the sphere of poetry and belles-

lettres? A successful lawyer might earn a sufficient fortune to retire from practice and devote himself to literature while he was still young enough to win fame therein: just as middle-aged men sometimes marry the sweethearts of their youth — with the happiest results.

Disappointed, but not cast down, John Hay accordingly began his legal training with his Uncle Milton in the spring of 1859. Before we describe his new life, however, we will conclude his self-revelations to Miss Perry.

He wrote the glowing letter just quoted, after he had settled in Springfield. "I am now at work," he added. "In work I always find rest. A strange paradox — but true. If my health returns, I do not question but that I shall work out of these shadows. If not, there is a cool rest under the violets, and eternity is long enough to make right the errors and deficiencies of time." [1]

Here is the familiar note which youth utters when bereavement or self-abnegation or contrition sweeps over it. "I can bear — but I am sure to die soon," says the young self-pitier, unaware that vanity and not fortitude is speaking, and that grief has its luxury which must be checked. In Hay's case, there seems no doubt that he suffered from poor health

[1] *Poet in Exile*, pp. 42–43.

that winter; possibly he thought that he had a disease
which would soon carry him off: but his yearning for
rest under the violets is so common among youths
who take Fate's rebuffs sentimentally that we need
not be alarmed by it. Nevertheless, we must not be-
little the burden of misery which a nature like his
actually feels under such conditions.

Nearly a year later, although he was then outwardly wrapped up in his new career at Springfield,
he replied regretfully to a letter from Miss Perry: —

"I hope you may never be placed in a situation where
you will be able to sympathize with my present habi-
tudes of mind, or appreciate the feelings of grateful
delight occasioned by a kindness like your last.

"When, in the midst of my laborious and intensely
practical studies, the current of my thoughts is
changed by a reminder of a state of existence so
much higher than mine, I feel for a moment as a
pilgrim might have felt, in the days when angels
walked with men, who, lying weary and exhausted
with his toilsome journey, has heard in the desert
silence faint hints of celestial melody, and seen the
desolate sands empurpled and glorified with a fleeting flash of spiritual wings.

"The splendor fades, but the ripples of memory
still stir the stagnant waters of the soul, and life is
less dreary that the vision has come and gone.

"It is cowardly in me to cling so persistently to a life which is past. It is my duty, and in truth it is my ultimate intention to qualify myself for a Western lawyer, *et præterea nihil*, 'only that and nothing more.' Along the path of my future life, short though it be, my vision runs unchecked. No devious ways. No glimpses of sudden splendor striking athwart. No mysteries. No deep shadows, save those in my own soul, for I expect prosperity, speaking after the manner of men. No intense lights but at the end. So my life lies. A straight path — on both sides quiet labor, at the end, Death and Rest.

"Yet though I know all this, though I feel that Illinois and Rhode Island are entirely antipathetic, though I am aware that thy people are not my people, nor thy God my God, I cannot shut my friends out of my memory or annihilate the pleasant past. I cannot help being delighted to receive a letter from you, and to know that the Doctor [Helme] sometimes remembers me. When I read 'After the Ball,' and when, going into the State House, the Secretary of State said to me, 'Hay, have you read the last *Atlantic?* there is the prettiest poem there this month it has ever published!' I could not help feeling a personal pride that I had heard it read, alive with the poet's voice and warm from the poet's heart.

"What more can I say than to confess that my friends are necessary to me, to ask you to give my love to the Doctor, and to write to me as soon as you will. How glad I am that the world is learning to love Mrs. Whitman as much as those who have sat at the feet of the revered Priestess." [1]

In this letter, even more than in the earlier, we perceive that Hay treats himself as he might any one else, whose plight he tries to describe in the finest literary style. He is not insincere; he is simply the artist, using his own emotions as stuff for his story. When this tendency becomes a habit, spontaneity gives way to artificiality: as in the case of Robert Louis Stevenson, who would spit blood in his handkerchief, and a few minutes later seize his pen and write — in a private letter intended for the world to admire — an account of the affair, so vivid, so correct, so "faultily faultless," that teachers of English might hold it up as a model to illiterate Freshmen.

Hay, however, was still far from this pitch of artistic self-intoxication, and, thanks to happy influences, which came to him in the disguise of disappointment, he never reached it. He believed that what he wrote to Miss Perry depicted, however faintly, the anguish of his soul. He wished also to free himself from the suspicion of having cravenly

[1] *Poet in Exile*, pp. 44-46: Springfield, Illinois, March 4, 1860.

deserted the ideal life. He still loved the Muse best, and only under the duress of necessity was he embarking on the worldly profession of the law. But though he might prosper, — and he expected "prosperity, speaking after the manner of men," — his heart would remain true to the ideal.

Just as a new life, of amazing inspiration, was opening for him, he thus pledged his devotion to the old: and he never wavered in it. Long afterward, when he appeared to strangers an accomplished man of the world, or when he staggered under the burdens of statesmanship, he heard again, and thrilled to hear, the poetic voices which captivated his youth. So, at certain seasons, dwellers on the Breton coast hear the pealing of the bells of the city which the waves submerged long, long ago.

CHAPTER IV

THE NEW LIFE

IN March or April, 1859, John Hay went to Springfield, to read law with his uncle, who was head of one of the oldest and most successful firms in the West. Fifteen years before, when Stephen T. Logan directed it, Abraham Lincoln had been a partner, and, besides him, two of his associates became Congressmen. Under Milton Hay, the office continued to be a nursery "for cradling public men": [1] for law and politics interlocked so closely that they often seemed merely two aspects of the same profession. It required far less acumen than young John Hay possessed to discern that the road to fortune lay through that office. The material expansion of Illinois — its railroads, its industries, its rapidly growing cities and towns, with the consequent fixing of titles and contracts and the adjusting of claims — made the lawyer the one indispensable member of the community. Men might manage to shift without the doctor, because Nature herself sometimes

---

[1] N. & H., I, 214, n. I. "John M. Palmer and Shelby M. Cullom left it to become Governors of the State, and the latter to be a Congressman and Senator."

worked a cure; and at a pinch they could do even without the minister, taking their chances as to the hereafter; but they needed the lawyer at every turn, and it was only a step from applying the laws to framing them. So Hay might hope, with reasonable diligence, either to prosper at the bar, or, if he preferred, to enter public life, which offered fame as well as fortune.

Far more important was it to the young apprentice, however, that both his position and his occupation threw him into relations, sometimes very friendly, with the leading men of Illinois. Such a privilege could come only in a community which, although small numerically, held the keys to vast enterprises. The material development of Illinois was at that period of incalculable significance. But it involved far more than the building up of the State itself; for the growth of the new Northwest and the exploitation of transcontinental projects were affected, directly or indirectly, by the attitude of Illinois, and this, in turn, depended upon the lawmakers at Springfield. And just at this time political concerns had begun to overshadow material. The crisis which had been preparing since the formation of the American Union could no longer be avoided, either by compromise, or threat, or ignoble subservience. In this crisis Fate summoned Illinois to play a pivotal part; and it happened that the providential man, not only for Illinois, but for the American Union, and for the maintenance of Anglo-Saxon civilization in the United States, occupied a shabby law office alongside of Milton Hay's, and practiced his profession during those intervals when politics did not utterly engross him.

This was Abraham Lincoln, now in his fiftieth year, who only recently, by his joint debates with Judge Stephen A. Douglas, had sent his reputation beyond the borders of the State. Even his neighbors and acquaintances, of whom he counted hundreds in central and northern Illinois, did not fully understand the genius which inspired Lincoln in that campaign. His speeches, whether in attack or rebuttal, stand alone in modern oratory: we must go back to the Socratic dialogues to find their parallels. He spoke so simply, he met his enemy's points so honestly and demolished them so easily, that his hearers, though entirely convinced, discovered nothing unusual in his performance. Eloquence still meant to them the Olympian dignity and the deep, sonorous voice of Daniel Webster, and the tidal ebb and flow of his periods, and the polish of his diction; or it meant the forceful declamation of Calhoun, or Wendell Phillips's invectives gleaming like bayonets in the sun.

Lincoln differed from all these. He had neither Webster's imperial presence, nor the rich, supple voice, nor the polished diction and gestures of the model orator. He breathed no echo of Burke or Chatham, no reminder of Cicero or Demosthenes. He was plain Abraham Lincoln, addressing crowds in the prairie towns as naturally as he would have talked to them one by one on his front porch. He had a power rarer than intellectual keenness or the zealot's fervor, or than intoxicating eloquence — the power to penetrate to fundamental principles. He saw the simple bases on which slavery and abolition, union and secession, finally rested; and in every debate he quickly stripped away confusing details and laid bare the essentials, which he presented so simply that they had the settled quality of scientific formulas. But he clothed his arguments in some parable or picturesque figure which everybody understood, and could not forget; and he spoke so sincerely that it was evident that he set truth above a political victory. Where Douglas evaded or straddled, Lincoln stood on principle; he resorted to no devices and wasted no time on quibbles, but squarely dislodged Douglas from one perch after another. Lincoln's good-nature, his humor, his wit, and large-hearted charity were as conspicuous as his trenchant logic — indeed, they sometimes blinded his hearers to the

extraordinary skill with which he upheld his cause.
We see now that while he was ostensibly working
for the success of the Republican Party in the next
election and his own choice as senator, he was really
proclaiming the impossibility that the nation should
continue half-bond, half-free, and he was restating
the fundamental principles without which civilization sinks into barbarism.

In November, 1858, the Republicans outvoted the
Douglas Democrats: when the legislature met, however, Douglas beat Lincoln for the senatorship by
eight votes; and while he went in triumph to the
United States Senate, Lincoln returned to his law
office in Springfield.   But the triumph was brief.
The Little Giant's prestige withered under the effect
of Lincoln's remorseless criticism, and although he
lived barely three years, at his death he had already
outworn his influence. History will not forget him,
however much he might pray to be forgotten; because he is as indissolubly bound up with Lincoln's
immortality as Brutus is with Cæsar's. He remains
as a warning to men of good intentions, much vanity, and no solid morality, who, in a national crisis,
when the differences between conflicting principles
stand out as uncompromisingly as life and death,
insist that it is only a matter of shading; that by
calling "black""white" and "white" "black" you

can make them so; that, after all, there are no immutable *things*, but only *adjectives*, which can be transposed or varied, like a girl's ribbons, to suit your fancy.

Abraham Lincoln believed that there are certain eternal distinctions between right and wrong, and he shattered Douglas's makeshifts as the Matterhorn shatters the troops of clouds which drive against it from one direction to another. And even though they should hide the mighty peak for a day, they never can be more than clouds, unsubstantial and evanescent, whereas the Matterhorn is granite and endures.

"I am glad I made the late race," Lincoln wrote to a friend. "It gave me a hearing on the great and durable questions of the age, which I could have had in no other way; and though I sink out of view, and shall be forgotten, I believe I have made some marks for the cause of civil liberty long after I am gone." [1]

To another correspondent he replied: "The fight must go on. The cause of civil liberty must not be surrendered at the end of one or even one hundred defeats. Douglas had the ingenuity to be supported in the late contest, both as the means to break down and to uphold the slave interest. No

[1] Lincoln to Henry, November 19, 1858.

ingenuity can keep these antagonistic elements in harmony long. Another explosion will soon come."[1]

When John Hay[2] began his career in his Uncle Milton's office, he found this strange figure next door, and it could not have been long before he, like every one else, was listening to Lincoln's stories and was feeling the indefinable fascination of his homely wit and moral fervor. Not that Hay at twenty-one suspected the heroic possibilities in the sad-eyed, ungainly pioneer, who uttered parables in language that might have been taken from the New Testament, or indulged in coarse jokes, or drew vivid word-portraits of the Western notables, or stated political issues with masterly clearness. Young Hay, still regretting his parting from the Muses, and still surreptitiously seeking their inspiration, could not be expected to recognize in Lincoln their substitute.

But even casual association with "Honest Abe," as his fellow citizens called him, could not fail to affect the impressionable youth. By nature sanguine and social, Hay was not of those who can nurse a life-long sorrow. His heart required time in order to be reconciled to the surrender of its poetic dreams, but his head acquiesced, and, acquiescing, took an eager

[1] Lincoln to Asbury, November 19, 1858. Both in N. & H., II, 169.
[2] On leaving Brown, Hay dropped his middle name, "Milton."

interest in the men with whom he was thrown; and
his intellectual curiosity kindled by degrees into passionate zeal.

Indeed, only a creature as emotionless as pumice-
stone could remain torpid in that crisis, when the
conflict — foreseen, dreaded, dodged, smothered, for
as far back as men could remember — was bursting
into flame. To be neutral then was to be an out-
cast. Every one must choose his side, for or against
slavery and secession. The question was compli-
cated, however, because a man who detested slavery might honestly believe that the preservation of
the Union, even with slavery allowed to continue in
the Southern States, was the chief concern. To destroy the Union would not free the slaves, but would
set up two hostile republics instead of one which,
although then torn by sectional differences, seemed
intended by destiny to remain one.

Brought up in a family which never swerved in
its devotion to freedom, John Hay absorbed his political opinions, as a boy does, from listening to his
elders. Owing to the loss of his early correspondence,
we have no means of tracing his opinions on national affairs; but this can hardly matter, because
he did not begin to think for himself until after he
returned to Springfield. He makes only one reference to politics in the letters which I have seen.

Writing to his mother from Providence on February 6, 1856, he says: "Banks is Speaker. There is very little enthusiasm here. But they rejoice in a quiet Yankee sort of way. How 'all-overish' I felt one evening when Mrs. Hunt was flaying the Abolitionists alive. Southern Chivalry is in the ashes at present. '*Sic semper Tyrannis*' says the North." [1]

Three years later, when Hay was studying law, the recently formed Republican Party had become powerful as the successor of the old Whigs and, still more, as the party of the zealous young men in the North, who were resolved to prevent further encroachments by the Southern slaveocracy. It was at that happy stage in the development of an institution when its ideals, unsullied as yet by selfish desires, justified the enthusiasm of its supporters. Its principles had the compulsion of religion; and rightly so, because they aimed at carrying out in the sphere of public life the behests of private conscience.

Despite his avowal that he was not suited for a reformer, and that he did not like to meddle with moral ills, John Hay enrolled himself as a Republican, and we cannot doubt that he soon felt the moral

[1] Unedited letter. On February 2, 1856, N. P. Banks, of Massachusetts, the Republican candidate, was elected Speaker of the House of Representatives by 103 votes to 100 for Aiken, of South Carolina.

stimulus of working with a party dedicated to human liberty. His sense of humor, always alert, kept him from being blind to the crudities of political action; but his zeal was stronger still.

Little record has come to hand of his apprenticeship in law. His uncle's office, which transacted all sorts of legal business, offered every opportunity for a thorough and well-rounded training. Hay was spasmodically diligent, and having made up his mind to be a lawyer, he exerted himself, as was his fashion, to succeed. In due season — February 4, 1861 — he was admitted to the bar.

On the surface, however, Hay appeared to his associates at this time as a young man of varied rather than serious interests. Quick at repartee and puns, lovable in disposition, he was a favorite at every social gathering. The girls delighted in him, and he in them; but, as one of the survivors writes me, "he found safety in numbers." They took French lessons together; they went to sociables and church fairs; they attended sermons and lectures and political rallies. Hay shone not only as the wittiest of the younger set, but as the winner of unusual distinction in an Eastern college, and as a reader and poet. His opinions on books made the rounds. His verses, sparkling or sentimental, were treasured by their recipients, and quoted. Even his sedate friend John

Nicolay, who had settled in Springfield to edit a newspaper, was enlivened by Hay's example.

Two specimens of Hay's fun, though but trifles, may be cited. The first is a note, sent to three sisters "with a huge bunch of wild, blue phlox, 1860":—

"I am lamentably ignorant as to whether Goldsmith is one of your favorite poets, but if he is, you have doubtless admired his beautiful and merciful lines: —

> "'No Phlox that range the valley free
>   To slaughter I condemn;
> Taught by the power that pities me,
>   I learn to pity them.'"

Another is from an invitation from Hay to one of these sisters to go with him to hear Lincoln speak in Cook's Hall. Like several of his notes, it is written in a French which gives it a more comical touch: —

"Je suis bien heureux que je puis annoncer a vous que M. Lincoln, l'honnête vieux Abe, va faire un discours a la salle du Cuisinier demain au soir. Voulez vous rappeler votre promesse et m'accompagner? J'espère d'entendre beaucoup de les choses bonnes, qui reposent comme Lazare après son mort, en 'Abraham's Bosom.'" [1]

Whatever regrets Hay buried in his heart, he faced the world so buoyantly that we may assume

[1] Printed as written.

that the wounds of disappointment were healing sooner than he imagined.

In the retrospect, even Warsaw gleamed with charms for him. On November 29, 1861, he wrote to a dear young friend there: —

"Warsaw dull? It shines before my eyes like a social paradise compared with this miserable sprawling village [Washington] which imagines itself a city because it is wicked, as a boy thinks he is a man when he smokes and swears. I wish I could by wishing find myself in Warsaw.

"I am cross because I am away from Warsaw. I believe honestly (if it is possible for me to believe anything honestly) that I shall never enjoy myself more thoroughly than I did that short little winter I spent at home. It was so quiet and so still, so free from anything that could disturb or bore me, that it seems in the busy days I am wearing out now like a queer little dream of contentment and peace, when I so obstinately and persistently left the dear old town that rainy, tearful, doleful Monday afternoon. I never before was so anxious to see Warsaw, or so reluctant to leave it. It is a good thing to go home. I seem to take a new lease on life; to renew a fast-fleeting youth on the breezy hills of my home. I feel like doing a marvelous amount of work when I return, and the dull routine of everyday labor is charmingly relieved by vanishing visions of green hills, grand rivers, and willowy islands that float between me and my paper." [1]

By the spring of 1860 he took a keen interest in the political campaign. The Republican State Convention, which met at Decatur on May 9 and 10, nominated Lincoln as Illinois' candidate for President. Then occurred that picturesque scene which illustrates how mankind is often more impressed by symbols than by what the symbols stand for. Before the vote was taken, word came from outside that an old Democrat had something he wished to give the convention. Presently, in came Lincoln's cousin, John Hanks, bearing two rails, and a banner with the inscription: "Abraham Lincoln, the rail candidate for President in 1860. Two rails from a lot of 3000 made in 1830 by Thomas Hanks and Abe Lincoln — whose father was the first pioneer of Macon County." Amid a rush of enthusiasm the convention voted for the "Rail-splitter," and this nomination the Republican National Convention confirmed at Chicago a week later, when, on the third ballot, Lincoln distanced Seward, New York's favorite son, and was declared the unanimous choice of the party (May 17, 1860).

From that moment, Springfield, Illinois, loomed

[1] *Century*, LXI, 453.

up in national importance. During the summer and autumn it seethed with politics. Every Republican politician, every friend of Lincoln, and even lukewarm partisans who, notwithstanding, desired to see him elected for the honor of the city and the State, joined in the campaign. The young men threw themselves into the cause with the ardor of Crusaders. Among them was Hay, who worked to enroll supporters and spoke at meetings as enthusiastically as if he had not deplored, in his letters to the poetesses at Providence, the hopeless materialism of the unshorn men of the prairies. He began to be electrified by the ideals which underlay the Republican movement. Nicolay served Lincoln as secretary in the campaign, and Hay helped Nicolay.

After his election as President, on November 6, Lincoln appointed Nicolay as his private secretary. His duties increased to such proportions that, although he was one of the most industrious of men, they soon exceeded his capacity, and he suggested that Hay be employed as assistant secretary. "We can't take all Illinois with us down to Washington," the President-elect said, good-humoredly; and then after a pause, as if relenting, he added: "Well, let Hay come."

Thus Fortune opened her door to the young man of twenty-two. Instead of condemning him to perpetual banishment in the "West," she led him to the East, to Washington, to the White House, to be the confidential helper of "the most sympathetic among all Americans, living or dead," at the most exciting national crisis since the American Union was founded. Hay knew that this experience could not fail to be a stepping-stone to whatever he might do later. President Lincoln, we may believe, saw more in him than a clerical assistant — clerks could be had anywhere: he saw the fresh, easy-mannered, sunny companion, who might relieve the tedium of routine life; the youth who, apparently understanding by intuition the ways of the world, might on occasion smooth over social roughnesses which the President himself would hardly have noticed. Nicolay, too, prized the frank nature and quick intelligence of the friend of his boyhood. It meant much for him to have an assistant who was at once congenial and willing and versatile.

So John Hay said good-bye to his uncle's law office, and to the young women who cherished his verses, and to his parents and friends at Warsaw; and on February 11, 1861, he started with Lincoln and the presidential party on their roundabout journey to Washington. The President's last words to his neighbors, before the train steamed out of Springfield, were full of sadness and affection, as became

one who realized the weight of the burden he was going away to take up, and the quick alternations of
life and death. What young Hay thought at that
moment we are not told; but it would be strange if
he were not thrilled at the prospect of plunging
into a new world, of unknown and alluring possibilities. Like many another poet in embryo, he was
soon to feel the exhilaration which comes from doing
after dreaming.

CHAPTER V

FIRST MONTHS IN THE WHITE HOUSE

ABRAHAM LINCOLN read his Inaugural Address at the Capitol on March 4, 1861. Since Washington's Farewell, no presidential utterance had moved the country so deeply as that, and of Lincoln's many stirring passages in it none equaled his concluding lines: "I am loth to close. We are not enemies, but friends. We must not be enemies. Though passion may have strained, it must not break our bonds of affection. The mystic chords of memory, stretching from every battlefield, and patriot grave, to every living heart and hearthstone, all over this broad land, will yet swell the chorus of the Union, when again touched, as they surely will be, by the better angels of our nature." [1] When John Hay's friends and classmates read that paragraph, they believed that he wrote it — so high was their estimate of his poetic talents and so little as yet did they discern the literary genius of Lincoln.

From that day Nicolay and Hay lived in the White House, within a moment's call of the President. The

[1] The passage was written by Lincoln, who transmuted Seward's suggestion into pure gold. N. & H., III, 336, 341 *n*.

small chambers assigned to them were shabby and scantily furnished; but the secretaries were young and used to roughing it, and they were soon too busy to heed passing discomforts. Nicolay had charge of the more official correspondence. Hay, who often took his share of this burden, wrote letters, saw callers, went on errands to the Departments, kept in touch with personages political, military, and social, and, in case of need, escorted Mrs. Lincoln when she drove out, or amused the Lincoln boys on a rainy day. He made himself very quickly a member of the family; and Lincoln, the most unconventional of men, welcomed his young, versatile, and trustworthy assistant, whose willingness and common sense could always be depended upon.

During the first weeks of the Administration, suspense prevailed in the White House and throughout the Government. Men realized that the relations with the Southern States were growing worse, not better, but they still regarded with incredulity the likelihood of a civil war. Lincoln had pledged himself not to be the aggressor: many anxious Northerners still hoped that even fanatical Secessionists would stop short before striking the irrevocable blow. News of the firing on Fort Sumter in Charleston Harbor, on April 12, and of its evacuation by the Union commander on April 14, dispelled

the last doubt. On April 15 President Lincoln issued his call for 75,000 volunteers.

Three days later Hay records in his Diary: "The
White House is turned into barracks. Jim Lane [1]
marshaled his Kansas warriors to-day at Willard's
and placed them at the disposal of Major Hunter,
who turned them to-night into the East Room. It
is a splendid company — worthy such an armory.
Besides the Western Jayhawkers it comprises some
of the best *material* in the East. Senator Pomeroy
and old Anthony Bleecker stood shoulder to shoulder
in the ranks. Jim Lane walked proudly up and
down the ranks with a new sword that the Major
had given him. The Major has made me his aid,
and I labored under some uncertainty, as to whether
I should speak to privates or not.

"The President to-day received this dispatch, 'We
entreat you to take immediate measures to protect
American Commerce in the Southern waters and
we respectfully suggest the charter or purchase of
steamers of which a number can be fitted from here
without delay.' Signed by Grinnell Minturn and
many others of the leading business men of the
place. The President immediately sent for the Cabinet. They came together and Seward [2] answered the

---

[1] James H. Lane, of Kansas, border-fighter, United States Senator, and brigadier-general of volunteers.

[2] William H. Seward, Secretary of State.

dispatch in these words: 'Dispatch to the President received and letter under consideration. W. H. Seward.'

"All day the notes of preparation have been heard at the public buildings and the armories. Everybody seems to be expecting a son or a brother or 'young man' in the coming regiments.

"To-night, Edward brought me a card from Mrs. Ann Stephens expressing a wish to see the President on matters concerning his personal safety. As the Ancient [1] was in bed I volunteered to receive the harrowing communication. Edward took me to a little room adjoining the Hall and I waited. Mrs. Stephens who is neither young nor yet fair to any miraculous extent, came in leading a lady — who was a little of both — whom she introduced to me as Mrs. Colonel Lander. [2] I was delighted at this chance interview with the Medea, the Julia, the Mona Lisa of my stage-struck days. After many hesitating and bashful trials, Mrs. Lander told the impulse that brought her. Some young Virginian — long-haired, swaggering, chivalrous, of course, and indiscreet friend — had come into town in great anxiety for a new saddle, and meeting her, had said that he and half a dozen others, including a daredevil guerrilla from Rich-

---

[1] One of the pet names which Hay and Nicolay gave the President.
[2] A popular actress of that generation.

mond, named F., would do a thing within forty-eight
hours that would ring through the world. Connect-
ing this central fact with a multiplicity of attendant
details, she concluded that the President was either
to be assassinated or captured. She ended by re-
newing her protestations of earnest solicitude mingled with fears of the impropriety of the step. Lander
has made her very womanly since he married her.
Imagine Jean M. Davenport a blushing, hesitating
wife.

"They went away, and I went to the bedside of
the Chief *couché*. I told him the yarn. He quietly
grinned.

"Going to my room, I met the Captain. He was
a little boozy and very eloquent. He dilated on the
troubles of the time and bewailed the existence of a
garrison in the White House 'to give *éclat* to Jim
Lane.'

"Hill Lamon came in about midnight saying
that Cash. Clay was drilling a splendid company at
Willard's Hall and that the town was in a general
tempest of enthusiastic excitement; which not being
very new, I went to sleep."

If John Hay had been able to continue during the
succeeding four years to write day by day the White
House Chronicle as amply as this first day of actual
war preparations, he would have left not only the

most complete, but the most varied and picturesque of records.

April 19 also was filled with business and alarms.

"Early this morning" (Hay writes), "I consulted with Major Hunter as to measures proper to be taken in the matter of guarding the House. He told me that he would fulfill any demand I should make. The forenoon brought us news of the destruction of government property at Harper's Ferry. It delighted the Major, regarding it as a deadly blow at the prosperity of the recusant Virginia.

"I called to see Joe Jefferson and found him more of a gentleman than I had expected. A very intellectual face, thin and eager, with large, intense blue eyes, the lines firm, and the hair darker than I had thought. I then went to see Mrs. Lander and made her tell the story all over again 'just by way of a slant.' Miss Lander the sculptor was there.

"Coming up, I found the streets full of the bruit of the Baltimore mob and at the White House was a nervous gentleman who insisted on seeing the President to say that a mortar battery had been planted on the Virginia heights commanding the town. He separated himself from the information and instantly retired. I had to do some very dexterous lying to calm the awakened fears of Mrs. Lincoln in regard to the assassination suspicion.

"After tea came Partridge and Petterbridge from Baltimore. They came to announce that they had taken possession of the Pikesville Arsenal in the name of the Government — to represent the feeling of the Baltimore conservatives in regard to the present imbroglio there — and to assure the President of the entire fidelity of the Governor and the State authorities. The President showed them Hicks [1] and Brown's [2] dispatch, which [read]: 'Send no troops here. The authorities here are loyal to the Constitution. Our police force and local militia will be sufficient.' Meaning, as they all seemed to think, that they wanted no Washington troops to preserve order, but, as Seward insists, that no more troops must be sent through the city. Scott [3] seemed to agree with Seward, and his answer to a dispatch of inquiry was: 'Governor Hicks has no authority to prevent troops from passing through Baltimore.' Seward interpolated: 'No right.' Partridge and Petterbridge seemed both loyal and hopeful. They spoke of the danger of the North being roused to fury by the bloodshed of to-day, and pouring in an avalanche over the border. The President most solemnly assured them that there was no danger. 'Our people are easily influenced by reason'(said he). 'They have

[1] Thomas H. Hicks, Governor of Maryland.
[2] George W. Brown, Mayor of Baltimore.
[3] General Winfield Scott, commanding the United States Army.

determined to prosecute this matter with energy, but with the most temperate spirit. You are entirely safe from invasion.'

"Wood came up to say that young Henry saw a steamer landing troops off Fort Washington. I told the President. Seward immediately drove to Scott's.

"Miss Dix called to-day, to offer services in the Hospital branch. She makes the most munificent and generous offers."

Events followed one another so rapidly that the White House had no repose, night or day. Alarmists, cranks, wiseacres beset the hall and corridors and strove to reach the President's office. The Potomac, according to rumors, was infested by suspicious-looking craft. Every one asked whether Washington could be held, in case the Secessionists should make a sudden dash upon it. Anxiety lest the mob should capture the White House itself and carry off the President, kept cropping up. Hay had under his special care the protection of both Mr. Lincoln and the Executive Mansion. "About midnight," he says, "we made a tour of the house. Hunter and the Italian exile, Vivaldi, were quietly sleeping on the floor of the East Room, and a young and careless guard loafed around the furnace fires in the basement. Good-looking and energetic young fellows, too good to be food for gunpowder, — if anything is."

The next day he "went up to see the Massachusetts troops quartered in the Capitol. The scene was
very novel. The contrast was very painful between
the gray-haired dignity that filled the Senate Chamber when I saw it last, and the present throng of
bright-looking Yankee boys, the most of them bearing the signs of New England rusticity in voice and
manner, scattered over the desks, chairs, and galleries, some loafing, many writing letters slowly and
with plough-hardened hands, or with rapid-glancing
clerkly fingers, while Grow [1] stood patiently by the
desk and franked for everybody."

The mobbing of the Sixth Massachusetts Regiment on its passage through Baltimore, on April 19,
and the break in that city of communications between Washington and the loyal North, caused
feverish agitation for several days. Unless the Union
troops could come through, the State of Maryland
might not only fall into the control of the Secessionists, but might send an invading force against the
Capital. If this were joined there by an attacking
column from Virginia, how could the town be saved?
Only when the Northern volunteers began to arrive
by roundabout routes did the alarm subside.

Through it all Lincoln seemed unruffled, though

[1] Galusha A. Grow, of Pennsylvania, Speaker of the House of
Representatives.

inwardly he was in great distress. A deputation of leading citizens of Baltimore waited on the President and begged him not to persist in sending troops by way of their city, because the mob was unmanageable; but these "whining traitors," as Hay calls them, promised that the loyal regiments should cross the State unmolested if they would avoid Baltimore. In the interest of conciliation, the President consented; but he declared that he would not again interfere with the war measures of the army.

Secretary Seward, more excited and less conciliatory, felt sure that the New York Seventh Regiment could cut their way through three thousand rioters; and he protested "that Baltimore *delenda est*, and other things," Hay adds with characteristic humor. But before Baltimore could be deleted, the Government must have at its disposal the very regiments to which Baltimore barred the way.

Old General Spinner, too, "was fierce and jubilant" at the news which seemed to him to hold out the pleasure of destroying traitors everywhere. "No frenzied poet," writes Hay, "ever predicted the ruin of a hostile house with more energy and fervor than he issued the rescript against Baltimore. . . . He was peculiarly disgusted with the impertinence of Delaware. 'The contemptible little neighborhood, without population enough for a decent country village, gets up on her hind legs and talks about armed neutrality. The only good use for traitors is to hang them. They are worth more dead than alive.' Thus the old liberty-loving Teuton raged."

At length, on April 25, the blockade was raised. The Seventh New York came through to the Capital without damage, and on the next day Massachusetts and Rhode Island troops arrived in large numbers. "Those who were in Washington on that Thursday, April 25," writes Hay, "will never during their lives, forget the event." [1] From that time on the transportation of Northern regiments across Baltimore ceased to be opposed.

On the 25th, Hay records that the President, who "seemed to be in a pleasant, hopeful mood," said: "I intend, at present, always leaving an opportunity for change of mind, to fill Fortress Monroe with men and stores; blockade the ports effectually; provide for the entire safety of the Capital; keep them quietly employed in this way, and then go down to Charleston and pay her the little debt we are owing her."

The President would not, however, countenance severity until conciliation had failed. Witness this memorandum, also dated April 25: —

"General Butler has sent an imploring request to the President to be allowed to bag the whole nest of

[1] N. &. H., IV, 156.

traitorous Maryland legislators and bring them in triumph here. This the Tycoon, wishing to observe every comity even with a recusant State, forbade."

Hay's hurried pen-portraits of the actors in this strange drama, as the examples I have cited show, possess the life-likeness of latter-day snap-shots. He has not only the knack of drawing vividly with a few strokes, but also a store of humor, which he sprays over them like a fixative. Thus, after calling on Governor William Sprague, of Rhode Island, he records: "A small, insignificant youth, who ——— his place; but who is certainly all right now. He is very proud of his company, of its wealth and social standing."

Carl Schurz, the German Liberal, who sought refuge as an exile to the United States, and in a few years was transformed into one of the most genuine American patriots of his time, is often referred to by Hay, who writes on April 26: "Carl Schurz was here to-day. He spoke with wild enthusiasm of his desire to mingle in the war. He has great confidence in his capability of arousing the enthusiasm of the young. He contemplates the career of a great guerrilla chief with ardent longing. He objects to the taking of Charleston and advises foraging on the interior States. . . . The Seventh Regiment band played gloriously on the shaven lawn at the south front of the

Executive Mansion. The scene was very beautiful. Through the luxuriant grounds, the gayly dressed crowd idly strolled, soldiers loafed on the promenades, the martial music filled the sweet air with vague suggestion of heroism, and C. Schurz and the President talked war."

On April 29 we have this entry: "Going into Nicolay's room this morning, C. Schurz and J. Lane were sitting. Jim was at the window, filling his soul with gall by steady telescopic contemplation of a Secession flag impudently flaunting over a roof in Alexandria. 'Let me tell you,' said he to the elegant Teuton, 'we have got to whip these scoundrels like hell, C. Schurz. They did a good thing stoning our men at Baltimore and shooting away the flag at Sumter. It has set the great North a-howling for blood, and they'll have it.'

"'I heard,' said Schurz, 'you preached a sermon to your men yesterday.'

"'No, sir! this is not time for preaching. When I went to Mexico there were four preachers in my regiment. In less than a week I issued orders for them all to stop preaching and go to playing cards. In a month or so, they were the biggest devils and best fighters I had.'

"An hour afterwards, C. Schurz told me he was going home to arm his clansmen for the wars. He has obtained three months' leave of absence from his diplomatic duties, and permission to raise a cavalry regiment. I doubt the propriety of the movement. He will make a wonderful land pirate; bold, quick, brilliant, and reckless. He will be hard to control and difficult to direct. Still, we shall see. He is a wonderful man."

A fortnight later, while the Marine Band played on the south lawn, Schurz sat with Lincoln on the balcony. "After the President had kissed some thousand children, Carl went into the library and developed a new accomplishment. He played with great skill and feeling, sitting in the dusk twilight at the piano until the President came by and took him down to tea. Schurz is a wonderful man. An orator, a soldier, a philosopher, an exiled patriot, a skilled musician! He has every quality of romance and of romantic picturesqueness."

The evident spell which Carl Schurz cast over John Hay was not accidental. Schurz, though less than ten years older than Hay, had seen and done many things. Uprooted from his native soil, he was flourishing in the land of his adoption. He embodied versatility, carried beyond the stage of the dilettante to that of the master; he was a cosmopolite. To be versatile and cosmopolitan were instincts which Nature had planted in John Hay at his birth —

ideals toward which he had been unconsciously grop-
ing since his earliest boyhood.

So Schurz fascinated him: but the person who
dominated him from his first day in the White House
was Lincoln. At the outset, the President's homeli-
ness, which was, in fact, primal simplicity, must have
amused him: for Hay had a keen eye for social distinctions and was already well versed in the lore of
manners which opens doors that neither birth, wealth,
nor genius can unlock. That the former rail-splitter
should occupy a position in which, among his other
functions, he was head of the official society of the
Capital of the Nation, must have tickled Hay's sense
of the comic. But soon Lincoln's great qualities —
his patience and love of justice, his readiness to listen, his fortitude — impressed the young secretary.
Lincoln's supreme naturalness, too, could not be resisted by any one who looked below the surface. Hay
loved humor, and here was Nature's master humor-
ist of that age; Hay loved wit, and here was a mind
of singular penetration and clearness, which saw
right to the heart of principles and could state them
in language that a child understood. One by one, the
best minds in Washington came into contact with
Lincoln; he met them squarely and seldom failed
to expose their fallacy, if there were one, or to uphold his own decision, if he approved it, by a phrase

or story not to be forgotten. The speeches of the famous orators at the Capitol have faded; Lincoln's remain. Thanks to his corrections, the State papers of the elegant Seward are still read; and Sumner also, the chief academic orator in Congress, might have profited if he had condescended to take the untutored Westerner for a schoolmaster.

Hay and Nicolay, drawn to Lincoln by his unusual geniality, little suspected at first that he was destined to be, through his unique combination of character and ability, the savior of the Republic. To each other they referred to him familiarly as "the Ancient," or "the Tycoon": and Hay, at least, though full of veneration, sometimes made merry over the Chief's oddities. The Diary abounds in glimpses of Lincoln during the critical month of April.

If ever a ruler had an excuse for showing anxiety, Lincoln had at that moment. Fort Sumter fell on April 15; on the 17th, Virginia seceded; on the 18th, the Union troops retired from Harper's Ferry and its arsenal; on the 19th, the Sixth Massachusetts was mobbed in Baltimore, and then followed the destruction of the railroad bridges and the cutting of the telegraphs; on the 20th, Robert E. Lee, whose appointment as commander of the Northern Army was pending, went over to Virginia, and drew a large number of army and navy officers with him to the

South; on the 20th, also, the Gosport Arsenal had to be abandoned. Yet in public Lincoln kept up his usual manner, and so successfully that strangers thought him either indifferent or shallow. Only once, in his private office, after peering long down the Potomac for the ships which were to bring the troops, believing himself to be alone, he exclaimed, " with irrepressible anguish, 'Why don't they come! Why don't they come!'"

The next day, when some battered soldiers of the Sixth Massachusetts called on him, he "fell into a tone of irony to which only intense feeling ever drove him: 'I begin to believe,' he said, 'that there is no North. The Seventh Regiment is a myth. Rhode Island is another. You are the only real thing.'" [1]

The young secretary, who overheard Lincoln's cry of anguish and was present at this interview, began to divine the depths of the President's nature.

In a few days, the tension being relieved, Hay writes: "Three Indians of the Pottawatomies called to-day upon their Great Father. The President amused them greatly by airing the two or three Indian words he knew. I was amused by his awkward efforts to make himself understood by speaking bad English; e.g., 'Where live now? When go back Iowa?'"

[1] N. & H., IV, 152–53.

Northern newspapers began to scold at the incompetence of the Administration, and the New York *Times* advised the immediate resignation of the Cabinet and warned Lincoln that he would be superseded: but that sort of hostility never worried him, and he joked about the *Times's* proposal to depose him.

On May 7 Hay writes: "I went in to give the President some little items of Illinois news, saying among other things that S. was behaving very badly. He replied with emphasis that S. was a miracle of meanness; calmly looking out of the window at the smoke of two strange steamers puffing up the way, resting the end of the telescope on his toes sublime."

Hay referred to Browning's suggestion that the North should subjugate the South, exterminate the whites, set up a black republic, and protect the negroes "while they raised our cotton."

"'Some of our Northerners seem bewildered and dazzled by the excitement of the hour,'" Lincoln replied. "'Doolittle[1] seems inclined to think that this war is to result in the entire abolition of slavery. Old Colonel Hamilton, a venerable and most respectable gentleman, impresses upon me most earnestly the propriety of enlisting the slaves in our army.' (I told him his daily correspondence was thickly inter-

[1] Senator James R. Doolittle, of Wisconsin.

spersed by such suggestions.) 'For my own part,'
he said, 'I consider the central idea pervading this
struggle is the necessity that is upon us of proving
that popular government is not an absurdity. We
must settle this question now, whether, in a free government, the minority have the right to break up
the government whenever they choose. If we fail,
it will go far to prove the incapability of the people to
govern themselves. There may be one consideration used in stay of such final judgment, but that is
not for us to use in advance: That is, that there exists
in our case an instance of a vast and far-reaching disturbing element, which the history of no other free
nation will probably ever present. That, however,
is not for us to say at present. Taking the government as we found it, we will see if the majority can
preserve it.'"

This statement, spoken offhand to his secretary,
reveals the foundation of Lincoln's judgment on the
War of the Rebellion: there was at stake something
more precious than the preservation of the Union,
something more urgent than the abolition of slavery,
— and that was Democracy. Two years and a half
later, in his address at Gettysburg, he put into one
imperishable sentence the thought of which this is
the germ.

Occasionally Hay jots down Lincoln's literary

preferences. One evening, he reports, there was much talk between him and Seward on Daniel Webster, "in which the financial *sanssoucism* of the great man was strikingly prominent. Seward thought he would not live, nor Clay, a tithe as long as John Quincy Adams. The President disagreed with him, and thought Webster will be read forever."

The President's unfashionable habits come in for playful mention. On hearing that the Honorable Robert Bourke, son of the Irish Earl of Mayo, was about to visit Washington, Hay writes to a friend: "I hope W. will find it out and, by way of showing him a delicate attention, take him to the observational settee whence, on clear afternoons, is to be seen, windows favoring, the Presidential ensarking and bifurcate dischrysalisizing." (August 21, 1861.)

It was well that Hay gave vent to his humor; because the burden of his work soon became oppressive, and before the summer was far advanced Washington, which, despite its unpaved streets and shanties and unhidden squalor, had been a holiday city, took on a gloomy air. Regiments poured in from all parts of the North and camped in the open spaces. Troops marched to and fro. Munitions and provisions were collected and despatched. On the Potomac naval preparations went forward. Civilians in government employ were actually busy, and their superiors, cabinet officers, and heads of bureaus, began to look careworn. With the heat, the fashionable residents, and the families of officials, fled as usual to Northern watering-places. At last the American Capital gave itself up in earnest to the grim business of war.

And yet, many persons still doubted whether the conflict would be either general or long drawn out. Optimists predicted that at the first reverse the Southern Confederacy would collapse; and, accordingly, influential newspapers clamored for action, while self-constituted advisers belabored the President with suggestions and berated him for not following them. The Administration had a foretaste of what a free press is capable of in time of war. The editor of a metropolitan daily would probably shrink from telling a dentist how to fill a tooth, and even the omniscient reporter of a country weekly might hesitate to instruct a surgeon in an operation for cancer; but both these gentlemen, and most of their neighbors and fellow citizens, feel wholly competent to direct lifelong experts in the highly specialized and intricate art of war. Yet it must be said that, as experts were few in 1861, advice had to come largely from novices; and why should the average man, who beheld the editor or politician of yesterday given command of a regiment to-day, consider his own

opinions on the conduct of the campaign as worth-
less?

Side by side with the importunities of amateur
strategists went the nagging of political wiseacres.
Happy Alexander and Cæsar and Hannibal, happy
Marlborough and Napoleon! Conducting their campaigns before the days of railroads or telegraphs,
they were not required to change their plans from
hour to hour in order to keep pace with the hysterical fluctuations of the public at home. In the American Civil War this malign influence marred the military plans to an extent till then unprecedented.
That such meddling was inevitable, however, seems
to be John Hay's opinion; for he approved, if he did
not actually write, the following lines: —

"Historical judgment of war is subject to an in-
flexible law, either very imperfectly understood or
very constantly lost sight of. Military writers love to
fight over the campaigns of history exclusively by
the rules of the professional chess-board, always sub-
ordinating, often totally ignoring, the element of
politics. This is a radical error. Every war is begun,
dominated, and ended by political considerations;
without a nation, without a government, without
money or credit, without popular enthusiasm which
furnishes volunteers, or public support which endures conscription, there could be no army and no

war — neither beginning nor end of methodical hos-
tilities. War and politics, campaign and statecraft are
Siamese twins, inseparable and interdependent; to
talk of military operations without the direction and
interference of an Administration is as absurd as to
plan a campaign without recruits, pay, or rations." [1]

In this forcible statement Hay filed his caveat
against the censure, which has been widespread and
weighty, of the direction of the Union campaigns
from Washington and of the sensitiveness of the Administration to political exigencies.

Both these conditions sprang up as soon as the
volunteer regiments were ready for service. General
Scott, the veteran head of the regular army, proposed his "anaconda plan," of blockading the coast
and establishing a cordon of garrisons down the
Mississippi, a device by which he thought the Confederacy might soon be strangled. He also counseled
delay till the autumn. The North, however, clamored for action. It felt the sting of the humiliation
of Sumter and Baltimore and of more recent rebuffs:
it believed that the Government was now strong
enough to crush the Rebellion; it remembered that
the term of the ninety-day men would soon run out.

Lincoln recognized the need of keeping public

---

[1] N. & H., IV, 359–60. This passage seems to me to bear Hay's
impress.

opinion enthusiastic, and, having made every military provision for a successful movement, he ordered an advance. Union General McDowell was to engage Rebel General Beauregard at Manassas, while Union General Patterson crushed Rebel General Johnston at Winchester. On July 21 the battle was fought at Bull Run; but the incompetent Patterson had allowed Johnston to slip by him, and McDowell, being confronted by both Beauregard and Johnston, was utterly beaten. His undisciplined troops, seized by panic, scampered as best they could through the darkness and the rain for Washington, nearly thirty miles off.

Hay describes how the President passed that eventful Sunday; he was anxious from the first, but reassured when frequent telegrams reported continued success. After dinner the President went to General Scott's office, only to find that burly old gentleman taking his afternoon nap. Scott roused himself long enough to declare that all must go well, and then, on the President's departure, he returned to sleep. But at six o'clock, while the President was out driving, Secretary Seward hurried over to the White House with a telegram announcing that the battle was lost and McDowell routed, and to urge that steps be taken to save the Capital from the pursuing enemy. All night long Lincoln stayed in his office giving directions, reading despatches, or listening to the reports of eye-witnesses, who began to reach the city about midnight.

Monday, the 22d of July, was one of the dismalest days Washington had ever seen. Before afternoon the news spread that the Rebels, having given up the pursuit, were not about to attack the outposts; but every one realized that the war, alternately dreaded and doubted for forty years, had come in earnest.

CHAPTER VI

WAR IN EARNEST

TO sketch, even in outline, the history of the Civil War, is not my purpose: for this is a life of John Hay, and the war interests us here only in so far as it concerns him, or as he sheds light on men and events, and especially on Abraham Lincoln. We have seen in the last chapter how quickly he adapted himself to his new situation. There is no more talk of his being doomed to waste his days in the materialistic, unshorn West; no suggestion of the poet in exile; no further reference to filling an early grave. He had neither deserted the Muse nor renounced his ideals: he had simply responded, as a healthy young man should, to the stimulation which comes with action in a supreme cause.

He was discovering that life transcended the fragments and echoes of it which passed for life in his books. He lay now under the spell of the Deed. Having among his many talents the gift of keen and enlightened curiosity, he watched men with the interest with which one follows the fortunes of the characters in a novel or a play. He was a sharp observer; sophisticated, chiefly through his reading, but not cynical: and he found unceasing amusement in human eccentricities.

Except at Paris during the French Revolution, there was never such a strange multitude, jumbled and incongruous, gathered in a modern city as that which swarmed in Washington from 1861 to 1865. It comprised men of every social class: toilers from farm and shop and clerks from counting-rooms; Eastern bankers and teachers; Western backwoodsmen, miners, and adventurers. It was swelled by office-seekers — a sordid gang, having one common instinct, the prehensile, among them; and by unnumbered contractors, sutlers, and speculators. Most conspicuous of all was the endless stream of volunteers, who flowed in at first by companies and battalions, next by thousands and tens of thousands, and so on up to hundreds of thousands — infantry, cavalry, artillery. You can still hear the incessant tramp of the foot-soldiers and the clatter of the horse, with the roll of drum and rumble of cannon, and the shrill, saucy call of the fifes: on they go over the bridges into Virginia, and many never come back.

Amid the brutal surge of life swept the ever-broadening torrent of Death: ambulances and wagons loaded and dripping with the wounded; hospitals bursting with bodies, mutilated but still alive, haunts of agony or delirium; surgeons, doctors, nurses, at work till they dropped exhausted; hearses, carts, caissons bearing coffins, attended by few or no mourners, on the hurried transfer to the cemetery, and then the lowering into the shallow grave, the clipped sentences of blessing from the minister or the volley of farewell; while day and night grief-stricken fathers and frantic mothers were searching for their sons, or at least for the maimed corpses of their sons. Through it all, the plot of the world-drama worked itself out.

And as if he were the privileged of Destiny, John Hay watches the unfolding of the spectacle from the White House, as from a proscenium box. Nor is he a mere looker-on. He is always at the President's right hand to do the President's bidding. What he sees and what he hears has due weight in shaping the President's decisions. For John Hay was a witness to be trusted: discreet, clear-sighted, businesslike, and, above all, sympathetic to Lincoln, who enjoyed equally his frankness and his humor.

After Bull Run, work at the White House re-doubled, the conduct of the war taking up the lion's share of energy. The capital question of choosing officers for the rapidly swelling army arose at every turn. Civilian troops had to be commanded by ci-vilian colonels, willing but necessarily ignorant. The higher grades were often filled for any other

reason except the military. Politicians, quick to
scent profit for themselves, secured commissions by
the same methods which brought them political
honors and lucre. If governors of States could not resist the pressure of aspiring statesmen, how could it
be expected that the President and his Secretary
of War should always select wisely among candidates of whom they had no personal knowledge?
And if battles were fought to appease public clamor,
why was it not logical to assign brigadierships to
gentlemen who controlled the political majority of
a large district, or even, it might be, of a doubtful
State? The problem of 1861, be it remembered, was
to secure, by hook or by crook, the loyalty of every
Northerner.

To the historian a conversation may be as important as a battle. Here, for instance, is Hay's minute
of a talk in which Mr. Lincoln disclosed quite can-
didly his conciliatory policy toward the South before
he became President.

"*October 22, 1861.* At Seward's to-night the President talked about Secession, Compromise, and other
such. He spoke of a committee of Pseudo-Unionists
coming to him before Inauguration for guarantees,
etc. He promised to evacuate Sumter if they would
break up their Convention, without any row or non-
sense. They demurred. Subsequently, he renewed

proposition to Summers [?], but without any result. The President was most anxious to prevent bloodshed."

On November 8, 1861, John Hay records that a "cheeky letter" has just been received from Benjamin F. Butler, of Massachusetts, who, with characteristic modesty writes the President: —

MY DEAR SIR, — Gen'l Wool has resigned. Gen'l Fremont must. Gen'l Scott has retired.

I have an ambition, and I trust a laudable one, to be Major-General of the United States Army.

Has anybody done more to deserve it? No one will do more. May I rely upon you, as you may have confidence in me, to take this matter into consideration?

I will not disgrace the position. I may fail in its duties.

Truly yrs.,

BENJ. F. BUTLER.

THE PRESIDENT.

P.S. I have made the same suggestion to others of my friends.

This was a specimen letter, illustrative of many.

How to deal with the rapaciously immodest is the special task of democracy. In earlier times they

throve by the monarch's favor, and dutiful subjects
sought no other explanation of their prosperity;
now, their promotion accuses the public itself.

Hay's early references to McClellan prepare us
for that commander's subsequent abysmal failure.
Called to Washington on July 26, McClellan took
charge of organizing into a fighting army the troops,
which were reaching the city at the rate of a regiment a day. For that work he possessed uncommon
ability, and to this was added the knowledge gained
from his West Point training, from service in the
regular army, and from inspection of the European
armies. He not only knew what was to be done, but
he had the art of persuading everybody that he was
the only man who could do it. His self-esteem, by
nature abnormally developed, swelled at last into
an elephantiasis of the ego. But among the hesitations, perplexities, and gropings of the summer of
1861, the value of McClellan's self-assurance was
quite as obvious as that of his technical competence.
The Army of the Potomac, moulded under his direction, felt for him an enthusiasm bordering on infatua-
tion and proof against the disillusion of subsequent
defeats. Though he was beaten in many fights, out-
generaled in his plans of campaign, and outmarched
and baffled by inferior forces, and though, through
a palsy of the will, he failed to convert Antietam

into a sweeping victory, — perhaps into a death-
blow of the Rebellion, — his infatuated supporters,
persisting in claiming that his primacy as a commander was still unrivaled, always threw the blame
on others.

Truth to tell, from the day he came to Washington,
McClellan was in danger of being smothered by adu-
lation. The North, frantic for a general to avenge its
defeats and to put down Secession, believed that in
McClellan it had the man. It imputed to him qualities he never possessed; it glorified his undoubted
points of excellence; it sought for happy parallels
and propitious signs to confirm its confidence. Napoleon was short of stature — so was "Little Mac";
Napoleon was young and self-reliant — so was
"Little Mac": what could be more logical than to
continue the parallel until it led to a Marengo and
an Austerlitz for "Little Mac"? McClellan was a
Democrat; and this enhanced his importance, because it advertised to the world that the Northern
Democrats would stand by the Union.

President Lincoln welcomed McClellan's coming,
and besides giving him every aid in forming the
army, deferred to his plans and methods. Hay, who
had a young man's impatience at too obtrusive conceit, was present at many of their interviews, and
seems very early to have doubted "Little Mac's"

omniscience. On October 22, 1861, he writes that
the President and the General talked over the death
of Colonel Baker at Leesburg.

"McClellan said: 'There is many a good fellow
that wears the shoulder-straps going under the sod
before the thing is over. There is no loss too great to
be repaired. If I should get knocked on the head,
Mr. President, you will put another man immediately
in my shoes.' 'I want you to take care of yourself,'
said the President. McClellan seemed very hopeful
and confident — thought he had the enemy, if in
force or not. During this evening's conversation,
it became painfully evident that he had no plan
nor the slightest idea of what Stone [1] was about."

In those early days the President used to call informally at McClellan's office to inquire how the
work was going or to make suggestions. At one of
these casual calls, on October 10, McClellan said:
"I think we shall have our arrangements made for
a strong reconnoissance about Monday, to feel the
strength of the enemy. I intend to be careful and to
do as well as possible. Don't let them hurry me is
all I ask." "You shall have your own way in the
matter, I assure you," said the President, and went
home.

[1] Brigadier-General Charles P. Stone. The battle of Ball's Bluff
was fought on the preceding day, October 21, 1861.

That refrain, "Don't let them hurry me!" was to be the burden of McClellan's talk and despatches throughout his service.

A few days later, McClellan traversed Senator B. F. Wade's opinion that an unsuccessful battle was preferable to delay, because a defeat could easily be repaired by the swarming recruits. [I] "would rather have a few recruits after a victory than a good many after a defeat." Lincoln regretted the popular impatience, but held that it ought to be reckoned with. "'At the same time, General,'" he said, "'you must not fight till you are ready.' 'I have everything at stake,' said the General; 'if I fail, I will not see you again or anybody.' 'I have a notion to go out with you, and stand or fall with the battle,'" Lincoln replied.

On November 1, McClellan succeeded Scott in command of the Army. The President in thanking him, said:—

"'I should be perfectly satisfied if I thought that this vast increase of responsibility would not embarrass you.' 'It is a great relief, sir! I feel as if several tons were taken from my shoulders to-day. I am now in contact with you and the Secretary. I am not embarrassed by intervention.' 'Well,' says the President, 'draw on me for all the sense I have, and all the information. In addition to your present command, the supreme command of the Army will entail a vast labor upon you.' 'I can do it all,' McClellan said quietly."

Hay evidently felt that this sublime assertion spoke for itself, but perhaps McClellan sounded more conceited than he intended. On November 11, Hay notes that McClellan promises to "feel" the Rebels on the next day — the first of many such promises. His entry for November 13 reads: —

"I wish here to record what I consider a portent of evil to come. The President, Governor Seward, and I went over to McClellan's home to-night. The servant at the door said the General was at the wedding of Colonel Wheaton at General Buell's and would soon return. We went in, and after we had waited about an hour, McClellan came in, and without paying particular attention to the porter who told him the President was waiting to see him, went up-stairs, passing the door of the room where the President and Secretary of State were seated. They waited about half an hour, and sent once more a servant to tell the General they were there; and the answer came that the General had gone to bed.

"I merely record this unparalleled insolence of epaulettes without comment. It is the first indication I have yet seen of the threatened supremacy of the military authorities. Coming home, I spoke to the President about the matter, but he seemed not to have noticed it specially, saying it were better at this time not to be making points of etiquette and personal dignity."

It was this invincible patience, called by some men vacillation and by others attributed to obtuseness, which proved in the end one source of Lincoln's mastery. Patience, the least showy of the virtues, works cumulatively; but what she does endures. There could be no finer example of the contrast between shadow and substance than appeared that winter in McClellan and Lincoln: Little Mac self-confident, idolized, showered with laurels *before* his battles, and barely condescending to listen to the advice of his chief; and the magnanimous President, bent on hearing all sides, suspending judgment until he had considered every fact, and loyally supplying the General with everything he demanded.

Winter passed, spring came, the nation longed to have the Army of the Potomac put to the test, but still McClellan delayed. The following extracts from Hay's brief notes to Nicolay, absent from Washington, to whom he wrote as confidentially as in his Diary, shows how the young secretary felt: —

"*March 31, 1862.* Little Mac sails to-day for down-river. He was in last night to see Tycoon.

He was much more pleasant and social in manner than formerly. He seems to be anxious for the good opinion of everyone."

"*Thursday morning* [April 3d]. McClellan is in danger, not in front, but in rear. The President is making up his mind to give him a peremptory order to march. It is disgraceful to think how the little squad at Yorktown keeps him at bay."

"*Friday, April 4, 1862.* McClellan is at last in motion. He is now moving on Richmond. The secret is very well kept. Nobody out of the Cabinet knows it in town."

"*April 9, 1862.* Glorious news comes borne on every wind but the South Wind. While Pope is crossing the turbid and broad torrent of the Mississippi in the blaze of the enemy's fire, and Grant is fighting the overwhelming legions of Buckner at Pittsburg, the Little Napoleon sits trembling before the handful of men at Yorktown, afraid either to fight or run. Stanton feels devilish about it. He would like to remove him, if he thought it would do."

At last the time came when even Lincoln's patience was exhausted. After McClellan's long series of blunders on the Peninsula, he was superseded by Pope, who, at the end of August, 1862, prepared to strike the Confederate Army. On August 30, the very day when Jackson and Longstreet were thrash-

ing Pope at Bull Run, Hay rode into Washington
from the Soldiers' Home with Lincoln.

"We talked," he says, "about the state of things
by Bull Run and Pope's prospect. The President was
very outspoken in regard to McClellan's present conduct. He said that really it seemed to him that Mc-
Clellan wanted Pope defeated. He mentioned to me
a dispatch of McClellan's in which he proposed, as
one plan of action, to 'leave Pope to get out of his own
scrape and devote ourselves to securing Washington.' He also spoke of McClellan's dreadful panic
in the matter of Chain Bridge, which he had ordered
blown up the night before, but which order had been
countermanded; and also of his incomprehensible interference with Franklin's corps, which he recalled
once, and then, when they had been sent ahead by
Halleck's order, begged permission to recall them
again; and only desisted after Halleck's sharp injunc-
tion to push them ahead until they whipped something, or got whipped themselves. The President
seemed to think him a little crazy. Envy, jealousy,
and spite are probably a better explanation of his
present conduct. He is constantly sending dis-
patches to the President and Halleck asking what
is his real position and command. He acts as chief
alarmist and grand marplot of the army."

Halleck, on the contrary, the President said, had

no prejudices. "[He] is wholly for the service. He does not care who succeeds or who fails, so the service is benefited.

"Later in the day we were in Halleck's room. Halleck was at dinner, and Stanton came in while we were waiting for him, and carried us off to dinner. A pleasant little dinner and a pretty wife as white and cold and motionless as marble, whose rare smiles seemed to pain her. Stanton was loud about the McClellan business. He was unqualifiedly severe upon McClellan. He said that after these battles there should be one court-martial, if never any more. He said that nothing but foul play could lose us this battle, and that it rested with McClellan and his friends. Stanton seemed to believe very strongly in Pope. So did the President, for that matter."

Nevertheless, after Pope's defeat at Second Bull Run the President concluded that McClellan must be restored to the command of the Army of the Potomac.

"'He has acted badly in this matter [the President admitted to Hay], but we must use what tools we have. There is no man in the army who can man these fortifications and lick these troops of ours into shape half as well as he.' I spoke of the general feeling against McClellan as evinced by the President's mail. He rejoined: 'Unquestionably he has acted

badly toward Pope. He wanted him to fail. That
is unpardonable. But he is too useful just now to
sacrifice.' At another time he said: 'If he can't fight
himself, he excels in making others ready to fight.'"

So "Little Mac" once more led the Army of the
Potomac; not for long, however, because after his
virtual failure at Antietam (September 17, 1862)
and his allowing Stuart to ride round the Army
of the Potomac and raid Chambersburg, popular
clamor demanded his dismissal. And Lincoln, the
long-suffering, convinced that the time had come,
relieved him.

Two years later McClellan was the Democratic
nominee for President. On September 25, Hay records that a letter had just come from Nicolay, who
was in New York, stating that Thurlow Weed, the
dominant Republican leader in New York State,
with whom Nicolay was to confer, had gone to Canada. When Hay showed the President the letter he
said: "I think I know where Mr. Weed has gone. I
think he has gone to Vermont, not Canada. I will
tell you what he is trying to do. I have not as yet
told anybody."

And then Lincoln proceeded to unfold the following story of a remarkable intrigue: —

"'Some time ago the Governor of Vermont came
to me "on business of importance," he said. I fixed

an hour and he came. His name is Smith. He is, though you would not think it, a cousin of Baldy Smith.[1] Baldy is large, blond, florid. The Governor is a little, dark sort of man. This is the story he told me, giving General Baldy Smith as his authority: —

"'When General McClellan was here at Washington [in 1862] B. Smith was very intimate with him. They had been together at West Point, and friends. McClellan had asked for promotion for Baldy from the President, and got it. They were close and confidential friends. When they went down to the Peninsula their same intimate relations continued, the General talking freely with Smith about all his plans and prospects, until one day Fernando Wood and one other [Democratic] politician from New York appeared in camp and passed some days with McClellan.

"'From the day this took place Smith saw, or thought he saw, that McClellan was treating him with unusual coolness and reserve. After a little while he mentioned this to McClellan, who, after some talk, told Baldy he had something to show him. He told him that these people who had recently visited him had been urging him to stand as an opposition candidate for President; that he had thought the thing over and had concluded to accept their

[1] General William F. Smith, the eminent Union commander.

propositions, and had written them a letter (which he had not yet sent) giving his idea of the proper way of conducting the war, so as to conciliate and impress the people of the South with the idea that our armies were intended merely to execute the laws and protect their property, etc., and pledging himself to conduct the war in that inefficient, conciliatory style.

"'This letter he read to Baldy, who, after the reading was finished, said earnestly: "General, do you not see that looks like treason, and that it will ruin you and all of us?" After some further talk the General destroyed the letter in Baldy's presence, and thanked him heartily for his frank and friendly counsel. After this he was again taken into the intimate confidence of McClellan.

"'Immediately after the battle of Antietam, Wood and his familiar came again and saw the General, and again Baldy saw an immediate estrangement on the part of McClellan. He seemed to be anxious to get his intimate friends out of the way and to avoid opportunities of private conversation with them. Baldy he particularly kept employed on reconnoissances and such work. One night Smith was returning from some duty he had been performing, and, seeing a light in McClellan's tent, he went in to report. He reported and was about to withdraw, when the General requested him to remain. After every one was gone he told him those men had been there again and had renewed their proposition about the Presidency: that this time he had agreed to their proposition, and had written them a letter acceding to their terms and pledging himself to carry on the war in the sense already indicated. This letter he read then and there to Baldy Smith.

"'Immediately thereafter B. Smith applied to be transferred from that army. At very nearly the same time other prominent men asked the same — Franklin, Burnside, and others.

"'Now that letter must be in the possession of F. Wood, and it will not be impossible to get it. Mr. Weed has, I think, gone to Vermont to see the Smiths about it.'"

Hay continues: —

"I was very much surprised at the story and expressed my surprise. I said I had always thought that McClellan's fault was a constitutional weakness and timidity, which prevented him from active and timely exertion, instead of any such deep-laid scheme of treachery and ambition.

"The President replied: 'After the battle of Antietam I went up to the field to try to get him to move, and came back thinking he would move at once. But when I got home he began to argue why he ought not to move. I peremptorily ordered him to advance. It was nineteen days before he put a man over the river. It was nine days longer before he got his army across, and then he stopped again, delaying on little pretexts of wanting this and that. I began to fear he was playing false — that he did not want to hurt the enemy. I saw how he could intercept the enemy on the way to Richmond. I determined to make that the test. If he let them get away, I would remove him. He did so, and I relieved him. I dismissed Major K. for his silly, treasonable talk because I feared it was staff-talk, and I wanted an example. The letter of Buell furnishes another evidence in support of that theory. And the story you have heard Neill tell about [Governor Horatio] Seymour's first visit to McClellan, all tallies with this story.' "

The last reference to McClellan in this Diary occurs on November 11, 1864, at the first meeting of the Cabinet after Lincoln's overwhelming reelection. The President brought out a sealed paper, which he had asked his Cabinet to indorse on August 23, and when Hay opened it they found it contained a brief memorandum in which Lincoln stated that, as it was extremely probable that he could not be reëlected, he intended "so to coöperate with the President-elect as to save the Union between the election and the inauguration."

"'I resolved,' he now told his Cabinet, 'in case of the election of General McClellan, . . . that I would see him and talk matters over with him. I would say, "General, the election has demonstrated that you are stronger, have more influence with the American people than I. Now let us together — you with your influence, and I with all the executive power of the Government — try to save the country. You raise as many troops as you possibly can for this final trial, and I will devote all my energy to assisting and finishing the war."'

"Seward said: 'And the General would answer you, "*Yes, yes*"; and the next day, when you saw him again and pressed those views upon him, he would say, "*Yes, yes*"; and so on for ever, and would have done nothing at all.'

"'At least,' added Lincoln, 'I should have done my duty, and have stood clear before my own conscience.'"

With that characteristic expression the record closes — a record which reveals Lincoln as invincibly patient, fair, and considerate toward even the general who caused him and the upholders of the Union so many poignant disappointments.

I have outrun the chronological order of events in order to give unity to Hay's memoranda on McClellan.

Some optimist has described man as a reasoning animal: "a creature with a passion for self-deception," would be more accurate; for animals do reason after their own fashion, whereas, so far as appears, they do not indulge in self-deception. On his being dismissed, McClellan's friends hinted that he was just about to win the decisive battle of the war, and his apologists, forgetful of his fifteen months of dawdling and disaster, perpetuate in history the legend that, if he had been given one more chance, he would have silenced his critics forever.

Hay's memoranda on McClellan, jotted down at the time, have the additional value of revealing Lincoln's attitude; and when Hay, twenty years later, wrote Lincoln's life, instead of softening or reversing his opinion of McClellan's conduct and incompetence, he repeated it with emphasis.

It is precisely such testimony as his that enables the historian to discover the state of mind, whether personal or collective, out of which came the motives which caused the events in any historical episode. We need to know the words actually spoken, the speech actually delivered, — not the expurgated or embellished revision, purveyed by Hansard or by the *Congressional Record*, — because those words were integral strands in the web of history. We need to know each actor's estimate of his fellows:

for however unjust, mistaken, or over-favorable that estimate may be, it determined action. Lee planned differently when he had to deal with Grant and not with McClellan. Nine persons out of ten in the North, including his Cabinet and Congress, underrated Lincoln during most of his presidential career. "Lincoln is a 'Simple Susan,'" wrote Samuel Bowles, editor of the Springfield *Republican*, only six days before the inauguration.[1] Had Mr. Bowles lived to edit his own letters by the light of subsequent events, he would doubtless have substituted his later opinions, and so would have figured as a successful prophet. Unless the historian comes to this knowledge, he can never show "the very age and body of the time his form and pressure"; the Past will be dead to him, an affair of mummies, a deciphering of mummy-cases, which no display of erudition concerning economics, commercial statistics or documents can bring to life.

John Hay's notes and letters serve as peep-holes through which, after these many years, we can look directly at the persons with whom he was thrown during the Rebellion at the moment of action, or we can hear their very voices. Fragmentary these records are: but they are usually so characteristic, so

[1] G. S. Merriam, *Life and Times of Samuel Bowles* (New York, 1885), I, 318.

vital, so symptomatic, that they reveal much. We often regret that this quick-eyed observer lacked the time to chronicle regularly each night, as the methodical Gideon Welles was doing, the happenings of the days. Still, the spontaneity of his minutes, enhanced by their frankness and vivacious language, counterbalances their fragmentariness.

Acute though Hay was in seeing and keen in judging, he did not turn cynic. In spite of the daily examples of unbridled selfishness that passed before him, his healthy trust in human nature was fortified by living close to Lincoln: and then — he was only twenty-three.

On September 5, 1862, he reports this bit of conversation with Seward: —

"'Mr. Hay,'" said the Secretary of State, "'what is the use of growing old? You learn something of men and things, but never until too late to use it. I have only just now found out what military jealousy is. . . . The other day I went down to Alexandria, and found General McClellan's army landing. I considered our armies united virtually and thought them invincible. I went home, and the first news I received was that each had been attacked, and each, in effect, beaten. It never had occurred to me that any jealousy could prevent these generals from acting for their common fame and the welfare of the country.'

"I said it never would have seemed possible to me that one American general should write of another to the President, suggesting that 'Pope should be allowed to get out of his own scrape his own way.'

"He answered: 'I don't see why you should have expected it. You are not old. I should have known it.' He said this gloomily and sadly."

There were, however, moments of elation, when good news came from the armies in the field, or the political prospect brightened. Thus, on the evening after Lincoln read his Emancipation Proclamation to the Cabinet, a party of ministers and their friends met at Secretary Chase's. "They all seemed to feel a sort of new and exhilarated life; they breathed freer; the President's Proclamation had freed them as well as the slaves. They gleefully and merrily called each other and themselves Abolitionists, and seemed to enjoy the novel accusation of appropriating that horrible name." (September 23, 1862.)

General Joseph Hooker — "Fighting Joe" — was another commander toward whom his contemporaries and posterity have had their reserves. Since the military history of the War has come to be studied dispassionately, Chancellorsville has risen into front rank among the critical battles, and, as Hooker commanded at Chancellorsville and was beaten, his reputation has, logically, suffered in proportion to the growing significance attached to that defeat.

Hay, however, evidently liked Hooker, of whose talks he made several notes. I cite the most important.

On September 9, 1863, he dined with Wise, where he met Hooker, Butterfield, and Fox.

"Hooker was in fine flow. . . . He says he was forced to ask to be relieved by repeated acts which proved that he was not to be allowed to manage his army as he thought best, but that it was to be manœuvred from Washington. He instanced Maryland Heights, whose garrison he was forbidden to touch, yet which was ordered to be evacuated by the very mail which brought his (Hooker's) relief. And other such many.

"At dinner he spoke of our army. He says: It was the finest on the planet. He would like to see it fighting with foreigners. . . . It was far superior to the Southern army in everything but one. It had more valor, more strength, more endurance, more spirit; the Rebels are only superior in vigor of attack. The reason of this is that, in the first place, our army came down here capable of everything but ignorant of everything. It fell into evil hands — the hands of a baby, who knew something of drill, little of organization, and nothing of the morale of the army. It was fashioned by the congenial spirit of this man into a mass of languid inertness, destitute of either dash or cohesion. The Prince de Joinville, by far the finest mind I ever met with in the army, was struck by this singular and, as he said, inexplicable contrast between the character of American soldiers as integers and in mass. The one active, independent, alert, enterprising; the other indolent, easy, wasteful, and slothful. It is not in the least singular. You find a ready explanation in the character of its original General. . . .

"Hooker drank very little, not more than the rest, who were all abstemious, yet what little he drank made his cheek hot and red and his eye brighter. I can easily understand how the stories of his drunkenness have grown, if so little affects him as I have seen. He was looking very well to-night. A tall and statuesque form — grand fighting head and grizzled russet hair, — red, florid cheeks and bright blue eyes, forming a strong contrast with Butterfield, who sat opposite — a small, stout, compact man, with a closely chiseled Greek face and heavy black mustaches, like Eugène Beauharnais. Both very handsome and very different."

"*September 10.* — I dined to-night at Willard's. . . . Speaking of Lee [Hooker] expressed himself slightingly of Lee's abilities. He says he was never much

respected in the army. In Mexico he was surpassed
by all his lieutenants. In the cavalry he was held
in no esteem. He was regarded very highly by General Scott. He was a courtier, and readily recom-
mended himself by his insinuating manner to the
General [Scott], whose petulant and arrogant temper had driven of late years all officers of spirit and
self-respect away from him.

"The strength of the Rebel army rests on the
broad shoulders of Longstreet. He is the brain of
Lee, as Stonewall Jackson was his right arm. Before
every battle he had been advised with. After every
battle Lee may be found in his tent. He is a weak
man and little of a soldier. He naturally rests on
Longstreet, who is a soldier born."

When we recall that only four months earlier
Hooker, having been beaten at Chancellorsville,
boasted of successfully withdrawing his army across
the river from Lee's army, which was not pursuing,
we shall find more humor in his depreciation of Lee
than he intended. From the frankness with which
Hooker and the others talked to Hay we may be
justified in suspecting that they thought they might
through him reach the President. Lincoln, who
never failed to give a man credit for his good qualities, remarked to Hay, "Whenever trouble arises I
can always rely on Hooker's magnanimity."

Hay has some characteristic references to another notoriety of that period — Benjamin F. Butler — whom he met at Point Lookout in January, 1864.

"In the dusk of the evening," he writes, "Gen'l Butler came clattering into the room where Marston and I were sitting, followed by a couple of aides. We had some hasty talk about business: he told me how he was administering the oath at Norfolk; how popular it was growing; children cried for it; how he hated Jews; how heavily he laid his hand on them; 'a nation that the Lord had been trying to make something of for three thousand years, and had so far utterly failed.' 'King John knew how to deal with them — fried them in swine's fat.'

"After drinking cider we went down to the *Hudson City*, the General's flagship. His wife, niece, and excessively pretty daughter . . . were there at tea. . . . At night, after the ladies had gone off to bed, — they all said *retired*, but I suppose it meant the same thing in the end, — we began to talk about some queer matters. Butler had some odd stories about physical sympathies . . . and showed a singular acquaintance with biblical studies. . . .

"At Baltimore we took a special car and came home. I sat with the General all the way and talked with him about many matters: Richmond and its long immunity. He says he can take an army within thirty miles of Richmond without any trouble; from that point the enemy can either be forced to fight in the open field south of the city, or submit to be starved into surrender. . . .

"He gave me some very dramatic incidents of his recent action in Fortress Monroe, smoking out adventurers and confidence men, testing his detectives, and matters of that sort. He makes more business in that sleepy little Department than any one would have dreamed was in it."

At that sort of work Butler undeniably excelled; at fighting, his achievements were restricted to the feats he boasted he could perform when the enemy was at an entirely safe distance. The proper comment on his airy capture of Richmond — by tongue — in this conversation with Hay, is to be found in Grant's statement of Butler's fiasco in commanding the Army of the James. "It was as if Butler were in a bottle. . . . He was perfectly safe against an attack; but the enemy had corked the bottle and with a small force could hold the cork in its place." [1]

Grant repeated this indelible epitaph on Butler's military career twenty years after the event. How Hay and Lincoln commented on him at the time appears in this entry in Hay's Diary of May 21, 1864: —

[1] U. S. Grant, *Personal Memoirs* (New York, 1910), II, 75. Grant borrowed the simile from General Barnard.

"Butler is turning out much as I thought he would — perfectly useless and incapable for campaigning. ... I said to the President to-day that I thought Butler was the only man in the army in whom power would be dangerous. McClellan was too timid and vacillating to usurp; Grant was too sound and cool-headed and unselfish; Banks also; Frémont would be dangerous if he had more ability and energy. 'Yes,' says the President; 'he is like Jim Jett's brother. Jim used to say that his brother was the d——dest scoundrel that ever lived, but in the infinite mercy of Providence he was also the d——dest fool.'"

The paragraph which immediately follows Lincoln's remark concerns another cause of anxiety: —

"The Germans seem inclined to cut up rough about the removal of Sigel from command in the Shenandoah," Hay writes. "They are heaping up wrath against themselves by their clannish impertinence in politics." [1] (May 21, 1864.)

Hay's close friend, during his four years in the White House, was Nicolay, who, although of a matter-of-fact nature himself, appreciated and enjoyed Hay's gleaming wit. Ill-health frequently

---

[1] General Franz Sigel, who had been defeated several times in May and June, 1864, was removed from his command, as a result of Early's raid against Washington in July.

caused Nicolay to go away for rest, and then his junior sent him racy letters.

"My dear George," he writes on August 21, 1861: "nothing new. An immense crowd that boreth ever. Painters who make God's air foul to the nostrils. Rain, which makes a man moist and adhesive. Dust, which unwholesomely penetrates one's lungs. Washington, which makes one swear."

On April 9, 1862: "I am getting along pretty well. I only work about twenty hours a day. I do all your work and half of my own now you are away. Don't hurry yourself. . . . I talk a little French too now. I have taken a great notion to the Gerolts.[1] . . . Madame la Baronne talked long and earnestly of the state of your hygiene, and said 'it was good intentions for you to go to the West for small time.'"

In August Nicolay took another vacation. "The abomination of desolation has fallen upon this town," Hay tells him. "I find I can put in twenty-four hours out of every day very easily, in the present state of affairs at the Executive Mansion. The crowd continually increases instead of diminishing. "(August 1, 1862.)

There are many references to chills and fever, which attacked Hay during his first summer, and kept

[1] Baron Gerolt was the Prussian Minister in Washington.

coming back to plague him. For exercise, he rides "on horseback mornings" the off horse, which "has grown so rampagious by being never driven (I have no time to drive) that no one else whom I can find can ride him." (August 27, 1862.)

A year later Hay reports that X. "and his mother have gone to the white mountains. (I don't take any special stock in the matter, and write the locality in small letters.) X. was so shattered by the idol of all of us, the bright particular Teutonne, that he rushed madly off to sympathize with Nature in her sternest aspects. . . . This town is as dismal now as a defaced tombstone. Everybody has gone. I am getting apathetic and write blackguardly articles for the *Chronicle*, from which W. extracts the dirt and fun, and publishes the dreary remains." (August 7, 1863.)

At the end of that month Hay felt so fatigued that he ran off for a few days to Long Branch, and to the Brown Commencement, where he "made a small chunk of talk." On his return, he found Washington as dull "as an obsolete almanac. . . . We have some comfortable dinners and some quiet little orgies on whiskey and cheese in my room. . . . Next winter will be the most exciting and laborious of all our lives. It will be worth any other ten." (September 11, 1863.)

And here is an item of a different kind. "My dear Nico: Don't, in a sudden spasm of good-nature, send any more people with letters to me requesting favors from Stanton. I would rather make the tour of a smallpox hospital." (November 25, 1863.)

That there were occasional rifts in the clouds of routine, the following playful note to Nicolay attests: —

"Society is *nil* here. The Lorings go to-morrow — last lingerers. We mingle our tears and exchange locks of hair to-night in Corcoran's Row — some half hundred of us. I went last night to a Sacred Concert of profane music at Ford's. Young Kretchmar and old Kretchpar were running it. Hs. and H. both sang: and they kin if anybody kin. The Tycoon and I occupied a private box, and both of us carried on a hefty flirtation with the M. girls in the flies. . . . I am alone in the White pest-house. The ghosts of twenty thousand drowned cats come in nights through the south windows. I shall shake my buttons off with ague before you get back." (June 20, 1864.)

"The world is almost too many for me," he confesses on September 24, 1864. "I take a dreary pleasure in seeing P. eat steamed oysters by the half-bushel. . . . S. must be our resource this winter in clo'. If you don't want to be surprised into idiocy, don't ask C. and L. the price of goods. A faint rumor has reached me and paralyzed me. I am founding a 'Shabby Club' to make rags the style this winter."

CHAPTER VII

ERRANDS NORTH AND SOUTH

SEVERAL times during his service at the White House, Hay went on political or military errands. The routine of a secretary's life, even under those varied conditions, sometimes wore upon him, and he longed for the excitement, and the sense of immediate accomplishment, which life in the field offered. The President, always considerate, granted leave of absence.

Hay's first trip was to South Carolina. He reached Stone River on April 8, 1863, the day after the Union fleet made a concerted attack on the forts which defended Charleston Harbor. At first he heard enthusiastic reports from some of the officers, especially from the army staff: but Admiral Du Pont judged more wisely that, although the commands of the ironclad had behaved gallantly "under the most severe fire of heavy ordnance that had ever been delivered," [1] the monitors themselves, if the attack had been persisted in, would have been sunk or captured by the enemy.

General Hunter created Hay a volunteer aide

[1] N. & H., VII, 72.

without rank. "I want my Abolition record clearly defined," Hay wrote Nicolay, "and that will do it better than anything else in my mind and the minds of the few dozen people who know me." Ever since the presidential campaign of 1860, Hay had been an unquestioning Republican: that meant a Unionist without compromise. When the Southern States forced the war, he regarded the Secessionists as plain rebels; in theory either criminals, scoundrels, or madmen, deserving neither charity nor quarter. As the war progressed, he accepted the abolition of slavery and Lincoln's plan of emancipation as essential to the restoration of peace.

Hay's mission did not bring him into actual fighting, but it gave him a view of an army and a fleet in operation, and it opened his eyes to the difficulty of taking Charleston by sea. An interview with Admiral Du Pont quickly revised the impression the army officer had made upon him, and he wrote the President that the Admiral, by refusing to persist in an impossible task, had saved the fleet. Lincoln, be it said, had not believed that the attack on Charleston could succeed.

He stopped first at Hilton Head, South Carolina, the headquarters of General Hunter. There he found his brother Charles dangerously ill.

"The doctor said he had a slight bilious attack,

and treated him on that supposition." John wrote
their mother on April 23.

"I was not satisfied and mentioned my ideas to the
General, who took the responsibility of dismissing
the physician and calling in another, a Dr. Craven,
who seems a very accomplished man. He at once
confirmed my suspicions and said it was a decided
case of pneumonia. . . . As soon as Craven took hold
of him, he commenced getting better and is now
entirely convalescent. . . . We will start for Florida this afternoon and remain there a few days.
The climate is cool and pleasant like the Northern
June.

"I never felt better in my life than I do now. I
ride a good deal, eat in proportion and sleep enormously. I hope to weigh about a ton when I return.

"As to our future military operations I know nothing. I do not believe the General does. We have
not force enough to take Charleston and we hear no
talk of reinforcements. The Admiral thinks it madness to attack again with the Ironclads. The Government at Washington think differently. They think
he is to blame for giving up so soon. I do not know
how it is to end.

"I am not despondent, however. If we rest on our
arms without firing another gun the rebellion will fall
to pieces before long. They are in a state of star-

vation from Virginia to Texas. All we have to do
is to stand firm and have faith in the Republic, and
no temporary repulse, no blunders even, can prevent
our having the victory. The elections in Connecticut have frightened the Rebels and disheartened
them more than the Charleston failure has discour-
aged us.

"We received Mary's letter last night, for which
thanks.

"JOHN HAY.
"*Colonel and A.D.C.*"

No doubt, Hay added his titles to his signature in
order to give satisfaction to his family at home,
which had every right to be proud of the patriotic
devotion of the "Hay Boys." Their father, writing
to one of his sisters early in the war, thus referred to
them:—

"Our family ranks are, as you remark, somewhat
scattered, but all I trust under the protection of a
kind Providence, as well as the prayers of anxious
parents. I have every reason to feel satisfied with
the careers so far of our young family. John has obtained a position, in a social and political point of
view, never before reached by a young man of his
age in this generation, as the son of the celebrated
Alexander Hamilton lately said to him. The guest

SCHOOLHOUSE AT WARSAW, ILLINOIS

JOHN HAY'S EARLIEST HOME AT WARSAW, ILLINOIS

of Cabinet Ministers [and] foreign Ambassadors, and occupying a position in the public mind, which causes a day's illness to be flashed across the Continent as a matter in which the nation felt an interest. His arrival in a city noticed in the dailies as much as General Jackson's would have been thirty years ago. But enough of self-gratulation. All the family I have no doubt share in the pleasant reflection that the honor of each one is the property of the whole.

"Augustus, if less conspicuous, is not less able to act his part respectably anywhere he may be placed. Charles E. is just now entering upon a career which if the balls of rebels do not cut [it] short, may be as splendid as that of his elder brother. He is now commissioned as aide-de-camp to Maj.-Gen. Hunter, who is now commander in Missouri, an honor never conferred on so young a man, as far as I know, since Alexander Hamilton was made aide to Gen. Washington. He was packed ready to leave Fort Leavenworth for Santa Fé when [they determined] to change his destination. His officer in command expressed surprise that such an honor should be conferred on a youth of his age, but told him he was deserving of it. He will be in St. Louis in a few days to get a new rig of regimentals suited to his new honor."

We cannot fail to sympathize with the honest pride of Dr. Hay, who saw his three sons serving their country as a matter of course in the crisis of the nation's life or death. The comparison of John's celebrity with that of General Jackson is not only delightfully naïf, but also indicates what an impression "Old Hickory" made on the imagination of his contemporaries.

As soon as his brother Charles was strong enough for the voyage, John took him to Florida.

"We visited all the posts of this department in that State," John wrote his grandfather on May 2, 1863, "and were gone more than a week. . . . I never saw a more beautiful country than Florida. The soil is almost as rich as our prairie land. All sorts of fruit and grain grow with very little cultivation, and fish and game of every kind abound. I found there a good many sound Union people, though the majority are of course bitter rebels."

To Nicolay, Hay wrote from Stone River: —

"I wish you could be down here. You would enjoy it beyond measure. The air is like June at noon and like May at morning and evening. The scenery is tropical. The sunsets unlike anything I ever saw before. They are not gorgeous like ours, but singularly quiet and solemn. The sun goes down over the pines through a sky like ashes of roses, and hangs for an instant on the horizon like a bubble of blood. Then there is twilight such as you dream about."

Hay returned to Washington during the critical interval between Chancellorsville and Gettysburg, when the Confederacy, flushed by the success which the incompetence of Hooker presented it, was preparing its astonishing invasion of Pennsylvania.

Months elapsed before Hay saw any direct result from his first trip south. Then, on December 28, 1863, he received letters from Unionists in Florida, asking him to go down there and run as their Representative for Congress. President Lincoln, in his annual message on December 8, had announced his intentions in regard to reconstruction of the Confederate States. He offered to guarantee a full pardon to all who had been connected with the Rebellion, provided they took an oath "to support, protect, and defend" the United States Constitution and the Union, and to abide by the recent legislation freeing the slaves. Only persons who had betrayed their trust by quitting offices under the United States Government in order to serve the Confederacy, or had maltreated the colored troops, were excluded from this amnesty. The President further promised that when citizens numbering a tenth of the voters in 1860 took this oath and established a republican government in any of the rebellious States, the

United States Government would protect them from foreign invasion and domestic violence.

When Hay consulted Mr. Lincoln in regard to the invitation from Florida, the President thought that this would be a good opportunity for testing his scheme. Accordingly, he commissioned Hay to start at once to Point Lookout, deliver the oath-books to General Marston, and then to go farther South.

"I went on board a little tug at the Seventh Street Wharf," he writes, "and rattled and rustled through the ice to Alexandria, where I got on board the *Clyde*, most palatial of steam tugs, fitted up with a very pretty cabin and berths, heated by steam, and altogether sybaritic in its appointments."

The next morning (January 3, 1864), on landing at Point Lookout, he was received by a pompous aide who led him through the bitter cold to General Marston's headquarters. "There stood in the attitude, in which, if Comfort were ever deified, the statues should be posed, — parted coat-tails, — a broad plenilunar base exposed to the grateful warmth of the pine-wood fire, — a hearty Yankee gentleman, clean-shaven, — sunny and rosy, — to whom I was presented, and who said laconically, 'Sit there!' pointing to a warm seat by a well-spread breakfast-table." Whilst they were eating, "the General told a good yarn on a contraband soldier who complained of a white man abusing him: 'I does n't object to de pussonal cuffin', but he must speck de unicorn.'"

Hay's description of the Southerners held as prisoners there throws light on the extent to which they were reduced.

"The General's flock are a queer lot," he writes. "Dirty, ragged, yet jolly. Most of them are still rebellious, but many are tired and ready to quit, while some are actuated by a fierce desire to get out of the prison, and, by going into our army, avenge the wrongs of their forced service in the Rebel ranks. They are great traders. A stray onion — a lucky treasure-trove of a piece of coal — is a capital for extensive operations in Confederate trash. They sell and gamble away their names with utter recklessness. . . . They sell their names when drawn for a detail of work, a great prize in the monotonous life of every day. A smallpox patient sells his place on the sick-list to a friend who thinks the path to Dixie easier from the hospital than the camp. The traffic in names on the morning of Gen'l Butler's detail of five hundred for exchange was as lively as Wall Street on days when Taurus climbs the zenith, or the 'Coal Hole' when gold is tumbling ten per cent an hour."

That evening General Butler came in, as described
in the preceding chapter, and took Hay back to
Washington.

On January 13, Hay received his commission as
Assistant Adjutant-General, and announced to the
President that he was ready to start. Mr. Lincoln
sent him off with a hearty, "Great good luck and
God's blessing go with you, John!"

At New York, he embarked on the *Fulton* with
the Fifty-fourth Colored Regiment. "Variety of
complexions," he notes; "red-heads — filing into
their places on deck — singing, whistling, smoking,
and dancing — eating candy and chewing tobacco.
Jolly little cuss, round, rosy, and half-white, singing: —

> "'Oh, John Brown, dey hung him!
> We're gwine to jine de Union Army.
> We're gwine to trabbel to de Souf
> To smack de Rebels in de mouf.'"

On the 19th, a cold raw day, they passed Charleston early in the morning, and saw Fort Sumter "lit
up by a passing waft of sunshine." Arrived at Hilton
Head, he reported to General Gillmore, who was
somewhat disconcerted, because he supposed that
Hay's mission would necessitate a military operation. Hay reassured him, and during the fortnight
of his stay there he visited the Union works round
Charleston.

On January 23, in company with Generals Gill-more and Terry, he "saw the scene of the crossing by Shaw; [1] crossed and went in ambulances to Wagner; spent some time there. From Gregg had a good view of Fort Sumter — silent as the grave — flag flying over it — a great flag flying over the battery on Sullivan's Island. The city, too, was spread out before us like a map; everything very silent; a ship lying silent at the wharf. No sign of life in Ripley, Johnson or Pinckney." [2]

Ten days later the silence was broken. Hay was again making a tour of inspection with General Terry.

"Just as we got in sight of Wagner a white smoke appeared in the clear air (the fog had lifted suddenly) and a sharp crack was heard. It seemed as if a celestial pop-corn had been born in the ether. 'There's a shell from Simkins,' said Turner. We went on and there were more of them. As we got to Wagner we got out and sent the ambulance to a place of safety under the walls. They were just making ready to discharge a great gun from Wagner. The Generals clapped hands to their ears. The gun was fired, and the black globe went screaming close to the ground

[1] Colonel Robert Gould Shaw, killed while leading the assault of his colored regiment, the Fifty-fourth Massachusetts, on Fort Wagner, July 18, 1863.
[2] Forts near Charleston.

over the island, over the harbor, landing and bursting near the helpless blockade-runner stranded halfway from Fort Beauregard to Fort Moultrie. We walked up the beach."

Hay observed acutely, not only sights but sounds.

"The shells have singular voices," he records of the cannonade; "some had a regular musical note like *Chu-chu-weechu-weechu-b r r r;* and each of the fragments a wicked little whistle of its own. Many struck in the black, marshy mud behind us, burying themselves, and casting a malodorous shower into the air. Others burrowed in the sand. One struck the face of Chatfield, while I was standing on the parapet, with a heavy thud, and in a moment afterwards threw a cloud of sand into the air. I often saw in the air a shell bursting, — fierce, jagged white lines darting out first, like javelins, — then the flowering of the awful bud into full bloom, — all in the dead silence of the upper air, — the crack and whistle of the fragments.

"Colonel Drayton took us to see the great 300-pounder Parrot. At a very little distance, an ugly-looking hole where a shell had just burst; beside the gun, traces in the sand of hasty trampling and wagon-wheels; dark stains soaking into the sand; a poor fellow had just had his leg taken off by a piece of a shell. I saw them putting a crushed and mangled mass into an ambulance. He was still and pale. The driver started off at a merry trot. A captain said: 'D—— you, drive that thing slower!'

"We walked back on the beach to Wagner. A shell exploded close behind us. I made a bad dodge. Walked all over Wagner and got a sympathetic view of the whole affair."

On February 9, Hay reached Jacksonville, from which point General Gillmore planned an expedition inland. Hay addressed the Confederate prisoners, explaining to them the nature of the amnesty and assuring them that, if they accepted it, the United States Government would protect them. Then he opened an office in the quartermaster's block, took out his oath-books, and waited.

"They soon came," he says, "a dirty swarm of gray coats, and filed into the room, escorted by a negro guard. Fate had done its worst for the poor devils. Even a nigger guard did n't seem to excite a feeling of resentment. They stood for a moment in awkward attitudes along the wall. . . . I soon found they had come up in good earnest to sign their names. They opened again a chorus of questions which I answered as I could. At last a big good-natured fellow said, 'This question's enough. Let's take the oath!' They all stood up in line and held up their hands while I read the oath. As I concluded, the negro sergeant came up, saluted, and said: 'Dere's one dat did n't hole up his hand.' They began to sign, — some still stuck and asked questions, some wrote good hands, but most bad. Nearly half made their mark."

Having secured sixty names, Hay was reasonably well satisfied with his first day's work. That more than half the prisoners of war were eager to desert showed how the spirit of the common people was broken. Everybody seemed tired of the war, and longed for peace on any terms. The political questions involved did not trouble them. "Some of the more intelligent cursed their politicians and especially South Carolina; but most looked hopefully to the prospect of having a government to protect them after the anarchy of the few years past. There was little left of what might be called Loyalty. But what I build my hopes on," he adds, "is the evident weariness of the war and anxiety for peace."

Though Hay abhorred the military and political leaders of the Rebellion, he pitied the many victims of their policy. Here is a vignette of a household to which he was introduced at Jacksonville: "I saw in a few moments' glance the wretched story of two years. A lady, well-bred and refined, dressed worse than a bound girl, with a dirty and ragged gown that did not hide her trim ankles and fine legs. A white-haired, heavy-eyed, slow-speaking old young man. A type of thousands of homes where punishment of giant crimes has lit on humble innocents."

War means kaleidoscopic contrasts. At Beaufort on Washington's Birthday, Hay attended a ball managed by the young officers. When the dancing began, he went to the hospital ship and "saw many desperately wounded; Colonel Reed mortally, clutching at his bedclothes and passing garments; picked up, bed and all, and carried away, picking out his clothes from a pile by shoulder-straps — 'Major?' 'No! Lieutenant-Colonel!'" General Saxton was so shocked by Reed's appearance that he returned to the ball and ordered lights out in half an hour. The dancers grumbled, but all had the heart to eat supper. The General "came back glowing with the triumph of a generous action performed, and asked us up to his room, where we drank champagne and whiskey, and ate cake."

Hay pursued his way to Fernandina, which added a few names to his roll; but some of the natives "refused to sign on the ground that they were not 'repentant Rebels.'" He already realized that his mission was premature. The necessary ten per cent of loyalists could not be secured, and "to alter the suffrage law for a bare tithe would not give us the moral force we want. The people of the interior would be indignant against such a snap-judgment taken by incomers, and would be jealous and sullen."

In order to complete his inspection, Hay went on to Key West, filling his Journal with pen-pictures of the sea and reefs and of the human derelicts. As you read the following passages, you might suppose that they were written, not by a young major on a politico-military errand, but by a Hearn or a Loti, twenty years later, recording leisurely his impressions of travel.

"*March 5.* . . . To-night the phosphorescent show is the finest I have yet seen. A broad track of glory follows the ship. By the sides abaft the wheels, the rushing waves are splendid silver, flecked here and there with jets of flame; while outside the silvery trouble, the startled fish darting from our track mark the blue waters with curves and splashes of white radiance. Occasionally across our path drifts a broad blotch of luminous brilliancy, a school of fishes brightening the populous waters.

"*March 6.* A beautiful Sunday; the purest Southern day; the air cool but cherishing and kindly; the distant shore fringed with palms and cocoanuts; the sea a miracle of color; on the one hand a bright vivid green; on the other a deep dark blue; flaked by the floating shadows cast by the vagrant clouds that loaf in the liquid sky.

"Leaning over the starboard rail, gazing with a lazy enjoyment at this scene of enchantment, at the fairy islands scattered like a chain of gems on the bosom of this transcendent sea, bathed in the emerald ripples and basking in the rosy effulgence of the cherishing sky; the white sails flitting through the quiet inlets; the soft breeze causing the sunny water to sparkle and the trees to wave, I thought that here were the Isles of the Blessed; within the magic ring of these happy islands the sirens were singing and the maids were twining their flowing hair with sprays of the coral. Anchored in everlasting calm, far from the malice of the sky, or the troubling eyes of men, they sported through the tranquil years of the everlasting summer, in the sacred idleness of the immortals."

And having laid on his colors in this luscious fashion, almost to the point of cloying, Hay, with characteristic humor, adds: —

"My friend, Canis Marinus, begged to differ. He said: 'There's the Ragged Keys; full o' mud-torkles and rattle-snakes; them little boats is full of Conks — come up for to sponge.'"

Hay found Key West "bathed in the quiet ripples of the pale green water, whitened by the coral. So bright green that I cannot describe the gem-like shine of the distant waters. The sea-gulls that soar above the sea have their white breasts and inside wings splendidly stained with green by the reflection of the gleaming water." As his business at the Key consumed little time, he devoted himself, as was his custom, to sight-seeing, which included, in this case, some of the queer inhabitants of the town. Except for "a very decent darky with a very decent buggy belonging to a v. d. Dr. S., the only blot of decency on the Key West escutcheon," he pronounced them "a race of thieves and a degeneration of vipers."

On the voyage North, the steamer ran into a fresh gale. "We all stood wide-legged and anxious on the forecastle as men will about little things on ships, — Joe heaving the lead, — the Captain leaning to the breeze, his alpaca coat bagging like a seedy balloon, — Old Reed confident and oracular, — till Stringer, who had been hanging like a pointer dog over the rail, sang out — 'Light ho! 4.' This was old Bethel, and we at once knew where we were. We anchored and lay there quietly. I finished my poem, 'Northward,' begun to-day on leaving Key West." [1]

On steaming into New York, after stopping at Fernandina and Hilton Head, three inches of snow covered the deck, where "effeminate Southerners

[1] At Camp Shaw, a little while before, he wrote "Lèse-Amour," one of his best love-lyrics.

of six months' standing" shivered "like Italian greyhounds." The next morning Hay reached the White House, and reported to the President, who thoroughly understood the state of affairs in Florida. (March 24, 1864.) [1]

Mr. Lincoln evidently approved Hay's discretion, tact, and alertness, because he soon sent him on another mission of a different kind.

Since the outbreak of the war, there had existed in the North a minority of sympathizers with the Rebellion who organized a secret society, with lodges, ritual, and ramifications after the pattern of the revolutionists in Continental Europe. They called themselves the Knights of the Golden Circle, and they had several aliases, — the Order of American Knights, the Order of the Star, and the Sons of Liberty, — to use, like criminals, in case of discovery. They intended to undermine the Union sentiment in the Northern States, by enrolling as many members as possible, who pledged themselves, not merely not to support the Union cause by enlisting in it, but actively to aid the Rebels by giving them information and other help. Where they safely could, they assailed the property and lives of loyal citizens. They collected arms and ammunition, they formed military bodies and drilled, and they prepared for a vast

[1] Hay summarizes his mission in N. &. H., VIII, 282–85.

exhibition of their powers when the right hour should strike. Till then, they worked underground.

The Northern High Priest of the Knights was Clement L. Vallandigham; the Southern head, Sterling Price, was a general in the Confederate Army. Vallandigham claimed that at its height the order numbered half a million, and though he probably exaggerated, the organization was large enough to be formidable. It flourished in Ohio, Indiana, Illinois, Kentucky, and Missouri, where its members, by voting in concert, might turn the scale in a close election. Their secrecy added tenfold to their presumed strength.

Late in the spring of 1864, General Rosecrans, commanding in Missouri, having unearthed the secrets of the Knights, imparted them to Governor Yates, of Illinois, who joined him in urging the President to allow Colonel Sanderson, of Rosecrans' staff, to go to Washington with the evidence. Lincoln, who from the first had looked upon the Knights with "good-humored contempt," was not inclined to create public alarm by sending for Sanderson. He suspected also that Rosecrans wished by this ruse to embroil the President with Secretary Stanton; and he therefore despatched Hay to St. Louis to ascertain what the revelations amounted to.

On the journey, Hay "sat and wrote rhymes in

the same compartment with a pair of whiskey smug-
glers." He describes Rosecrans as "a fine, hearty,
abrupt sort of talker, heavy-whiskered, blond, keen
eyes, with light brows and lashes, head shunted forward a little; legs a little unsteady in walk." Coming to business after dinner, he offered Hay a cigar.
"'No? Long-necked fellows like you don't need
them. Men of my temperament derive advantage
from them as a sedative and as a preventer of corpu-
lence.'" Then, puffing away, and looking over his
shoulder from time to time, as if fearing he might be
overheard, he disclosed his discoveries about the
"O.A.K." as the Order of American Knights was
called for short. Detectives who had joined their
lodges in Missouri, reported that the whole order
was in a state of intense activity; that it had committed many recent massacres; that it proposed to
elect Vallandigham, then in exile in Canada, a
delegate to the Democratic Convention in Chicago,
and that if the Government rearrested him when he
came, the conspirators would "unite to resist the
officers and to protect him at all hazards."

Having listened attentively to Rosecrans, Hay
called on Sanderson, heard his statements, and then
went back to finish the evening with the General.
The discreet secretary neither made suggestions nor
asked for a copy of Sanderson's voluminous report.

He, too, surmised that Rosecrans wished by this means to "thwart and humiliate Stanton," and that Sanderson, naturally proud of his success as a ferret, would like to impress the President with his worth; and he suspected that they wanted money for the secret service fund.

These things he duly related to Lincoln, who "seemed not over-well pleased that Rosecrans had not sent all the necessary papers" by Hay. As for the General's urging secrecy, the President remarked that a secret which had already been confided to the Governors of Illinois, Indiana, and Ohio, and to their respective staffs, "could scarcely be worth keeping now." He thought the Northern section of the conspiracy a negligible quantity—"a mere political organization, with about as much of malice and as much of puerility as the Knights of the Golden Circle."

Events confirmed Lincoln's view: for although Vallandigham returned to Ohio unmolested, and took a vehement part in the Democratic Convention, the O.A.K. kept still, and, if they exerted any influence on the election in November, that influence was undeniably puerile.

Not only downright traitors, but political opponents of President Lincoln and peace-at-any-price men strutted and fretted their hour upon the stage, during that summer of 1864. In some respects the most notable of these annoying critics was Horace Greeley. No one disputed that his organ, the New York *Tribune*, was then the most authoritative newspaper in the United States. It had the widest circulation among farmers and rural readers, "the plain people" whom Lincoln regarded as the backbone of the country. It was taken with equal favor in the counting-room and offices and in the stores and homes, of the large cities and towns. Scores of thousands of Northerners turned to it every day, not only for its news but for its opinions. Its editorial page set forth, as in a serial story, the Gospel according to St. Horace, which his devotees, untroubled by its inconsistencies, came to accept without question.

The *Tribune* was what Greeley made it; the embodiment of his virtues, his defects, his prejudices. He shed his personality through it from the first column to the last, and the thousands to whom he appealed admired him as much in his weakness as in his strength. He was a New England Yankee, honest, shrewd, enterprising, resourceful, believing that the Lord helped those who helped themselves, and that, as he had prospered exceedingly, the Lord was on his side. Nature gave him the racy speech, the tart phrase. What he saw, he stated clearly; but this does not imply that he saw either far or deep. Though he spent all his mature life in New York City, his mind retained the schoolmasterish quality of his youth. So his person, with its ill-fitting clothes, and his face stamped by a countrified expression and encircled by flowing locks and a shaggy, diffuse throat beard, suggested — no matter where you met him — the rusticities of Vermónt.

For more than twenty years, Greeley had been the autocrat of the *Tribune*. When the war broke out the multitudinous public that had been taught by him in their ordinary affairs turned to him for guidance. The loose habits of reasoning, and of snap-judgments, which confirmed journalists seldom escape, Greeley not merely did not struggle against, but he cultivated. He dipped his pen of infallibility into his ink of omniscience with as little self-distrust as a child plays with matches. Conscious of the utter rectitude of his intentions, he found it hard not to suspect those who differed from him of moral crookedness. Doomed, as editors must be, to express opinion on insufficient evidence, he seemed at times to regard evidence in general as finical if not superfluous. Assuming that Abraham Lincoln, though well-meaning, was inexperienced and possessed of only a mediocre capacity, Greeley made it his duty to advise him; and when his advice was not taken, he berated the advisee. With equal assurance he criticized the conduct of international relations by Seward, the financial measures of Chase, and the operations of every commander afloat or ashore. From his editorial chair in the *Tribune* office, it cost him no more effort to tell Grant or Farragut what to do than to discuss the pumpkin crop with an up-state farmer.

A list of Greeley's misjudgments, from the days when, after he had supported Lincoln's candidacy, he upheld peaceable secession, down to the summer of 1864, when he labored frantically to stop the war, would serve as a warning against the deteriorating effects of journalism upon even a ready intellect and a well-developed conscience. It ought also to show the folly of trying to play the rôle of infallibil-ity without sufficient preparation. Greeley was not the only editor to whom this would apply; he was simply the most conspicuous, because the most in-fluential; therefore I have paused to describe him. Eventually, posterity may remember Horace Greeley only as the man who, with unusual power of scold-ing, harassing, irritating, with ingenuity in uncandid criticism, with exasperating self-righteousness and petulance, never succeeded in exhausting the pa-tience or in shaking the magnanimity of Abraham Lincoln.

On July 7, 1864, Greeley wrote Lincoln that he

had received word from a person who called himself William C. Jewett, that two ambassadors of
"Davis & Co." were then in Canada, with full power
to negotiate a peace, and that Jewett requested that
either Greeley should go at once to Niagara Falls
to confer with them, or a safe-conduct should be sent
to take them to Washington to talk with the Presi-
·dent himself. Greeley says: —

"I venture to remind you that our bleeding,
bankrupt, almost dying country also longs for peace;
shudders at the prospect of fresh conscriptions, of
further wholesale devastations, and of new rivers of
human blood. And a widespread conviction that the
Government and its prominent supporters are not
anxious for peace, and do not improve proffered opportunities to achieve it, is doing great harm now,
and is morally certain, unless removed, to do far
greater in the approaching elections."

After further lecturing the President, Greeley suggests the following terms: —

"1. The Union is restored and declared perpetual.
2. Slavery is utterly and forever abolished throughout the same. 3. A complete amnesty for all political offenses. 4. Payment of $400,000,000 to the
Slave States, *pro rata*, for their slaves. 5. The Slave
States to be represented in proportion to their population. 6. A National Convention to be called at once."

The letter concludes quite in Greeley's best vein:—

"Mr. President, I fear you do not realize how intently the people desire any peace consistent with the national integrity and honor, and how joyously they would hail its achievement and bless its authors. With United States stocks worth but forty cents in gold per dollar, and drafting about to commence on the third million of Union soldiers, can this be wondered at? I do not say that a just peace is now attainable, though I believe it to be so. But I do say that a frank offer by you to the insurgents, of terms which the impartial will say ought to be accepted, will, at the worst, prove an immense and sorely needed advantage to the National cause; it may save us from a Northern insurrection."

President Lincoln was skeptical in the premises, but he thought it wise to put Greeley's proposal to the test, and accordingly he appointed Greeley himself his agent to interview the negotiators.

"If you can find any person, anywhere," the President wrote on July 9, "professing to have any proposition of Jefferson Davis in writing, for peace, embracing the restoration of the Union, and abandonment of slavery, whatever else it embraces, say to him he may come to me with you, and that if he really brings such proposition he shall at least have safe-conduct with the paper (and without publicity, if he chooses) to the point where you shall have met him. The same if there be two or more persons."

To this downright message Greeley replied querulously, declaring that he had little heart in the task imposed upon him and that he thought the negotiators would not "open their budget" to him. Still hesitating, he wrote on the 13th that he had definite information that "two persons,[1] duly commissioned and empowered to negotiate for peace," were at that moment not far from Niagara Falls in Canada, and desirous of conferring with the President himself or with such agents as he might designate.

As Horace Greeley had received the President's terms and promise of a safe-conduct for the Confederates four days before, this note was, to say the least, astonishing. The President cut short the deliberate vacillation by telegraphing, "I was not expecting you to send me a letter, but to bring me a man or men." At the same time he despatched Major Hay to New York with the following letter: —

"Yours of the 13th is just received, and I am disappointed that you have not already reached here with those commissioners, if they would consent to come, on being shown my letter to you of the 9th inst. Show that and this to them, and if they will

[1] "Hon. Clement C. Clay, of Alabama, and Hon. Jacob Thompson, of Mississippi."

come on the terms stated in the former, bring them.
I not only intend a sincere effort for peace, but I
intend that you shall be a personal witness that it is
made." [1]

This letter Hay delivered to Greeley in New York
on the 16th. Greeley "didn't like it, evidently;
thought that he was the worst man that could be
taken for that purpose; that as soon as he arrived
there [Niagara] the newspapers would be full of it;
that he would be abused, blackguarded, etc., etc."
Still, if the President insisted, he would go, provided
he received an absolute safe-conduct for four persons. This Hay arranged, and Greeley agreed to be
in Washington on Tuesday morning, the 19th, with
the negotiators, if they would come.

"He was all along opposed to the President pro-
posing terms," Hay adds in his Diary. "He was in
favor of some palaver anyhow; wanted them to propose terms which we could not accept, if no better,
for us to go to the country on; wanted the Government to appear anxious for peace, and yet was
strenuous in demanding as our ultimatum proper
terms."

So Greeley journeyed to Niagara, petulant, un-
easy, vaguely suspecting, perhaps, that the President had turned the tables on him, and feeling some

[1] N. & H., IX, 189.

doubts as to the authority of the agents whom he was going to meet.

Arrived at Niagara, he sent word, through "Colorado" Jewett, to the representatives of "Davis & Co.," that he was "authorized by the President of the United States to tender [them] his safe-conduct on the journey proposed" [to Washington], and to accompany them at their earliest convenience. He omitted to state Mr. Lincoln's two conditions — "the restoration of the Union, and abandonment of slavery"; perhaps the omission was intentional, because Greeley was fixed in his purpose that the Confederates should propose their terms first. He soon learned, however, that they lacked credentials, yet he failed to realize that through Jewett they had deceived him as to their authority. Here was a bizarre contradiction: the infallible editor of the *Tribune* tricked by very common adventurers, who now assured him that they knew the views of the Confederate Government and that, if they were given a safe-conduct to Richmond, they could easily procure credentials.

By this clever turn they hoped to have it appear to the world that Lincoln was suing the Confederates for peace. Greeley, instead of repudiating them on discovering that they had duped him, telegraphed to Washington the new proposal of Clay and Holcombe (the fourth of the schemers). In reply, the President wrote the following note, and sent it by Major Hay on the first train to Niagara: —

EXECUTIVE MANSION, WASHINGTON
July 18, 1864.

To whom it may concern: Any proposition which embraces the restoration of peace, the integrity of the whole Union, and the abandonment of slavery, and which comes by and with an authority that controls the armies now at war against the United States, will be received and considered by the Executive Government of the United States, and will be met by liberal terms on other substantial and collateral points, and the bearer or bearers thereof shall have safe-conduct both ways.

ABRAHAM LINCOLN.

This paper Major Hay handed to Greeley at the International Hotel, Niagara, about noon on July 20. Greeley was "a good deal cut up at what he called the President's great mistake in refusing to enter into negotiations without conditions." He seemed "nettled and perplexed," possibly because he began to suspect that he had been too credulous. Hay finally persuaded Greeley to go with him to the Canadian side and deliver the President's letter.

"We got to the Clifton House," Hay records, "and

met George N. Sanders at the door. . . . Sanders is a seedy-looking Rebel, with grizzled whiskers and a flavor of old clo'. He came up and talked a few commonplaces with Greeley while we stood by the counter. Our arrival, Greeley's well-known person, created a good deal of interest, the bar-room rapidly filling with the curious, and the halls blooming suddenly with wide-eyed and pretty women. We went up to Holcombe's room, where he was breakfasting or lunching — tea and toasting, at all events. He was a tall, solemn, spare, false-looking man, with false teeth, false eyes, and false hair.

"Mr. Greeley said: 'Major Hay has come from the President of the United States to deliver you a communication in writing and to add a verbal message with which he has been entrusted.' I handed him a note, and told him what the President and Seward had told me to say, and I added that I would be the bearer of anything they chose to send by me to Washington, or, if they chose to wait, it could go as well by mail. He said: 'Mr. Clay is now absent at St. Catherine's. I will telegraph to him at once, and inform you in the morning.'

"We got up to go. He shook hands with Greeley, who 'hoped to see him again'; with me; and we went down to our carriage. He again accosted Greeley; made some remark about the fine view from the

House, and said, 'I wanted old Bennett [1] to come up, but he was afraid to come.' Greeley answered: 'I expect to be blackguarded for what I have done, and I am not allowed to explain. But all I have done, has been done under instructions.' We got in and rode away. As soon as the whole thing was over, Greeley recovered his spirits and said he was glad he had come, — and was very chatty and agreeable on the way back and at dinner."

Before taking the train, Greeley, unknown to Hay, had an interview with the shabby go-between, "Colorado" Jewett, whom "he seems to have authorized to continue to act as his representative." Jewett informed his accomplices at the Clifton, and they wrote Greeley arraigning the President for his breach of faith. Jewett at once gave their letter to the press, and its effect was just what the enemies of the Union desired. So far as appears, Greeley never informed the negotiators of Lincoln's promised safe-conduct. Pretending that the President's later note canceled the earlier, he supported the denunciation of the agents of "Davis & Co."

On being himself attacked by the loyal newspapers, he threw the blame on Lincoln. There was a call for the correspondence, and the President, by publishing it, could have given the Infallible One his

[1] James Gordon Bennett, editor of the *New York Herald*.

quietus: but as usual he would not seek a personal vindication at the risk of depressing public opinion. He feared that it would be "a disaster equal to the loss of a great battle," if it were known that the autocrat of the most influential newspaper in the North "was ready to sacrifice everything for peace," and was "frantically denouncing the Government for refusing to surrender the contest."[1]

The President, in his desire to soothe the enraged patriot, or at least to make him understand the purpose of the earlier notes, invited Greeley to go to Washington. This he declined in a ranting letter: "The cry [of the Administration]," he wrote, "has been steadily, No truce! No armistice! No negotiation! No mediation! Nothing but surrender at discretion! I never heard of such fatuity before. There is nothing like it in history. It *must* result in disaster, or all experience is delusive." And then, after insinuating that the effort for a tolerable peace might have succeeded if it had been honest and sincere, Mr. Greeley added: "I beg you, implore you, to inaugurate or invite proposals for peace forthwith. And in case peace cannot now be made, consent to an *armistice for one year*, each party to retain, unmolested, all it now holds, but the Rebel ports to be opened. Meantime, let a national convention be

[1] N. & H., IX, 198.

held, and there will surely be no more war at all events." [1]

To paraphrase Greeley's own expression: in the history of the Rebellion there is nothing "for fatuity" like this outburst by the political sage, who counted more readers than any other editor in the United States.

Even after Lincoln was dead, slavery abolished, the war ended, and the Union saved, Greeley stuck to his false statement with all the tenacity of the self-righteous when they are caught erring.[2] But Hay, who took part in the negotiations and had access to the documents, lived on to tell the truth.[3]

This mission, more important in its bearing than in its immediate results, was the last on which Lincoln sent him. As on the earlier ones, he acquitted himself well — was quick to see and hear, trusty in obeying instructions, discreet in dealing with strangers, unstartled by emergencies.

[1] N. & H., ix, 197.
[2] See his brief and disingenuous account of the transaction in his *American Conflict* (New York, 1866), ii, 664–65, in which he throws all the blame on Lincoln.
[3] N. & H., ix, chap. 8.

CHAPTER VIII

THE GREAT COMPANION

FOR Hay, during those four years, the daily and often hourly companionship of Abraham Lincoln was the most important influence of all. His position as private secretary not only gave him a knowledge from the inside of military and political plans, and an acquaintance with thousands of persons whose collective motives and deeds were woven into the fabric of the Drama, but it enabled him to observe, at closest range, the working of the mind, and the movement of the heart and character of the ruler who has had no peer in the Anglo-Saxon world.

John Hay has himself described, in a genial chapter,[1] the daily routine of life in the White House. The rush of office-seekers began on the first day of Lincoln's administration and continued, with slight fluctuations, until the last afternoon of Lincoln's life. Nicolay, Hay, and the others near the President tried to screen him from this drain on his time and strength; but he would not be screened. He felt that as the Head of the Nation belonged to the whole peo-

[1] *Century Magazine*, November, 1890; XLI, 33-37.

ple, he ought to be accessible to every one. He understood, also, the value of hearing opinions, though only in a moment's talk, from every quarter, and he could usually get something, if it were only a quaint phrase, even from cranks.

He was too shrewd a politician not to avail himself of such opportunities for personal interviews as arose. The spoils system inevitably flourished, because, with the coming in of a new party, offices under the Government, from top to bottom, were filled by new men. The outbreak of war created myriads of other posts, departmental, military, and naval. Under these conditions, fitness was not seldom overlooked: for Lincoln could not afford to estrange the influential backers of greedy place-seekers. The unfathomable Irony which manifests itself everywhere in human affairs, seemed bent on making sport of Democracy when it obliged Lincoln to turn aside from business of incalculable importance, while Senators urged upon him the claims of their poor relatives to the postmasterships of insignificant villages.

But "although the continual contact with importunity which he could not satisfy, and with distress which he could not always relieve, wore terribly upon him and made him an old man before his time, he would never take the necessary measures to defend himself," says Hay. ". . . Henry Wilson once remonstrated with him about it: 'You will wear yourself out.' He replied, with one of those smiles in which there was so much of sadness, 'They don't want much; they get but little, and I must see them.'"

President Lincoln rose early. In summer he spent the night at the Soldiers' Home where the heat was less intense than in the city; but by eight o'clock he had ridden to the White House and was at his desk. Long before ten o'clock, the stream of visitors poured in. The Cabinet met ordinarily on Tuesdays and Fridays. "At luncheon time," Hay writes, "he had literally to run the gauntlet through the crowds who filled the corridors between his office and the rooms at the West end of the house occupied by the family. The afternoon wore away in much the same manner as the morning; late in the day he usually drove for an hour's airing; at six o'clock he dined. He was one of the most abstemious of men; the pleasures of the table had few attractions for him. His breakfast was an egg and a cup of coffee; at luncheon he rarely took more than a biscuit and a glass of milk, a plate of fruit in its season; at dinner he ate sparingly of one or two courses. He drank little or no wine . . . and never used tobacco."[1]

"That there was little gayety in the Executive

[1] *Century*, XLI, 34.

House during his time," hardly needs to be hinted. The two younger boys, William and Thomas, enlivened it with their good-natured, unrestrained, and unconventional ways; but William died in less than a year, leaving "Tad" the only offshoot of young life in that somber household. Lincoln himself would give free play to his humor if a few friends were with him; and he was apt, at any time, to flash out one of the racy comments, or stories with an application, which his hearers never forgot. Lincoln "read Shakespeare more than all other writers together," and he went occasionally to the theater. His favorite plays were *Hamlet, Macbeth*, and the Histories, especially *Richard II*. He often quoted from the last the amaranthine passage beginning, —

> "Let us sit upon the ground,
> And tell sad stories of the death of Kings."

For relaxation he turned to Thomas Hood, and to Artemus Ward, Nasby, and other professional jokers of the time. But most of his evenings he spent in his office, unless there was a dinner-party.

"Upon all but two classes," Hay adds, "the President made the impression of unusual power as well as unusual goodness. He failed only in the case of those who judged men by a purely conventional standard of breeding, and upon those so poisoned by political hostility that the testimony of their own eyes and ears became untrustworthy. . . . The testimony of all men admitted to his intimacy is that he maintained, without the least effort or assumption, a singular dignity and reserve in the midst of his easiest conversation."

As I have noted earlier, Lincoln's young secretaries came sooner than the public to appreciate his greatness, and, in so far as it can be said of any one, they shared the confidence of that deep, patient, reticent nature. Lincoln discussed freely every topic except himself. Hay's Journal, from which many pithy extracts have already been made, furnishes us some of the most vivid flashlight pictures of Lincoln in personal moments or on historical occasions that exist.

Hay records that on January 27, 1862, the President issued his General War Order, No. 1. "He wrote it without any consultation, and read it to the Cabinet, not for their sanction but for their information. From that time he influenced actively the operations of the campaign. He stopped going to McClellan's and sent for the General to come to him. . . . His next order was issued after a consultation with all the Generals of the Potomac Army in which, as Stanton told me next morning, 'we saw ten Generals afraid to fight.' The fighting Generals were

McDowell, Sumner, Heintzelman and Keyes, and Banks. These were placed next day at the head of the Army Corps. So things began to look vigorous."

"Sunday morning, the 9th of March [1862], the news of the *Merrimac's* frolic came here. Stanton was fearfully stampeded. He said they would capture our fleet, take Fort Monroe, be in Washington before night. The President thought it was a great bore, but blew less than Stanton. As the day went on, the news grew better. And at four o'clock the telegraph was completed, and we heard of the splendid performance of the *Monitor*."

Lincoln acted so simply, not only dispensing with the forms of command but often seeming to wait on advice, that it took some time for his Cabinet officers to understand that he was, indeed, master. Thus before issuing his Order No. 3, deposing McClellan, he purposely omitted to consult Blair, who was opposed to the treatment of Frémont. Blair published a letter discourteous to the President, but when he went to explain it, Lincoln, instead of disciplining him, "told him he was too busy to quarrel with him," adding that if Blair "did n't show him the letter, he would probably never see it."

Patient though he was, and charitable in finding excuses for the shortcomings of the generals in the field, Lincoln felt the reverses keenly. Witness this reference to him at the time of the Second Battle of Bull Run.

"Everything seemed to be going well and hilarious on Saturday" (August 30, 1862), writes Hay, "and we went to bed expecting glad tidings at sunrise. But about eight o'clock the President came to my room as I was dressing, and calling me out, said: 'Well, John, we are whipped again. I am afraid. The enemy reinforced on Pope and drove back his left wing, and he has retired on Centreville, where he says he will be able to hold his men. I don't like that expression. I don't like to hear him admit that his men need holding.'

"After a while, however, things began to look better, and people's spirits rose as the heavens cleared. The President was in a singularly defiant tone of mind. He often repeated, 'We must hurt this enemy before it goes away.' And this morning, Monday [September 1], he said to me, when I made a remark in regard to the bad look of things: 'No, Mr. Hay, we must whip these people now. Pope must fight them; if they are too strong for him, he can gradually retire to these fortifications. If this be not so — if we are really whipped, and to be whipped — we may as well stop fighting.'"

The North, indignant at Pope's disaster, which

the public attributed to McClellan's lack of support, demanded that McClellan be cashiered. The Cabinet was unanimous against him. But Lincoln would not be persuaded. "He has acted badly in this matter," he said to Hay, "but we must use what tools we have. There is no man in the army who can man these fortifications and lick these troops of ours into shape half as well as he. Unquestionably he has acted badly toward Pope. He wanted him to fail. That is unpardonable. But he is too useful just now to sacrifice."

There spoke the man of sober second thought, whom neither popular clamor nor personal pique could move.

Under date, September 23, 1862, we have a still more memorable entry. "The President wrote the [Emancipation] Proclamation on Sunday morning, [September 21] carefully. He called the Cabinet together on Monday, September 22, made a little talk to them, and read the momentous document. Mr. Blair and Mr. Bates made objections; otherwise the Cabinet was unanimous. The next day Mr. Blair, who had promised to file his objections, sent a note stating that, as his objections were only to the time of the act, he would not file them lest they should be subject to misconstruction."

News traveled with desperate slowness to those

kept in suspense at the White House during a crisis. The battle of Gettysburg ended at dark on July 3, 1863; and yet for more than a week following, doubt and hope alternated in Lincoln's mind as to whether the Union general would complete his victory by destroying Lee's army. Hay writes:

" *Saturday, July 11, 1863*. The President seemed in specially good humor to-day, as he had pretty good evidence that the enemy were still on the North side of the Potomac, and Meade had announced his intention of attacking them in the morning. The President seemed very happy in the prospect of a brilliant success. . . .

" *Sunday, 12th July*. Rained all the afternoon. Have not yet heard of Meade's expected attack.

" *Monday, 13th*. The President begins to grow anxious and impatient about Meade's silence. I thought and told him there was nothing to prevent the enemy from getting away by the Falling Waters if they were not vigorously attacked. . . . Nothing can save them if Meade does his duty. I doubt him. He is an engineer.

" *14th July*. This morning the President seemed depressed by Meade's despatches of last night. They were so cautiously and almost timidly worded — talking about reconnoitring to find the enemy's weak places, and other such. . . . About noon came the despatches stating that our worst fears were true. The enemy had gotten away unhurt. The President was deeply grieved. 'We had them within our grasp,' he said; 'we had only to stretch forth our hands and they were ours. And nothing I could say or do could make the army move.'

"Several days ago he sent a despatch to Meade which must have cut like a scourge, but Meade returned so reasonable and earnest reply that the President concluded he knew best what he was doing, and was reconciled to the apparent inaction, which he hoped was merely apparent.

"Every day he has watched the progress of the army with agonizing impatience, hope struggling with fear. He has never been easy in his own mind about General Meade since Meade's General Order in which he called on his troops to drive the invader from our soil. The President says: 'This is a dreadful reminiscence of McClellan. The same spirit that moved McClellan to claim a great victory because Pennsylvania and Maryland were safe. The hearts of ten million people sunk within them when McClellan raised that shout last fall. Will our Generals never get that idea out of their heads? The whole country is our soil.'"

"*15th July.* Robert Lincoln says the President is silently but deeply grieved about the escape of Lee.

He said: 'If I had gone up there I could have whipped them myself.'"

And Hay adds: "I know he had that idea."

To picture Lincoln commanding at Gettysburg, crushing Lee's army, and with it the Rebellion, in the most significant battle of the nineteenth century, dazzles the imagination. More than one of the Union generals regarded Lincoln as possessing unusual qualifications as a commander: but could he have compassed that?

On July 16th: "General Wadsworth came in. He said in answer to Abe's question, 'Why did Lee escape?' 'Because nobody stopped him,' rather gruffly. Wadsworth says that a council of war of corps commanders, held on Sunday, the 12th . . . on the question of fight or no fight, the weight of authority was against fighting. French, Sedgwick, Slocum, and Sykes strenuously opposed a fight. Meade was in favor of it. So was Warren, who did most of the talking on that side, and Pleasonton was very eager for it, as also was Wadsworth himself. The non-fighters thought, or seemed to think, that if we did not attack, the enemy would, and even Meade thought he was in for action, had no idea that the enemy intended to get away at once. Howard had little to say on the subject.

"Meade was in favor of attacking in three col-

umns of 20,000 men each. Wadsworth was in favor
of doing as Stonewall Jackson did at Chancellorsville, double up the left, and drive them down on
Williamsport. I do not question that either plan
would have succeeded. Wadsworth said to Hunter,
who sat beside him: 'General, there are a good many
officers of the regular army who have not yet entirely lost the West Point idea of Southern superior-
ity. That sometimes accounts for an otherwise un-
accountable slowness of attack.'

"*19th July, Sunday.* The President was in very
good humor; ... in the afternoon he and I were
talking about the position at Williamsport the other
day. He said: 'Our army held the war in the hollow
of their hand, and they would not close it.' Again
he said: 'We had gone all through the labor of till-
ing and planting an enormous crop, and when it was
ripe we did not harvest it! Still', he added, 'I am
very, very grateful to Meade for the great service he
did at Gettysburg.'"

Characteristic is this last sentence of Lincoln's
indefectible sense of justice!

Another characteristic trait — his mercifulness —
appears in this episode: —

"To-day [July 18] we spent six hours deciding
on Court Martials, the President, Judge Holt and
I. I was amused at the eagerness with which the

President caught at any fact which would justify
him in saving the life of a condemned soldier. He
was only merciless in cases where meanness or cruelty
was shown. Cases of cowardice he was specially
averse to punishing with death. He said it would
frighten the poor fellows too terribly to shoot them.
. . . One fellow who had deserted, and escaped, after
conviction, into Mexico, he sentenced, saying, 'We
will condemn him as they used to sell hogs in Indiana,
as they run.'"

Without extraordinary power of resilience, Lincoln
could hardly have stood up against the disappointments and failures of the army, combined with the
unremitted attacks of political opponents and the
fault-finding of nominal friends, which he had to
endure day by day and year by year. His misunderstood liking for humor was one of the signs of his
fundamental health. In the summer of 1863, politicians were already discussing whom to elect to succeed him as President. In his own Cabinet he had
competitors. Yet he was neither angered by such
disloyalty nor exasperated by the readiness of party
leaders to throw him over. He saw the irony of being
the victim of such a conspiracy.

On August 7, 1863, only a month after Gettysburg, Hay writes to Nicolay: —

"The Tycoon is in fine whack. I have rarely seen

him more serene and busy. He is managing this war, the draft, foreign relations, and planning a reconstruction of the Union, all at once. I never knew with what a tyrannous authority he rules the Cabinet till now. The most important things he decides, and there is no cavil. I am growing more convinced that the good of the country absolutely demands that he should be kept where he is till this thing is over. There is no man in the country so wise, so gentle and so firm."

On August 9, 1863, Hay says: "This being Sunday and a fine day I went down with the President to have his picture taken at Gardner's. He was in very good spirits. He thinks that the Rebel power is at last beginning to disintegrate; that they will break to pieces if we only stand firm now. Referring to the controversy between two factions at Richmond, one of whom believed still in foreign intervention, Northern treason and other chimæras; and the other, the administration party, trusts to nothing but the army, he said: '[Jefferson] Davis is right. His army is his only hope, not only against us, but against his own people. If that were crushed, the people would be ready to swing back to their old bearings.'"

Hay accompanied Lincoln to inspect the statuary of the East pediment of the Capitol, and the President, with the eye of an expert, objected to the statue of the Woodchopper, by Powers, "as he did not make a sufficiently clean cut." On two evenings they tried a new repeating rifle, with which "the President made some pretty good shots." An irrepressible patriot came up and, "seeing the gun recoil slightly, said it would n't do; too much powder; a good piece of audience should n't rekyle; if it did at all, it should rekyle a little forrid." On another evening, they visited the Observatory, while "the President took a look at the moon and Arcturus. I went with him to the Soldiers' Home, and he read Shakespeare to me, the end of *Henry V* and the beginning of *Richard III*, till my heavy eyelids caught his considerate notice, and he sent me to bed."

Of Lincoln's unconventional ways these two extracts tell: —

"The President came in last night in his shirt and told me of the retirement of the enemy from his works at Spottsylvania, and our pursuit. I complimented him on the amount of underpinning he still has left, and he said he weighed 180 pounds. Important if true." (May 14, 1864.)

"A little after midnight as I was writing those last lines, the President came into the office laughing, with a volume of Hood's Works in his hand, to show Nicolay and me the little caricature, 'An Unfortunate Bee-ing'; seemingly utterly unconscious that he, with his short shirt hanging about his long legs, and setting out behind like the tail feathers of an enormous ostrich, was infinitely funnier than anything in the book he was laughing at. What a man it is! Occupied all day with matters of vast moment, deeply anxious about the fate of the greatest army of the world, with his own plans and future hanging on the events of the passing hour, he yet has such a wealth of simple *bonhommie* and good fellowship that he gets out of bed and perambulates the house in his shirt to find us, that we may share with him the fun of poor Hood's queer little conceits." (April 30, 1864.)

The late Richard Watson Gilder once said that amid all his trials Lincoln had one compensation in the White House — John Hay. Incidents such as these confirm him.

On September 11, 1863, Hay writes to Nicolay, not yet returned from a trip to the Rocky Mountains: "You may talk as you please of the Abolition Cabal directing affairs from Washington; some well-meaning newspapers advise the President to keep his fingers out of the military pie and all that sort of thing. The truth is, if he did, the pie would be a sorry mess. The old man sits here and wields, like a backwoods Jupiter, the bolts of war and the machinery of government with a hand especially steady and equally firm.

"His last letter [1] is a great thing. Some hideously bad rhetoric—some indecorums that are infamous—yet the whole letter takes its solid place in history as a great utterance of a great man. The whole Cabinet could not have tinkered up a letter which could have been compared with it. He can rake a sophism out of its hole better than all the trained logicians of all the schools. I do not know whether the nation is worthy of him for another term. I know the people want him. There is no mistaking that fact. But politicians are strong yet, and he is not their 'kind of a cat.' I hope God won't see fit to scourge us for our sins by any one of the two or three most prominent candidates on the ground."

On September 23, bad news came from General Rosecrans, who was expected to defeat the Confederate army round Chattanooga. Hay was at the War Department when "they were trying to decipher an intricate message from Rosecrans giving reasons for the failure of the battle. The Secretary [Stanton] says: 'I know the reason well enough. Rosecrans ran away from his fighting men and did not stop for thirteen miles. . . . No, they need not shuffle it off

[1] Dated August 26, 1863, to James B. Conkling, to be read at the Illinois Republican Convention. N. & H., VII, 380–84.

on McCook. He is not much of a soldier. I never was in favor of him for a Major-General. But he is not accountable for this business. He and Crittenden both made pretty good time away from the fight to Chattanooga, but Rosecrans beat them both.'"

Then Hay hurried "out to the Soldiers' Home through the splendid moonlight" to ask the President to attend a council at the War Department that night. "[I] found the President abed. I delivered my message to him as he dressed himself, and he was considerably disturbed. I assured him as far as I could that it meant nothing serious, but he thought otherwise, as it was the first time Stanton had ever sent for him. When we got in, however, we found a despatch from Rosecrans stating that he could hold Chattanooga against double his number; could not be taken until after a great battle; his stampede evidently over."

The loyal secretary, on returning from a visit to New York, told the President of the evidence he had seen there of the conduct of Secretary Chase "in trying to cut under" for the Republican nomination. Mr. Lincoln said, "it was very bad taste, but he had determined to shut his eyes to all these performances; that Chase made a good Secretary, and that he would keep him where he is: if he becomes President, all right! I hope we may never have a worse man.

I have all along seen clearly his plan of strengthen-
ing himself. Whenever he sees that an important
matter is troubling me, if I am compelled to decide
it in a way to give offence to a man of some influence,
he always ranges himself in opposition to me, and
persuades the victim that he [Chase] would have
arranged it very differently. It was so with Gen'l
Frémont, — with Gen'l Hunter, when I annulled his
hasty proclamation, — with Gen'l Butler, when he
was recalled from New Orleans, — with the Missouri
people, when they called the other day. I am entirely
indifferent to his success or failure in these schemes,
so long as he does his duty as the head of the Treasury Department."

Magnanimity such as this has had few parallels.
It would be unthinkable in the case of a Richelieu or
a Frederick or a Bismarck.

Lincoln continued to appoint, at Chase's suggestion, officials who would work in Chase's interest.
When Hay remonstrated, "he laughed on, and said
he was sorry the thing had begun, for though the
matter did not annoy him, his friends insisted that it
ought to." But by an adroit turn of the tables, the
President, supporting Seward in the raid which the
Senate made on him, caused the too impetuous
Chase to resign. Chase supposed that he would
thereby bring the President to terms. Far from it.

"When Chase sent in his resignation," the "backwoods Jupiter" confided to Hay, "I saw that the
game was in my own hands, and I put it through.
When I had settled this important business at last
with much labor and to my entire satisfaction, into
my room one day walked D. D. Field and G. Opdycke, and began a new attack upon me to remove
Seward. For once in my life I rather gave my temper
the rein, and I talked to those men pretty d——d
plainly. Opdycke may be right in being cool to me.
I may have given him reason this morning." (October 30, 1863.)

Memorable is Hay's account of the trip to Gettysburg, where President Lincoln spoke at the consecration of the Soldiers' Cemetery. The Presidential
party left Washington on November 18, 1863. "On
our train were the President, Seward, Usher and
Blair; Nicolay and myself; Mercier and Admiral
Raymond; Bertinatti and Capt. Isotta, and Lieut.
Martinez and C. M. Wise; W. McVeagh[1]; McDougal
of Canada; and one or two others. At Baltimore,
Schenck's staff joined us.

"Just before we arrived at Gettysburg, the President got into a little talk with McVeagh about Missouri affairs. McVeagh talked radicalism until he
learned he was talking recklessly. . . .

[1] Wayne MacVeagh.

"At Gettysburg the President went to Mr. Wills, who expected him, and our party broke up. McVeagh, young Stanton and I foraged around for a while — walked out to the College, got a chafing dish of oysters, then some supper, and, finally, loafing around to the Court House, where Lamon was holding a meeting of marshals, we found Forney,[1] and went around to his place, . . . and drank a little whiskey with him. He had been drinking a good deal during the day, and was getting to feel a little ugly and dangerous. He was particularly bitter on M[ontgomery] Blair. McVeagh was telling him that he pitched into the President coming up, and told him some truths. He said the President got a good deal of that, from time to time, and needed it.

"He says, 'Hay, you are a fortunate man. You have kept yourself aloof from your office. I know an old fellow over seventy, who was Private Secretary to Madison. He thought there was something solemn and memorable in it. Hay has laughed through his term.' . . .

"We went out after a while, following the music to hear the serenades. The President appeared at the door, said half a dozen words meaning nothing, and went in. Seward, who was staying around the corner

[1] John W. Forney, a notorious journalist in Washington and Philadelphia.

at Harper's, was called out, and spoke so indistinctly
that I did not hear a word of what he was saying.
Forney and McVeagh were still growling about
Blair. We went back to Forney's room, having
picked up Nicolay, and drank more whiskey. Nicolay
sang his little song of the 'Three Thieves,' and we
then sang ' John Brown.' At last we proposed that
Forney should make a speech, and two or three
started out . . . to get a band to serenade him. I
staid with him; as did Stanton and McVeagh. He
still growled quietly, and I thought he was going to
do something imprudent."

Then follows an account of the serenade, and of
the bibulous Forney's speech, in which, in tipsy
fashion, he mingled drollery and gravity. When the
crowd greeted him with shouts, he said: "My friends,
these are the first hearty cheers I have heard to-
night. You gave no such cheers to your President
down the street. Do you know what you owe to that
great man? You owe your country — you owe your
name as American Citizens." After "very much of
this," Hay adds, "W. McVeagh made a most touch-
ing and beautiful spurt of five minutes, and Judge
Stevenson of Pennsylvania spoke effectively and
acceptably to the people. 'That speech [of Forney's] must not be written out yet,' says Young.
'He will see further about it when he gets sober,' as

we went upstairs. We sang 'John Brown' and went home."

Quite Shakespearean is this low comedy interlude, coming just before the stately, dramatic scene of consecration. Perhaps, after all, Nature sometimes emulates Shakespeare.

"In the morning," of the 19th, Hay continues, "I got a beast and rode out with the President and suite to the Cemetery in procession. The procession formed itself in an orphanly sort of way, and moved out with very little help from anybody; and after a little delay Mr. Everett took his place on the stand, — and Mr. Stockton made a prayer which thought it was an oration, — and Mr. Everett spoke as he always does, perfectly; and the President, in a firm, free way, with more grace than is his wont, said his half-dozen lines of consecration, — and the music wailed, and we went home through crowded and cheering streets.

"I met Gen'l Cameron after coming in, and he, McVeagh and I, went down to dinner on board the N. C. R. R. car. I was more than usually struck by the intimate jovial relations that exist between men that hate and detest each other as cordially as do those Pennsylvania politicians.[1]

[1] General Simon Cameron's daughter became, in 1866, the second wife of Wayne MacVeagh.

In the morning I got a horse, and rode out with
the President's suite to the cemetery in the procession. The
procession formed itself in an orderly sort of way
& moved out with very little help from anybody &
after a little delay Mr. Everett took his place on the
stand — and Mr. Stockton made a prayer which
thought it was an oration — and Mr. Everett spoke as
he always does perfectly — and the President in a
firm free way, with more grace than is his wont said
his half dozen lines of consecration and the
music wailed and we went home through
crowded and cheering streets. And all the
particulars are in the daily papers.

I met John Cameron & Wyatt coming in and W. McV.
and I went down to dinner on board the
U.C. R.R. Car. I was more than usually struck
by the intimate jovial relations that exist between
men that hate and detest each other as
cordially as do these Pennsylvania politicians.

We came home the night of the
19th.

PAGE OF HAY'S DIARY RELATING TO THE CONSECRATION OF THE
MILITARY CEMETERY AT GETTYSBURG, NOV. 19, 1863

"We came home the night of the 19th."

Though brief, Hay's description of the delivery of the Gettysburg address serves. In the "History," he and Nicolay devote a dozen pages to the occasion, and, writing by the focused light of a quarter of a century, they assign to it an immediate recognition which very few of those who heard it were aware of. It was Edward Everett's monumental oration — which he did " perfectly, as he always does " — that carried the day. After that, Lincoln's few sentences seemed almost inadequate; or, at best, they came like the benediction, which you forget, after an impressive sermon, which you remember. To-day, however, Everett's marmoreal periods move no-body, while Lincoln's words of living flame bid fair to light and heat many generations. Emotion, not marble, is the medium of enduring eloquence.

The Diary, in spite of gaps, when Hay was too busy to write, reflects the variety of experiences which came to him day by day at Lincoln's elbow.

On November 22, 1863, he notes that " the Presi-dent is very anxious about Burnside." On the 24th, the tone changes. "To-night the President said he was much relieved at hearing from Foster that there was firing at Knoxville yesterday. He said anything showing that Burnside was not overwhelmed was cheering: Like Sallie Carter, when she heard one of her children squall, would say, 'There goes one of my young ones, not dead yet, bless the Lord!'"

On December 10, we learn that Sumner spoke with great gratification of Lincoln's recent message to Congress. "The President repeated, what he has often said before, that there is no essential contest between loyal men on this subject, if they consider it reasonably. The only question is: Who constitute the State? When that is decided, the solution of subsequent questions is easy. He says that he wrote in the Message originally that he considered the discussion as to whether a State has been at any time out of the Union, as vain and profitless. We know that they were — we trust they shall be — in the Union. It does not greatly matter whether in the mean time, they shall be considered to have been in or out. But he afterwards considered that the 4th Section, 4th Article of the Constitution, empowers him to grant protection to States in the Union, and it will not do ever to admit that these States have at any time been out. So he erased that sentence as possibly suggestive of evil. He preferred, he said, to stand firmly based on the Constitution rather than work in the air."

Another turn in the whirligig of experiences! On December 13, 1863, Hackett, the actor, spent the evening at the White House, and in their talk the President showed "a very intimate knowledge of those plays of Shakespeare where Falstaff figures. He was particularly anxious to know why one of the best scenes in the play — that where Falstaff and Prince Hal alternately assume the character of the King — is omitted in the representation. Hackett says it is admirable to read, but ineffective on the stage." Two nights later the President took his secretaries to Ford's Theatre to see Hackett as Falstaff in *Henry IV*. He thought that Hackett misread the line, "mainly *thrust* at me," which should be "mainly thrust at *me*." Hay dissented. "The President thinks the dying speech of Hotspur an unnatural and unworthy thing — and who does not?" [1]

And here is the first record of a famous saying. "The President to-night [December 23, 1863] had a dream: He was in a party of plain people, and as it became known who he was, they began to comment on his appearance. One of them said: 'He is a very common-looking man.' The President replied: 'The Lord prefers common-looking people. That is the reason he makes so many of them.'"

Among other duties, it fell to Hay to act as guide

---

[1] Lincoln's letter of August 17, 1863, to Hackett is well known. In it he says: "I think nothing equals *Macbeth*." Also that he thinks the King's soliloquy in *Hamlet*, "Oh, my offence is rank," surpasses Hamlet's own, "To be or not to be."

to persons of importance. One such service he described under the date of April 24, 1864.

"The President, loafing into my room, picked up a paper and read the *Richmond Examiner's* recent attack on Jeff Davis. It amused him. 'Why,' said he, 'the *Examiner* seems about as fond of Jeff as the [New York] *World* is of me.'

"E. L. Stanley, son of Lord Stanley, has been here for a week. I took him over to Arlington and showed him the African. He asked more questions than I ever dreamed of in similar circumstances. He applied a drastic suction to every contraband he met with, and came back with brain and note-book crammed with instructive miscellany. He has been exhausting everybody in the same way, till his coming is dreaded like that of the schoolmaster by his idle flock. He is a most intelligent gentleman — courteous and ready — a contrast to most Englishmen in his freedom from conceit and prejudice. He leaves town to-day. I gave him my autograph book; we exchanged cartes 'like two young shepherds, very friendly and pastoral.'"

During the late spring and early summer of 1864 the watchers in the White House followed anxiously General Grant's invasion of Virginia. On May 9 the first despatches from him came in, and the President was highly pleased. "It is the dogged pertinacity of Grant that wins," said he. The story was told that "Meade observed to Grant that the enemy seemed inclined to make a Kilkenny fight of the affair; and Grant answered, 'Our cat has the longest tail.'"

"*June 23*. The President arrived to-day from the front, sunburnt and fagged, but still refreshed and cheered. He found the army in fine health, good position, and good spirits; Grant quietly confident; he says, quoting the Richmond papers, it may be a long summer's day before he does his work, but that he is as sure of doing it as he is of anything in the world. Sheridan is now on a raid, the purpose of which is to sever the connection at junction of the Richmond and Danville Railroads at Burk's, while the army is swinging around to the south of Petersburg and taking possession of the roads in that direction."

Significant was Grant's remark to the President, that "when McPherson or Sherman or Sheridan or [James H.] Wilson is gone on any outside expedition, he feels perfectly secure about them, knowing that, while they are liable to any of the ordinary mischances of war, there is no danger of their being whipped in any but a legitimate way." Grant "seems to arrive at his conclusions without any intermediate reasoning process — giving his orders with the greatest rapidity and with great detail. Uses the

theoretical staff-officers very little," one of his subordinates told Lincoln.

Excitement over operations in the field was hardly
more intense than over the political campaign. Lincoln had been renominated by the Republicans; Mc-
Clellan, resenting his deposition from the command
of the Army of the Potomac, accepted the nomination of the Democrats. With fatal propriety the platform on which he ran declared that the war had been
a failure and that overtures for peace ought to be
made without delay. The issue was squarely posed.

Lincoln's friends saw dangers in every quarter.
No doubt a large minority in the North was tired
of war: no doubt many who had a sentimental regard for the Union thought that the emancipation
of the slaves had been wrongly given prominence.
Every discontented officer — every disgruntled politician — every merchant whose business was bad —
— every civilian who dreaded the draft — the ambitious leader like Chase — the party boss — the
army of unappeased office-seekers — the jealous —
the vindictive — all these, and everyone else with a
greed or a grievance, would unite to defeat Lincoln.
Thus, at least, it appeared to his foreboding lieutenants.

Even Hay, who was no alarmist, felt little confidence. "There is a diseased restlessness about men

in these times," he wrote Nicolay on August 25, 1864, "that unfits them for the steady support of an administration. It seems as if there were appearing in the Republican Party the elements of disorganization that destroyed the Whigs. If the dumb cattle are not worthy of another term of Lincoln, then let the will of God be done, and the murrain of McClellan fall on them."

Lincoln himself never lost his poise. Whatever his thoughts, his comments were humorous. He was charitable towards the disloyal. But he understood the danger: Democracy was at stake.

How subtle were the temptations presented to him appears from the following note in Hay's Diary:

"*September 23, 1864.* Senator Harlan thinks that Bennett's [1] support is so important, especially considered as to its bearing on the soldier vote, that it would pay to offer him a foreign mission for it, and so told me. Forney has also had a man talking to the cannie Scot, who asked plumply, 'Will I be a welcome visitor at the White House if I support Mr. Lincoln?' What a horrible question for a man to be able to ask! So thinks the President apparently. It is probable that Bennett will stay about as he is, thoroughly neutral, balancing carefully until the October elections, and will then declare for the side

[1] Senator James Harlan; J. G. Bennett, of the *New York Herald.*

which he thinks will win. It is better in many respects to let him alone."

The October elections went far to relieve anxiety. The President, with Hay, heard the returns at the War Department. Early news from Indiana and Ohio was cheering, but that from Pennsylvania was "streaked with lean." "The President in a lull of despatches took from his pocket the Nasby papers, and read several chapters of the experiences of the saint and martyr, Petroleum V. They were immensely amusing. Stanton and Dana [1] enjoyed them scarcely less than the President, who read on, *con amore*, until nine o'clock." Reports from the hospitals and camps showed wide differences of opinion among the voters. The Ohio troops voted about ten to one for Union, but "Carver Hospital, by which Stanton and Lincoln pass every day, on their way to the country," gave the heaviest opposition vote — about one out of three. Lincoln said, "That's hard on us, Stanton, they know us better than the others."

The Presidential election took place on November 8. Throughout the day, Hay reports, the White House was still and almost deserted. The President said to him: "It is a little singular that I, who am not a vindictive man, should have always been before

[1] Charles A. Dana, Assistant Secretary of War.

the people for election in canvasses marked for their bitterness: always but once. When I came to Congress it was a quiet time. But always, besides that, the contests in which I have been prominent have been marked with great rancor."

That evening they spent at the War Department. From the first, the returns were most encouraging and Lincoln's good humor added to the gayety of the company. When somebody (Eckert) came in "very disreputably muddy," the Tycoon was reminded of a story. "'For such an awkward fellow,' he said, 'I am pretty sure-footed. It used to take a pretty dexterous man to throw me. I remember, the evening of the day in 1858, that decided the contest for the Senate between Mr. Douglas and myself, was something like this, dark, rainy, and gloomy. I had been reading the returns and had ascertained that we had lost the legislature, and started to go home. The path had been worn hog-backed, and was slippery. My foot slipped from under me, knocked the other one out of the way, but I recovered myself and lit square; and I said to myself: " *It's a slip and not a fall.*"'"

When Fox, Assistant Secretary of the Navy, said that retribution had overtaken Hale and Winter Davis, "two fellows that have been specially malignant to us," Lincoln replied: "'You have more of that feeling of personal resentment than I. Perhaps I may have too little of it, but I never thought it paid. A man has not time to spend half his life in quarrels. If any man ceases to attack me, I never remember the past against him.'"

"Towards midnight," Hay adds, in his memorandum of this historic occasion, "we had supper. The President went awkwardly and hospitably to work shovelling out the fried oysters. He was most agreeable and genial all the evening. . . . Capt. Thomas came up with a band about half-past two, and made some music. The President answered from the window with rather unusual dignity and effect, and we came home."

At the Cabinet meeting on the 11th, "The President took a paper from out his desk, and said: 'Gentlemen, do you remember last summer I asked you all to sign your names to the back of a paper, of which I did not show you the inside? This is it. Now, Mr. Hay, see if you can get this open without tearing it.' He had pasted it up in so singular style that it required some cutting to get it open. He then read as follows: —

"'EXECUTIVE MANSION,
"'WASHINGTON, Aug. 23, 1864.

"'This morning, as for some days past, it seems exceedingly probable that this Administration will

not be re-elected. Then it will be my duty to so
co-operate with the President elect as to save the
Union between the election and the inauguration;
as he will have secured his election on such ground
that he cannot possibly save it afterwards.[1]

"'A. LINCOLN.'"

Lincoln went on to say, as I have quoted in an
earlier chapter, that he had resolved, if McClellan
were elected, to talk matters over with him.[2]

"The speeches of the President at the last two
serenades are very highly spoken of," Hay continues.
"The first I wrote after the fact, to prevent the
'loyal Pennsylvanians' getting a swing at it themselves. The second one, last night, the President
himself wrote late in the evening, and read it from
the window. 'Not very graceful,' he said; 'but I am
growing old enough not to care much for the manner
of doing things.'"

On November 12, 1864, Hay, with a large party,
went down to Grant's headquarters at City Point.
They found him occupying a little wall-tent. "At
our first knock he came to the door. He looked
neater and more careful in his dress than usual; his

---

[1] This paper was indorsed: "William H. Seward, W. P. Fessenden, Edwin M. Stanton, Gideon Welles, Edw. Bates, M. Blair, J.
P. Usher."

[2] See *ante*, pp. 133, 134.

hair was combed, his coat on, and his shirt clean, his long boots blackened till they shone." He thought that the Rebels were "about at the end of their tether; that Lee and Early had received their final re-inforcements"; that the negro troops are admirable in many respects, but "that an army of them could [not] have stood the week's pounding at the Wilderness or Spottsylvania as our men did; 'in fact, no other troops in the world could have done it.'" Grant was "deeply impressed with the vast importance and significance of the late Presidential election." The orderliness of it "proves our worthiness of free institutions, and our capability of preserving them without running into anarchy or despotism."

During the ensuing months we have only sparse records of Hay's life. In March, Secretary Seward, without solicitation and to his surprise, appointed him Secretary of Legation at Paris. "It is a pleasant and honorable way of leaving my present post, which I should have left in any event very soon," he writes his brother Charles. "I am thoroughly sick of certain aspects of life here, which you will understand without my putting them on paper, and I was almost ready, after taking a few months' active service in the field, to go back to Warsaw and try to give the Vineyard experiment a fair trial. . . . The President requested me to stay with him a month or so longer to get him started with the reorganized office, which I shall do, and shall sail probably in June. . . . I very much fear that all my friends will disapprove this step of mine, but if they knew all that induced me to it they would coincide." (March 31, 1865.)

A fortnight after Hay sent this letter, his life at the White House and his association with the Great Companion came to a tragic end.

On Good Friday, April 14, 1865, President and Mrs. Lincoln, accompanied by Miss Harris and Major Henry R. Rathbone, went to Ford's Theatre to see *Our American Cousin*. At about ten o'clock John Wilkes Booth crept to the door of their box, opened it, leveled a pistol at the back of the President's head, and fired point-blank. Mr. Lincoln never spoke again. They carried him unconscious to the house across the street — No. 453 Tenth Street — and laid him on a "bed in a small room at the rear of the hall, on the ground floor."

In a few moments Washington was alarmed, stunned. "A crowd of people rushed instinctively to the White House and, bursting through the doors, shouted the dreadful news to Robert Lincoln and Major Hay, who sat gossiping in an upper room. . . . They ran downstairs. Finding a carriage at the door, they entered it and drove to Tenth Street."

Before they crossed the threshold of the house they were prepared for the worst.

Hay watched near the head of the President's bed throughout the night. Gradually the slow and regular breathing grew fainter, and the "automatic moaning" ceased. "A look of unspeakable peace came upon his worn features. At twenty-two minutes after seven he died. Stanton broke the silence by saying, 'Now he belongs to the ages.'" [1]

[1] N. & H., x, 292.

CHAPTER IX

HAY was twenty-seven years old when the Civil War ended, bequeathing to him the memory of an astonishing experience which had called into play all his talents except the literary. In knowledge of the world, in acquaintance with men, in trial by the most daunting modern forms of ordeal, he had little to learn. He had kept his head and his temper, and his capacity to take adverse fate ironically, almost blithely. But except to the professional soldier, war offers no permanent career; and the war, which ripened Hay, left him with his fortune still unmade.

To have been Lincoln's private secretary during four years was privilege enough for one lifetime, but the recollection of it would neither feed nor clothe him; and Hay, with a constitutional inability to make money, found himself almost as poor when he quitted Washington in 1865 as when he went there with Lincoln in 1861. A few parcels of unprofitable land in Florida and an undeveloped vineyard in Warsaw represented the savings from his meager salary. Gladly, therefore, he accepted the post of Secretary of Legation at Paris, which promised him an imme-

diate living wage and a much needed change of
scene. Perhaps it might lead to something better.

Having visited his home, he reached Paris early
in the summer. Nicolay went also, to serve as American Consul there. "Mr. Nicolay is an intelligent,
honorable man, with a bilious temperament," wrote
Thurlow Weed, the Republican boss of New York
State, to John Bigelow, who was in charge of the
American Legation. "I *think* you will like him. Hay
is a bright, gifted young man, with agreeable manners and refined tastes. I don't believe he has been
spoiled, though he has been much exposed. If he
remains the modest young man he was, I am *sure*
you will like him." That was the time when tem-
peraments were classified as bilious, sanguine, nervous, or phlegmatic, and Weed would doubtless have
defined Hay as sanguine.

John Bigelow, the American Minister, had served
during nearly Lincoln's entire administration, and
upon him had fallen the task of preventing the Emperor Napoleon III from openly supporting the cause
of the Confederate States. Next to Charles Francis
Adams in London, whose work in helping to preserve
the Union can never be overestimated, Bigelow was
the most valiant defender abroad of the American
Republic. A vigorous writer, a scholar, a man of the
world whose courtliness suggested the traditions of

the Saint-Germain Quarter, he combined also in rare measure dignity and democratic downrightness.

Hay reached his post in June, 1865. For Mr. Bigelow he soon felt an affectionate admiration, which never slackened through life, while Mrs. Bigelow's inexhaustible vivacity now amused and now fascinated him. *"Mon Dieu! qu'elle est vive, qu'elle est vive!"* he records in his Diary, quoting "Old Plon," whom I take to be Prince Napoleon — "Plon-Plon."

The conclusion of the American Civil War left France and the United States face to face over an international question of grave menace. The French Emperor, taking advantage of the American upheaval, had sent an army to Mexico, conquered a part of that discord-ridden country, established an empire there under French protection and given the imperial crown to Archduke Maximilian, brother of the Austrian Emperor, Francis Joseph. Napoleon's purpose could not be misunderstood. He intended, if the American Republic were split into two separate and mutually hostile nations, that French influence should not stop at the Rio Grande.

One of the first acts of the Government at Washington after the Union had been saved, was to serve notice on the French Emperor that he must withdraw his army from Mexico; and while the American troops were massed in great numbers on the Mexican frontier to give point to this notice, it fell to Mr. Bigelow at Paris to carry on the diplomatic negotiations between the two governments. The Mexican difficulty was, indeed, the chief official business at the American Legation during John Hay's stay in Paris; but although he watched it intently from the inside, we cannot suppose that he shaped the course of events. After discharging his duties as secretary, he chiefly occupied himself with social life. His happy gift of riveting acquaintances, his quick interest in all sorts of persons and things, and his determination to make himself proficient in that Book of Paris which has fascinated the world since the days of Louis the Fourteenth, secured to him constant entertainment. He perfected himself in speaking French; he visited the art galleries, the theaters, the opera; and he found time to write poetry.

From 1865 to 1868 the Paris of the Second Empire stood at its zenith, surpassing in fashion and luxury its own earlier brilliant days. To observers who looked below the surface it seemed milliner-made, and even the soldiers, who were always on parade and lent color to every function, seemed soldiers in uniform only. But Napoleon III, the center from which all splendors radiated, was still the acknowledged arbiter of Europe, although there were already doubters who whispered that he too would collapse at the first shock with reality. He had lost prestige in Syria and in Italy, and now the United States blocked his ambitions in Mexico. Jesuit-led Clericals claimed greater and greater privileges from him, while the mutterings of Republicans from their hiding-places penetrated even to his study in the Tuileries. Never a keen reader of character, he set down Bismarck, who visited him at Biarritz, as "a not-serious man" — Bismarck the terrible, in whose brain was already matured the plan to Prussianize Germany and to fix German despotism upon Europe, after having bled France — and any others who opposed him — white.

Hay, fresh from the four years' struggle which had determined that Democracy should not perish from the earth in America, fostered the dream, dear to many persons at the time, that a Golden Age of Freedom was about to dawn. Even in England men predicted that the Republic would come after Queen Victoria's death, if not before; and that on the Continent, as soon as the French autocrat could be curbed, the unification of Italy would be completed and that of Germany achieved. Then the peoples of Europe, united at last according to the principle of nationality, would be peace-loving and peace-keeping, liberal in their political methods, and bound together by a sense of mutual interdependence and of common ideals.

Towards Napoleon III, the despot who prevented the immediate realization of this dream, Hay felt aversion mingled with scorn, for he half suspected that the Emperor was more than half a charlatan.

Being not only a diplomat but a discreet diplomat, he kept his opinions to himself. In private, however, he gave vent to them in poems which he did not publish until after his return from France. These poems are interesting, not only because they have their place in Hay's literary development, but also because they show us his innermost convictions at this time.

The first, "Sunrise in the Place de la Concorde," he wrote in August, 1865, shortly after his arrival in Paris, and whilst the views or prepossessions concerning Napoleon III which he had brought with him from America were still fresh. It opens with a description apparently slight and yet vivid.

> I stand at the break of day
> In the Champs Elysées.
> The tremulous shafts of dawning
> As they shoot o'er the Tuileries early,
> Strike Luxor's cold gray spire,
> And wild in the light of the morning
> With their marble manes on fire
> Ramp the white Horses of Marly.

But the Place of Concord lies
Dead hushed 'neath the ashy skies.
And the Cities sit in council
With sleep in their wide stone eyes.
I see the mystic plain
Where the army of spectres slain
In the Emperor's life-long war
March on with unsounding tread
To trumpets whose voice is dead.
Their spectral chief still leads them, —
The ghostly flash of his sword
Like a comet through mist shines far, —
And the noiseless host is poured,
For the gendarme never heeds them,
Up the long dim road where thundered
The army of Italy onward
Through the great pale Arch of the Star!

And then the poet goes on to describe earlier scenes
which the Place de la Concorde witnessed.

There is one that seems a King,
As if the ghost of a Crown
Still shadowed his jail-bleached hair;
I can hear the guillotine ring,
As its regicide note rang there,
When he laid his tired life down
And grew brave in his last despair.

Other figures rise in his imagination: Madame
Dubarry —

Who weeps at leaving a world
Of love and revel and sin. . . .
For life was wicked and sweet
With kings at her small white feet!

and Marie Antoinette, "every inch a Queen,"—

> Whose blood baptized the place,
> In the days of madness and fear, —
> Her shade has never a peer
> In majesty and grace.

And so on to the glorious promise of 1848: —

> As Freedom with eyes aglow
> Smiled glad through her childbirth pain,
> How was the mother to know
> That her woe and travail were vain?
> A smirking servant smiled
> When she gave him her child to keep;
> Did she know he would strangle the child
> As it lay in his arms asleep?
>
> .   .   .   .
>
> The treasure of 'Forty-Eight
> A lurking jail-bird stole,
> She can but watch and wait
> As the swift sure seasons roll.
>
> And when in God's good hour
> Comes the time of the brave and true,
> Freedom again shall rise
> With a blaze in her awful eyes
> That shall wither this robber-power
> As the sun now dries the dew.

In another poem, "The Sphinx of the Tuileries,"
Hay speaks even more scornfully —

> Of the Charlatan whom the Frenchmen loathe
> And the Cockneys all admire.
>
> .   .   .   .

Afraid to fight and afraid to fly,
   He cowers in an abject shiver;
The people will come to their own at last, —
   God is not mocked forever.

These and similar indictments of the Third Napoleon the young diplomat confided, temporarily,
to his portfolio. By inheritance and choice he loathed
despotism; and when he found it personified in a
man whose resource was craft and not strength, his
loathing was doubled. He believed so heartily that
Democracy could cure political evils of every degree
of malignity, that he underestimated the advantage
which the element of readiness gave to the partisans
of Reaction, solidaire, and propped by their standing armies and their churches.

Whatever the Poet's convictions, however, the
Secretary of Legation seemed not to know of them.
He mixed with Imperialists as smoothly as with every
one else, and although he may have abhorred their
principles, he found his instinct for refinement enjoying the elegance of the Imperial Court. "One tor-
ment of diplomatic life," he writes, "is that you never
know the names of these agreeable fellows," — the
imperial Chamberlains. "They lose all identity in
their violet coats and Imperial moustaches. You do
not hear their names when you are presented to
them, and if you look upon the official list of the

officers of the Emperor's household you only find
that you may take your choice of a dozen names
for the man you are looking after."

Among Hay's notes is a report of a conversation he
had on September 25, 1866, with the Reverend Dr.
Smith, Professor of Dogmatic Theology in Propa-
ganda Fide College at Rome. That was the interval
when the Pope's Temporal Power was being bol-
stered up, somewhat unsteadily, by a French garrison. "I got one idea," Hay says, "which was definite
enough, to wit, the absolute uncertainty in which
the Roman politicians are as to the future. The
Professor declared that "the Pope is really not fixed
in any plan. It seems now certain that the French
will withdraw in December. Then, what will happen,
remains to be seen. If the enemies of the Temporal
Power are willing to allow him to exercise the sov-
ereignty over the little patch of earth around the
Eternal City, he can still retain his position and
prestige in the Catholic World. If, on the contrary,
he is made the object of violent attack from without,
he will retire from Rome."

The Professor admitted that there were many
revolutionists in the city, but he added that both
they, and the Pope's friends, were "too weak, too
destitute of enterprise to accomplish anything. . . .
The only thing to be feared is the flood swelling in

from Italy and submerging Rome. But, I asked, is it considered impossible, among reasonable men around the Pope, to treat with the King of Italy and to obtain from him the protection he would doubtless gladly accord? The Doctor shook his head and said slowly, 'I do not see how it can be done. There are some compromises which would destroy the very essence of the principle in question. These cannot be made. Such compromises are different from merely accepting the logic of events.'"

The Doctor further related that several years before, when the Curia was much perturbed, Pius IX said to Lord Odo Russell, the English Envoy: "'I suppose, if I am driven out of Rome, you will let me come to Malta, would you not?'" Lord Odo consulted the British Foreign Secretary,[1] his uncle, who "immediately answered that whenever his Holiness desired it an English man-of-war would be at his service at Civita Vecchia to take him to Malta. This despatch still exists, and Dr. Smith says it is the only document that has passed between the two governments on the subject."

That the Catholic Pope should turn in private for protection to the Protestant power which he reviled in public, is among the humors of that decade of insincerities.

[1] Lord John Russell.

When Hay referred to the hope of the Catholics in America to see the Pope among them, the Doctor said "the matter had sometimes been thought of, but that it seemed impracticable; as the Pope should occupy a more central position in reference to Christendom."

"The Emperor never was the meekest of men," Hay records in another place, "but his temper is sour this autumn [1866] as the disappointed vintage of Burgundy . . . just before going to Biarritz. . . . [he] went to see the Palais de l'Exposition. He seemed to be very bilious. On coming in sight of the Champ de Mars, he said: 'Call that a palace! Looks like a gasometer!' When he came to the high, closed fence, surrounding the park, he says: 'What does this mean? Tear it down! The people have a right to see the building.' They explained, and he compromised by tearing holes in the fence at intervals. On each side of the North entrance were neat brick structures for the officers of the Exposition. Here his bile boiled over. '*Otez moi ça!* What the Devil do you spoil the view so for? Tear them down!' And this week you see workmen demolishing with pick and shovel what they built laboriously last week with chisel and trowel."

In contrast to this glimpse of Napoleon in peevish mood, is Hay's description of an Imperial reception at the Tuileries. In November, 1866, Mr. Bigelow was succeeded as Minister by General John A. Dix, — former Secretary of the Treasury, who, when Secession became active, telegraphed to New Orleans, "If any one attempts to haul down the American flag, shoot him on the spot." Soon after his arrival in Paris, Marquis de Moustier, the Imperial Grand Master of Ceremonies, informed him that the Emperor would receive him on Sunday, December 23, at two o'clock.

"I hired a carriage and two servants, in the Rue Boissy d'Anglas, for Hoffman [1] and myself," writes Hay. "It was a highly respectable looking affair, not fresh enough to look hired, with a couple of solemn flunkies that seemed to have been in the family for at least a generation. We went to the General's [Dix] and in a few moments came in the Baron de Lajus. He said he was very much crowded to-day with *besogne*, that he had five Ministers to bring to the Palace, and that therefore we would please excuse his hurry. Upon which we all rose and went to the door, where we found a court carriage, the Imperial arms blazing on the panels and the harness, drawn by four horses and accompanied by two mounted outriders. Everything covered with tawdry, tarnished gold lace. It seemed like the

[1] Under secretary at the Legation.

Triumphal Car in a flourishing circus. Into this
vehicle mounted the General and the Chamberlain,
Hoffman and I following in our sham-private *remise;*
and we had all the honors of a stare from the *badauds*
on the asphalt of the Champs Elysées as the party
lumbered down to the Tuileries. We were all in our
Army uniform.

"Arrived there, we were shown to a warm, cheery
ante-room, with a superb wood fire and a fine view
of the Tuileries gardens, the Avenue and the Arch
of Triumph." "We waited some time, while other
dignitaries gathered — the Colombian Minister;
Fane, the British Minister *ad interim;* the long,
gaunt Bavarian, Perger de Paglas and his secretary,
who seemed moved by rusty springs"; a "thin, wiry,
blue-blooded Brazilian; a Peruvian; and some more."
Then some of the "violet people" moved the party
into a larger saloon. They "were presented to the
Duc de Cambacérès, a jaunty old gentleman, lean
and shaven and wigged — long also. He bowed lavishly and seemed distressed that nobody would sit
down." Then Mr. Bigelow was called for, and "he
entered the next room where the blaze of the Imperial Presence dazzled us through the opening door.
His audience of leave was soon over.

"Gen'l Dix, followed by me and Hoffman, was
then ushered into The Presence. The General

looked anxiously around for the Emperor, advancing undecidedly, until a little man, who was standing in front of the Throne, stepped forward to meet him. Everybody bowed profoundly as the Duc de Cambacérès gave the name and the title of the General. The little man bowed, and the General, beginning to recognize in him a dim likeness to the Emperor's portrait, made his speech to him."

Here follows a characteristic digression. "I looked around the room for a moment," Hay continues, "admiring as I always do on ceremonial occasions in France the rich and tasteful masses of color which the various groups of Great Officers of the Crown so artistically present. Not a man's place is left to accident. A cardinal dashes in a great splash of scarlet. A *cent-garde* supplies an exquisite blue and gold. The yellow and the greens are furnished by the representatives of Law and Legislation, and the Masters of Ceremonies fill up with an unobtrusive violet. Yet these rich lights and soft shadows are accessory to the central point of the picture — the little man who is listening or seeming to listen to the General's address. If our Republican eyes can stand such a dazzling show, let us look at him.

"Short and stocky, he moves with a queer, side-long gait, like a gouty crab; a man so wooden looking that you would expect his voice to come rasping out

like a watchman's rattle. A complexion like crude
tallow — marked for Death, whenever Death wants
him — to be taken sometime in half an hour, or left,
neglected by the Skeleton King for years, perhaps,
if properly coddled. The moustache and imperial
which the world knows, but ragged and bristly, concealing the mouth entirely, is moving a little nervously as the lips twitch. Eyes sleepily watchful —
furtive — stealthy, rather ignoble; like servants
looking out of dirty windows and saying 'nobody at
home,' and lying as they say it. And withal a wonderful phlegm. He stands there as still and impas-
sive as if carved in oak for a ship's figurehead. He
looks not unlike one of those rude inartistic statues.
His legs are too short — his body too long. He never
looks well but on a throne or on a horse, as kings
ought."

In all his writing, Hay never did better than that.
As a historical portrait in the gallery of nineteenth-
century celebrities, it will take its place. If it seems
malign, its malignity may be compared with the acid
which bites in the etching.

Hay goes on to tell how General Dix, raising his
voice and grown a little oratorical, closes his speech
and hands the Emperor his sealed letter of credence.
The Emperor gives it to the Duc de Bassano, who
stands at his right. The Emperor's "face breaks up

splash of scarlet. A cent-garde supplies an exquisite blue and gold. The yellows and the greens are furnished by the representatives of law & legislation and the Masters of Ceremonies fill up with an unobtrusive violet. Yet these rich lights and soft shadows are accessory to the central point of the picture — the little man who is listening or seeing to listen to the General's address. If our Republican eyes can stand such a dazzling show, let us look at him.

Short and stocky; he moves with a queer sidelong gait like a gouty crab: a man so wooden looking that you would expect his voice to come rasping out like a watchman's rattle. A complexion like crude tallow — marked for Death, whenever Death wants him — to be taken some time in half an hour or left neglected by the Skeleton King, for years perhaps, if properly coddled. The moustache and imperial which the world knows, but ragged and bristly concealing the mouth entirely is moving a little nervously as the lips twitch. Eyes sleepily watchful — furtive, stealthy.

DESCRIPTION OF NAPOLEON III IN JOHN HAY'S DIARY

with ungainly movements of the moustache and the eyelids. You can imagine it a sort of wooden clock preparing to strike. When he speaks you are sure of your theory. His voice is wooden; it is not so strong and full as a year ago. He speaks rather rapidly and not distinctly. He slurs half his words, as rapid writers do half their letters. He makes his set speech, which, with the General's, will appear to-morrow in the *Moniteur*, and then comes sidling up and says (smilingly, he evidently thinks, but the machinery of smiles at the corners of his mouth is apparently out of repair), 'You expect many of your countrymen in Paris this year?'

"'A great many, doubtless.'

"'There will be a regiment of your *milice?*'

"'There has been some talk of it, etc., etc., but your Majesty will not expect them to compare with your veterans.'

"'But you have shown that it does not take long to make good troops.'"

After further gracious trivialities, Hay and Hoffman were presented to the Emperor, who, "clearly wishing to be very civil, as it is most rare that a monarch addresses a Secretary of Legation, said, 'But you are very young to be Col-o-nel. Did you make the war in America?'

"I wanted to insist that older and wickeder men

than I were responsible for that crime, but I thought best to answer the intention rather than the grammar, and said I had had an humble part in the war.

"'Infanterie or cavalerie?'

"'The general staff!'

"'And you?' he said, turning to Hoffman, and received the same answer. We bowed and backed out of the Presence."

Upon leaving the Emperor, the party was taken to the Empress Eugénie.

"She was charmingly dressed in a lilac walking dress with an almost invisible bonnet," says the observant Hay. "She had doubtless been to church like a good, pious lady, as she is, and received afterwards in her promenade costume. Time has dealt very gently with her. [Eugénie was born May 5, 1826.] She is still full of those sweet, winning fascinations that won her a crown. There are few partisans so bitter as not to be moved by her exquisite manner. Even the little stories at which men smile, her subjection to priests, her hanging up over old Baciocchi's deathbed the holy rag from the baby linen of John Baptist, which extorted from the tormented old sinner his last grim smile, her vestal lamp in the Church of Our Lady of Victories, and all that mummery is not unfeminine, and people do not care to be bitter about it.

"To the General she was charming. She talked about the President [Johnson] and his trip to Chicago (which the General explained was purely a personal visit of friendship to the tomb of a friend! ! !). When we were presented, she made the identical remark made by the Emperor, 'You are young to be Colonel?' People after a dozen years of intercourse get the same ideas and ways of looking at things. She asked if the grade of Colonel was the same in our army as in the French. She spoke English with a charming Castilian accent, which is infinitely prettier than the French. She is so winning and so lovely that one feels a little guilty in not being able in conscience to wish her eternal power for herself, her heirs and assigns.

"So we left the gracious blonde Spaniard and passed down through the avenue of flunkies to the door where our own sham flunkies received us and drove us to the Rue de Presbourg. The ceremony is concluded by giving to the Chief Piqueur a present of 250 francs."

With the resignation of John Bigelow and the coming of General Dix, Hay's term as Secretary of Legation expired. The new Minister wished to have his own subordinates; and, according to the haphazard diplomatic practice of the American Government, even the most important posts, instead of being

guarded by permanent officials who knew the business traditions and ceremonial, were from time to
time swept clean of experts and handed over to a
new batch of novices.

As this was the well-understood procedure, Hay
did not complain. "I am going home, as the papers
have stated, in a strange paroxysm of truthfulness,"
he wrote to his friend Albert Rhodes in December,
1866. "I leave the service of the ungrateful Republic
in a week or two more.

Vain pomps and glories of this world I hate ye. (Shakes.)

I shall try to find a place behind some respectable
counter. I do not care what I sell — candles or
stocks — so that profits shall accrue. I shall pull off
my coat and roll up my sleeves, but I don't believe
Jordan will be so hard a road to travel as it is cracked
up to be. . . . I am falling into the sere, the yellow
leaf."

Before Hay quitted Paris, he had a final view of the
Emperor, at the Diplomatic Reception on January
1, 1867. Ever since the New Year's Day eight years
before, when Napoleon's remark to the Austrian
Ambassador was construed as a hint of impending
war, that annual occasion had caused some trepidation to European politicians. Hay's description of
one of the last of these ceremonies, sketched with

sont bien compliquées là-bas!' The poor devil, who doubtless feels himself lost by his advocacy of the Imperial cause in Mexico, had no reply to this insolent remark from his angry and ungrateful tempter. The Emperor bowed, the Prince Imperial bowed, and Almonte bowed. I did not dare to look at him.

"I looked at the Emperor instead, who came to Gen'l Dix and was very gracious — speaking French this time — asked the General where he lived and said it was a *beau quartier* — the General said yes, thanks to His Majesty — and His Majesty pulled the corners of his mouth into a sort of smile and bowed to the General and bowed to me and passed to Brazil — and put a malicious little question to Brazil about its war — and then walked almost hastily past the small Powers — pausing an instant with Fane (who was below us, having been presented five minutes later the day we were) — then passed out; and we loafed down to the door and waited in the uncomfortable entry for our carriages, till we were blue and ill-natured. Then made calls on the necessary nobs by writing our names in a book at their door, and at last went home and took off our livery and were glad it was over."

Before the end of that month of January, John Hay was on his way home. His year and a half in

Paris had made him what he had instinctively yearned to be since boyhood — a cosmopolite. His life at Washington had given him a knowledge of all sorts of Americans in war-time; at Paris, the world capital, he saw society in Imperial form, — elegant, luxurious, cynical, sophisticated, — but he also saw, behind the "blazing hedges of tinsel," the unlovely machinery of despotism. So he came home a man of the world, but an unalloyed American whom the seductions of an Empire only left a more zealous believer in a Republic.

CHAPTER X

WASHINGTON DURING RECONSTRUCTION

HAY reached New York on February 1, 1867, spent the day and evening with some of his cronies, and took the Owl Train for Washington. "Met on the cars a lame darkey in trouble, and paid his fare to Washington." The Diary during the succeeding weeks throws many side-lights on life at the Capital at an interesting moment.

The conflict between President Andrew Johnson and Congress was becoming angry. The Radical Republicans had begun to push the fighting to the point where a trial for impeachment could not be avoided. The Reconstruction of the Southern States, lately in rebellion, called out the worst passions of extremists of both sides, who would not learn that rancor can never do the work of justice, much less of generosity, in cementing a peace.

Many of the Republicans believed that, unless the vanquished Southerners were sternly watched, they would foment insurrection, and so denature, if they did not actually nullify, the results attained by the Civil War. Others supposed that they had the best of warrants for making the way of the transgressor as hard as possible. The desire to atone for the immemorial persecution of the Black Man by suddenly proclaiming him the political equal of the White Man, and even by setting him up to rule over the White Man, moved many zealots. The politicians, as usual, traded on the enthusiasm of the unwise, or availed themselves of the scoundrel's last refuge — patriotism.

To the immense misfortune of the country, and to his own, President Johnson had neither the temperament, training, nor tact to meet such a crisis. History has justified many of his measures, and has applauded his resistance to the fire-eaters who cried for vengeance on the stricken Rebels; but his opponents saw nothing but ill-masked craft or patent treachery in his acts, and his friends felt no loyalty to his person. Never was the patience of Lincoln, never were his fairness and spirit of conciliation, so sorely needed. For lack of him the wounds of war did not cicatrize and the process of Reconstruction became an ignoble tragedy, long drawn out.

"I drove to Willard's," Hay writes; "saw the same dead beats hanging around the office, the same listless loafers moving gloomily up and down, pensively expectorating. Several shook hands with me cordially; the Radical fellows wanting to sympathize with me as a martyr and a little disappointed when

they found I was none. Lamon picked me up and
I went to his office; saw Judge [Jeremiah S.] Black
and talked politics for a while. The terrible defeats
of the past year have sobered and toned down the
Conservatives. They talk very quietly and very
sensibly."

Then he drove to the State Department. Secretary Seward "came swinging in, saying, 'Well, John
Hay, so you got tired of it and came home.' 'Yes,'
I said, 'it was time. I had enough of the place and
the place had enough of me.'

"He then went into a long and very clever dis-
quisition on the dangers of a man holding office —
the desiccation and fossilizing process — illustrating
it by Mr. Hunter and saying he feared Nicolay was
getting into that way. I assured him Nicolay was
not; that he was single-heartedly pursuing 10,000
dollars, and that when he got it he would come home
and go to his ranch. He was glad to hear that, he
said.

"He talked of the Motley business, which was new.
He explained his letter to Motley, which to me
needed no explanation; being the same as he sent
to Nicolay, and which Nicolay and I thought was
meant to call out a denial simply of the charges made
against him. The Copperheads and Democrats who
now form almost the entire support of the President,

are continually boring him for offices and accusing
Mr. Seward of wickedly keeping in their places the
old Radical Lincoln appointees. They make charges
against these, and Mr. Seward sends them notifica-
tions thereof. Everybody but Motley has considered
them as kindly intended, and answered them in that
sense."

Since Motley's recall from Vienna directly shaped
John Hay's career, and is often referred to in his
Journal, we may describe it briefly. It caused a
fuming scandal at the time, added to popular indignation against President Johnson, disturbed Seward's friends, and cut deeply into the proud nature
of Motley himself.

A nondescript person named George W. Mc-
Crackin, of New York, wrote from Paris to President Johnson complaining that the American diplomatists abroad were disloyal to the Administration.
He charged that Motley not only did not pretend to
conceal his disgust at the President's "whole conduct," but despised American democracy and pro-
claimed "loudly that an English nobleman" was
"the model of human perfection." "There is not in
all Europe," McCrackin added, "a more thorough
flunkey or a more *un*-American functionary." Perhaps McCrackin hankered after a diplomatic position, for he noted enviously that Massachusetts

monopolized the lion's share of the consulates; perhaps Mrs. Motley, never having heard of Mrs. McCrackin (if that lady existed), neglected to invite her to tea; perhaps McCrackin was simply an austere patriot of the Catonic variety — let us give him the benefit of the doubt.

President Johnson, already at odds with his party and with Congress, and irritated by the popular insinuations against his own integrity, handed McCrackin's letter to Seward, and bade him to send formal inquiries to the diplomats arraigned by McCrackin as to their attitude. Seward supposed that Motley would make light — as he himself did — of the random accuser. Motley, however, was thoroughly incensed, and instead of sleeping over the matter, he hurried off a long disavowal of the charges, and closed by handing in his resignation. When Seward received this, he replied that, of course, the resignation could not be accepted; but on giving the President the summary of Motley's letter, Johnson said, "with a not unnatural asperity, 'Well, let him go.'" So Seward had to recall his despatch by cable, and Motley resigned. After hearing Seward's story, Hay wrote to Nicolay: "He [Motley] becomes a high-priced martyr and has the sure thing on a first-class mission two years hence. It is hard for Seward to save Lincoln's friends from being pushed off their stools by hungry Copperheads; he defends them when he can."

In the Diary there follows the rest of Seward's conversation on February 2, which illuminates both Seward himself and the situation as he saw it.

"He told me Frederick Seward had gone to St. Domingo to buy a harbor and bay for a naval station for the United States. Not having heard a word since they sailed — Admiral Porter and he — he was a little anxious about him.

"He talked a great deal of the present position of politics and of his own attitude. He never seemed to me to better advantage. His utter calmness and cheerfulness, whether natural or assumed, is most admirable. He seems not only free from any political wish or aspiration, but says distinctly that he cares nothing for the judgment of history, so that he does his work well here.

"He speaks utterly without bitterness of the opposition to him and the President. He thinks the issue before the country was not fairly put, but seems rather to admire the cleverness with which the Radical leaders obscured and mis-stated the question to carry the elections. He says the elections in short amount to this: —

"*Congress to the North.* Do you want rebels to rule the Government? — No.

"Do you want more representation than the South? — Yes.

" Do you want negroes to vote in the South and not in the North? — Yes.

"Do you want to give up the fruits of victory to the South? — No.

"*Congress to the South.* Do you want your negroes to vote, and not Northern negroes? — No.

" Do you want to lose fifty members of Congress? — No.

"Do you want to be deprived of a vote yourselves? — Not by a damned sight.

"And so the issue is clearly presented in such a style as to decide the question beforehand.

"He asked me if I wanted anything — if I would like to go back to Europe. I said I would like anything worth having, if it could be given to me without any embarrassment to him or the President at the present time."

Hay spent the evening with his old friend, Harry Wise, who, he records, "is disgusted with Johnson. His first words to me were, 'Everything is changed — you find us all Copperheads.' Painter said, 'You will find the home of virtue has become the haunt of vice.' [Henry] Adams said, 'A man asked me the other day if I had been at the White House lately, and I told him No. I want to remember that house as Lincoln left it.' Every one I met used some such expression. It is startling to see how utterly without friends the President is."

On Sunday, Hay "went to church alone. Walked home with Miss L. and listened a half hour to her clever Washington gossip — the most spirituel in the world. Then made several visits; saw Hooper[1] and Agassiz."

Hay dined with Secretary Seward at four o'clock — an hour commended to the attention of epicures. Doolittle[2] and Thurlow Weed came in. Their talk was on populations, ancient and modern, Weed having most to say about Rome and Italy, and Seward about the East, Babylon and Palestine. "His pictures of the desolation of those countries, which once nourished [their] millions, and where now a rat would starve, were very graphic."

"He suddenly said to me: 'And now, John Hay, if it were not that Weed is continually in the way, I would make you a Minister. But it seems Mr. Harris[3] is a very good man and has been defeated, and the President is fond of him and so a mission must be kept for him. There is a vacancy in Sweden, and I suppose Weed will insist on Harris having it.'

[1] Samuel Hooper, member of Congress from Massachusetts.
[2] James R. Doolittle, Senator from Wisconsin.
[3] Ira Harris, Senator from New York.

"'Would Harris take such small change?' I asked.

"Here Weed, who had not much relished Seward's badinage, broke out, 'It is too good for him. He would take anything. He deserves nothing.'

"This led to some conversation on Cowan's[1] chances. They all thought them rather slim. Seward said it ought to be known in justice to Cowan that he had asked for nothing and knew nothing of the appointment until it came to the Senate. Doolittle said he would try to persuade Sumner to report upon the nomination without a recommendation and let the Senate act upon it in that way.

"Seward asked Doolittle if he had any influence left in the Committee on Foreign Relations? 'Scarcely any,' said Doolittle. 'If there were anybody there you could depend on,' said Seward, 'I would like to have mischievous and annoying questions about our foreign policy prevented. When a private negotiation is begun and not finished, a blast of publicity destroys it; there is nothing more to be done. The attention and jealousy of the world outside is attracted to us and obstacles spring up in an hour. I have an understanding with Banks and have always had such a one with Sumner, until he has of late become hopelessly alienated. Conness[2] is especially

[1] Senator Edgar Cowan of Pennsylvania nominated as Minister to Austria, but not confirmed.
[2] John Conness, Senator from California.

troublesome. I could manage him by giving him all the offices in the Department, but he is so greedy and unreasonable that one cannot talk sensibly with him."

Thurlow Weed having left for New York just after dinner, Doolittle and Seward canvassed the situation. The former "thought the public temper was calming a little. Seward agreed with him — thought every day was a day gained for the cause of reason. Doolittle said Wade [1] was very ambitious for the place of President of the Senate, — that he had great strength; but that Fessenden [2] was beginning to be spoken of; that Fessenden evidently desired to be elected — which was a little unexpected, as Fessenden had never for a moment occupied the chair, but had always avoided taking it. The same is true of Wade.

"Seward said that Morgan [3] had called upon him that afternoon and had said the same thing of Fessenden. Seward told him he was for Fessenden; though that would probably injure Fessenden's chances if it were known; that Fessenden was by nature and habit of mind a safe and reasonable man; 'though he has more temper than I, for I have none; he would bend and make concessions for the sake of

[1] Benjamin F. Wade, Senator from Ohio.
[2] William P. Fessenden, Senator from Maine.
[3] Edwin D. Morgan, Senator from New York.

retaining his power to do good, which I could never do. I am satisfied that Fessenden wants that place for the good he can do and the harm he can prevent.'"

Here Hay interjects an interesting comment: "The whipped-out, stunned way of talking that I have seen in all the Conservatives, is very remarkable. No bitterness, no energetic denunciation, no threats; but a bewildered sort of incapacity to comprehend the earnest deviltry of the other side, characterizes them all — but Seward, who is the same placid, philosophic optimist that he always was, the truest and most single-hearted Republican alive.

"As [Doolittle] rose to go, Seward said, 'You must somehow help me to do something for John Hay.' I was touched and astonished at this kind persistence of the Secretary in my favor.

"I staid an hour or so. He told me that it seemed as if they would prove General Dix to have been in receipt of the two salaries of the Minister and Naval Officer [of the port of New York]. He seemed much disgusted at this. He said, 'It almost makes me determined never to give up a prejudice again.' He ran over General Dix's history, showing how consistently the General had always pursued his bread and butter in every conjuncture, always getting on pretty well, but always losing the great prizes of his ambition by an unlucky lack of political principle and an over-greed of office, in every period of party crisis. He had always been opposed to him, but had taken him up and stood by him since the beginning of the War, in spite of the General's attempt to 'cut under' from time to time. Seward got him into Buchanan's Cabinet through Stanton. When Bigelow's place [at Paris] fell vacant by his resignation last July, Seward kept it for Dix. And now it seems he is to fall by this ignoble charge of avarice.

"We had some comforting optimist talk. I believe so utterly in Republicanism that I am never troubled long about the future. Baron Gerolt came in and we talked Napoleon and Bismarck and *fusil à aiguille*."

This last reference reminds us how recent the mounting of Prussia, and of Germany dominated by Prussia, has been. In 1867 the world was beginning to perceive that, by the crushing of Austria at Sadowa the year before, a power of the first order had come to the front. Men were already speculating as to the time of the inevitable contest between France and Prussia for mastery, and as to the relative merits of the French *chassepot* and the Prussian needle-gun.

The investigation of General Dix's alleged drawing of two salaries, which the Senate made a pretext for harassing him, resulted in his favor. Meanwhile, Hay was directly affected because Seward seems to have intimated that he would send him to Paris as *Chargé d'Affaires*, in case Dix were forced to resign. Hay enlivened the days of waiting by making the rounds of official and social life, in each of which he was welcome.

"I went to see Charles Eames — found there Ashton and. Chandler. Eames was unusually sesquipedalian over the Motley correspondence — denounced Seward's letter as one 'from which every element of tolerableness had been carefully eliminated'; and the Treasury men came in with the same style of thing, till I got loud and oratorical also."

On "one of God's own days" he joined Mrs. Sprague and Miss Hoyt, "doing a constitutional," and "walked with them in the blessed sunshine and shopped and rode in street cars (they paying, for I found the Fenians at Willard's had stolen all my money, which, like an idiot, I had left lying on my table. The curse of Donneraile be on them!) They took me in the afternoon to the President's to make a bow to Mrs. Patterson and Mrs. Stover. The [White] House is much more richly and carefully furnished than in my time. But the visitors were not quite up to the old mark, which itself was not hard to reach."

Another morning Hay went to Congress, and sent his card in to his old Springfield acquaintance, Shelby M. Cullom. "[He] brought me in on the floor, where I staid an hour or two and shook many hands. Everybody said something about the better days gone and nobody spoke of the better days coming. Yet in those better days they mourned, a million fine fellows were slaying each other with swords and guns, and the widows and the orphans were increasing faster than the babies."

On February 6 Mr. Seward told Hay that he had appointed him a temporary employé in the Department of State, to act, for the present, as Seward's private secretary; but Hay declined, knowing how quickly the men who were caught in the treadmill of routine ceased to be thought of as within reach of an independent career. He told Mr. Seward that "if he wished my personal services in the Department that of course they were entirely at his service; but that if he had done this out of his own usual kindness for me, that I thought best to decline; that I had better go home and see my parents for the present. He agreed with me and left me perfectly free to do as I liked, saying the place in the Department was open whenever I wanted it. He said he had proposed my name to the President the day before as Minister to Sweden. The President said he had another man for it — General [Joseph J.] Bartlett, of New York. We are doing all we can for the soldiers, you know, etc. He said the matter was strictly confidential as yet.

"I told him I had business proposals under consideration — they were not what I wanted but would probably support me and give me in time a competence. He said he had no doubt that a good position in business was worth very much more to me than any appointment I could hold under the Government. I agreed, but said that, after being Minister, I could make better arrangements. He said he would not forget me. I thanked him for all his goodness and took leave.

"Now the real reason I declined this thing was, I believe, a motive I did not suspect or acknowledge to myself: the note and telegram I had received the night before. I went to Mrs. Sprague's and she had slept on it and said no. So I determined to stay here till after Monday anyhow."

To what the "note and telegram" referred, I have no clue: presumably, to some business offer, about which Hay had asked Mrs. Sprague's advice.

The Diary now introduces us to a personage who has been often mentioned in the White House Journal — Charles Sumner, the senior Senator from Massachusetts.

"I dined with Sumner. The party was Mr. and Mrs. Sumner,[1] who looks very sweet and matronly in her *secondes noces*, Miss H., Mr. Field[2] of Philadelphia, George Wm. Curtis and myself. I like Sumner better since his marriage. He should have been married long ago. Every man should who can afford it. His ready-made family is very taking. Little Bel H. came running in for dessert and rated Curtis soundly for not giving her the largest bonbon. It was quite startling to see Sumner in the bosom of his family.

"The conversation was entirely political. The debate of the day in the Senate. Sherman's speech against including Cabinet Ministers in the Tenure of Office bill was rather severely criticized by Sumner, who thought he had been too magnanimous in allowing it to pass unanswered. Sumner thought the power of appointing and removing members of the Cabinet more properly belonged to the Senate as a permanent body than to the President. He said the Senate was less liable to become depraved and bad than the President. He said, 'for instance, I can scarcely imagine a Senate that would now confirm Mr. Seward.'

"As to the argument in favor of harmony in the

[1] Mrs. Sumner was the young widow of Samuel Hooper's son.
[2] John W. Field.

Cabinet, he scouted that altogether. He said that in every constitutional government in the world the head of the Government was frequently obliged to accept ministers that were personally and politically obnoxious. That it was the duty often of a patriotic Minister to remain in the counsels of a perverted administration as a 'privileged spy.' He referred to Stanton and said it should be made impossible for Johnson to remove him.

"In all this ingenious and really clever and learned talk of Sumner's, I could but remark the blindness of an honest, earnest man, who is so intent upon what he thinks right and necessary that he closes his eyes to the fatal consequences of such a course in different circumstances and different times. The Senate is now a bulwark against the evil schemes of the President; therefore, he would give the Senate a power which might make it the most detestable engine of anarchy or oppression. Had this law that he now demands existed in 1861, the Rebellion would have had its seat and center in Washington, and loyalty would have worn the bloody color of Revolution. I told him so, but he would not see it, saying if the South had taken that course they would by that act have abnegated their rebellion — which to me seems absurd.

"Gen'l Dix was discussed. Curtis favored letting

him slide for his two years. Field thought the 'hoary old place-hunter should be marked and punished.' Sumner treated with contempt the charge of cumulation against Gen'l Dix. His crime of presiding at the Philadelphia Convention [1] is capital. How can the Senate reject the small fry of renegade Unionists and permit to go unscathed the man who gave to that wicked scheme all its momentary respectability?

"Sumner's account of the rejection of McGinnis [2] was very amusing. 'The Senate's answer to Master Seward.' He said Bartlett had come in in McGinnis' place. 'He is an old-fashioned Copperhead — did good service in our war, they say, but that won't save him.'" ("Bartlett was at last confirmed," Hay adds in the margin.)

"*February 7, Thursday.* Went to the House. The bill for the military government of the Rebel States was up. Brandegee [3] made a little flourish of the eagle with a long Latin quotation that made the Western members grin. Banks [4] I talked with some time. He was really despondent about the course things were taking — deprecating most earnestly

[1] A convention of "conservative" Republicans, held in August, 1866.

[2] George F. McGinnis, rejected by the Senate as Minister to Sweden.

[3] Augustus Brandegee, member of Congress from Connecticut.

[4] N. P. Banks, member from Massachusetts.

this abdication of the civil power in favor of the irresponsible military. I thought the case was not hopeless—bad as it was—as Congress could at any time resume the powers it now delegates for a temporary purpose. He said the people would more likely acquiesce in a bad thing done than work for its repeal. I talked with Boutwell [1] five minutes afterwards. He was confident that the measure was a good one and that the Army could be trusted. I think there never was an army that could be trusted, as an army. It is un-Anglo-Saxon to perpetuate this state of things. I recognize the miserable situation of the South, and perhaps this bill is necessary —but it is a bad thing to do for all that. Woe be to him by whom this offence cometh."

In the evening, after calling on Seward, who showed him a superb set of Chinese chessmen, Hay went to a reception at the White House.

"The President was very cordial to me: said I must come and see him. Mrs. Johnson received for the first time; a quiet, invalid old lady. The crowd not choice, but as good an average as ever; scarcely any distinguished people and none squalid. We used to have plenty of both."

Following Seward's advice, Hay went to see

[1] George S. Boutwell, of Massachusetts, one of the Republican Radicals.

Browning,[1] who was very cordial and promised at
once. "He feels very gloomy," notes the diarist.
"Thinks we are going to the devil. He is a brighter
man and older man than I, but I know we are not."

February 8. "Dined with the Hoopers. There
heard of Banks' unexpected and dramatic heading
off of Overseer Thad[2] in the House. Enormously
clever man is Banks. Too moderate and wise just
now — a doomed Girondin, I am afraid. Raymond[3]
is as clever, but not as good and strong.

"Doolittle said the other night to Seward that
Banks had told him a few days before that he saw
no earthly power that could prevent the impeachment of the President. This impressed Doolittle
very much, as he said, Banks being himself against
impeachment. Seward said that it would impress
him more if it was not that he remembered that
Banks had thought there was no salvation out of
Knownothingism — when in fact there was none
in it.

"Went to Secretary Welles's reception. Sheridan[4]
was the lion, looking, as Miss Hooper says, as if he

[1] Orville H. Browning, Secretary of the Interior, the department
before which the Southern land claims which Hay held would come.
[2] Thaddeus Stevens, of Pennsylvania, fire-eater, leader of the Republicans in the House.
[3] Henry J. Raymond, M. C. from New York, editor of the *New
York Times*.
[4] General Philip H. Sheridan.

would blow up on short provocation. A mounted torpedo, somebody once called him — inflammable little Jack of Clubs — to whom be all praise. Then a German Cotillon at Reverdy Johnson's [1] — very ill led by a booby . . . , who danced in a straddling sort of way, 'wide between the legs as if he had gyves on.'"

"*February 9.* Went up to the House again. Talked with C.[2] about the affair of the day before. Saw another instance of the curious intolerance of the majority, and the feebleness of individual judgment when opposed to the decisions of the caucus. C. was heartily for Banks and his motion, and was full of delighted admiration of the way he carried it against Stevens — but acknowledged he had voted the other way. He says Boutwell is jealous of Banks and anxious to discredit him before the people of Massachusetts. I got the end of Boutwell's speech, which was very fine and nervous. Boutwell always shows to good advantage when thoroughly roused and excited. Raymond talked a little — clever and fluent as ever, and impressing nobody.

"In the evening there was a German Cotillon at Baron Gerolt's. Kasserow led, and very well. I danced with Miss Haggerty. Invitations were for 6½, being Saturday. People accepted and went early.

[1] Senator from Maryland.   [2] Presumably Cullom.

We dispersed to bed at midnight with a queer sense of its being the next morning.

"*Sunday, February 10.* At breakfast, Drake Dekay handed me Nasby's last letter about the legal lynching of a negro in Kentucky. The wit and satire of Locke [1] was growing so earnest and savage that it is painful to read him. This article is as pathetic as it is grotesque.

"I told Sumner what I conscientiously believe, that Seward has done all in his power to save Mr. Lincoln's appointees from being displaced by the Copperhead pressure; that he had spoken of giving a place to me without demanding or suggesting any adhesion to the present administration as the condition of the appointment.

"I asked Sumner if he did not intend to write a history of these times. He answered in a way to convince me that he had thought a great deal of the matter. He greatly regretted the absence of jottings to fix in his mind the incidents of his daily intercourse with the President, the Ministers of Government and the leading Congressmen. He considers himself the most highly qualified man in America to write an exhaustive political history of this great period, on account of his great and unusual facilities of inter-

---

[1] D. R. Locke, political satirist, who wrote over the pseudonym of "Petroleum V. Nasby."

course with every branch of government and opinion.
He said 'it was impossible to do anything of the kind
so long as he remained in the Senate.' I suggested
that he might find the necessary leisure in the representation of the country for a few years in Europe. This suggestion was by no means novel to
him.

"He told me that several months ago, when he
spoke to Seward about the Harvey [1] matter, Seward
had said that every Minister in Europe was with the
President as against Congress. He said he did not
answer, as he might have done, that he had at that
moment in his pocket a letter from Motley and one
from Hale disproving that assertion.

"Sumner has grown very arrogant with success.
He feels keenly the satisfaction of being able to bind
and loose at his free will and pleasure. There is no
selfish exultation in it, or too little for him to recognize — it is rather the fierce joy of a prophet over
the destruction of the enemies of his Lord. He speaks
with hearty enjoyment of what is to happen to
Cowan; referred to Doolittle's 'sleek, purring attempt' to soften him in that matter so far as to have
Cowan's name referred to the Senate without recommendation — and his snort of rejection."

Hay, as we have seen, interspersed his political

[1] James E. Harvey, Minister to Portugal.

conferences with fashionable engagements. His life in Paris had made him more than ever at his ease in society. He was always a favorite with women.

"*February 11*. Mrs. Sprague gave a beautiful ball. The ladies who danced the Cotillon, and many who did not, had their hair powdered *à la marquise*. I have never seen so beautiful and picturesque a roomful. Some of the most striking were the Hostess herself (with whom I danced), the Hoyts, Miss Romain Goddard, Miss Haggerty, and Mrs. Banks, who was very correctly dressed, even to the extent of the blue ribbon around the neck, a little refinement in which she was alone — Miss Kinzie, a fresh Western beauty and a superb *danseuse*. Mrs. Sumner and Miss Hooper, though not powdered, were beautifully dressed."

During the evening, Hay talked with the Chief Justice, who showed him Carpenter's engraving of the Reading of the Proclamation. "He objects to the whole picture being made subsidiary to Seward, who is talking while every one else either listens or stares into vacancy. He thinks it would have been infinitely better to have taken the 22d of September, when the Proclamation was really read to the Cabinet. I referred to Seward's criticism that the subject was not well chosen — that the really decisive Cabinet meeting was that at which it was decided to provision and reinforce Fort Sumter. He said there was no such meeting; that Mr. Lincoln asked the opinion of the Cabinet in writing; that there were but two of the Cabinet who favored the reinforcement, himself and Blair; that Blair was more decided than he in favor of reinforcing the fort; that *he* (Chase) thought some strong and decided assertion or proclamation of the intention of the Government should have been made at that time. Chase was always a little addicted to *coups de théâtre*.

"I said I thought an exaggerated importance was often ascribed to the manner in which events were accomplished; that in great revolutionary times events accomplished themselves not by means of, but in spite of, the well-meant efforts of the best and wisest men. The Girondins nearly monopolized the brains of France; yet they were crushed out, as it was probably necessary they should be — that the destiny of the people should be accomplished through their fever and their struggles.

"He quite agreed with this, insisting, however, upon the individual responsibility of each one to do what seems best in his sight for the commonwealth.

"Of course this was also my view. I am obstinately optimist, but not fatalist. Every man should do what he thinks is right, but he should know also that what the Republic does is right — in the largest sense."

The Dix case, on which hung Hay's prospects of a diplomatic post, was delayed from day to day in the Senate. Charles Sumner, the dominating influence in the Committee on Foreign Relations, held out against confirming him with the stubbornness of a virtuous fanatic, basing his opposition, not on the charges of cumulation of offices, but on Dix's having presided over the Philadelphia Convention. Sumner said: "It is the only ground I can stand on. I once reported against a man because he had delirium tremens. Saulsbury and McDougall [1] denounced me as a water-drinking fanatic. I once objected to a candidate that he could not read. I was accused of searching an impossible Boston ideal of scholarship for public service. So now, if I say of a man that he supports the policy of the President, and that I will not send him abroad to misrepresent me and the Senate, that is intelligible and satisfactory."

Writing to Nicolay at this time Hay says: "Sumner has blood in his eye. He is splendid in his present temper — arrogant, insolent, implacable — thoroughly in earnest — honest as the day."

---

[1] Senators Willard Saulsbury, of Maryland, and James A. McDougall, of California.

Whilst the appointment hung fire, Hay cast about for an alternative occupation. He received offers to join a firm of lawyers, or to become a claim agent. Either promised a good income in those days, when the American citizen who could not think up some claim against the national Treasury was either hopelessly dull or singularly honest. Hay himself had bought in 1864 seven pieces of land in Florida, which he now got patents for; but this speculation never bore fruit for him.

"*February 12.* After dinner went in to say goodnight to the Chief Justice. His guests had just gone; it was eleven o'clock. I walked up and down the deserted salon with him a few moments. He said there had been a good many Southern people there that evening; that he made it a point to treat them always with especial courtesy. I agreed that this was a good thing to do, even where they abused you for it and called it Yankee subserviency and charged it to mean motives. They know it is not true; they feel their inferiority, and their bluster is the protest of wounded pride. Chase said he felt kindly towards the people of the South. He only demanded that no man of any color should suffer for having been loyal during the war; which is little enough to ask, and which must be insisted on, *ruat cœlum.*"

"*February 21.* Dined with the Hoopers. . . . Mr.

Hooper came in disgusted with the action of the House on the bill to redeem the 7-30 notes and 'for the inflation of the currency.' He could not help being a little amused, even in his disgust, at the neat way in which they had taken advantage of his success in getting the bill introduced 'by turning it wrong-side out and handing it back to him passed.'

"During this week saw very much of Chase and his family; played a combination of billiards and 10 pins in the parlor, which kept us out of politics."

Tired at last of waiting, Hay went to New York on February 23. There he talked over various business projects, and saw Guernsey, editor of *Harper's Magazine*, who said he would like some short stories, but "did not encourage the novel nor the Lincoln book." As usual, Hay called on many friends. "Thurlow Weed," he writes, "has spoken to me about going into the redaction of a newspaper, the *Commercial Bulletin*, which he "intends buying and running as a Republican paper, he assures me. I don't much like the idea of Hurlbert [1] in it, and the whole thing looks to me hopeless. This is no time for reactionary measures."

On March 3, Forney telegraphed that Dix had been at last confirmed. Hay at once wrote Secretary

---

[1] William H. Hurlbert, a brilliant but untrusted New York editorial writer.

Seward a long letter, full of gratitude for his benev-
olent intentions. "I have come to regard you," he
added, "as I know the world will, when the smoke
has risen from the battlefields of to-day, as nearly
as one may reach it, the ideal of the Republican
workingman — calm without apathy, bold without
rashness, firm without obstinacy, and with a patriotism permeated with religious faith."

There being nothing further to expect from Washington, Hay journeyed to Warsaw.

CHAPTER XI

THE ROVING DIPLOMAT — VIENNA

HAY returned to Warsaw as poor in purse as when he set out for Paris; for a diplomatic secretaryship was ill paid and led nowhere. In spite of his fondness for the great world, he always went home gladly. He loved his parents; he delighted in the old familiar places; and as he grew older he found more and more refreshment and delight in nature herself.

"I am safely lodged at last among my Lares and Penates," he wrote Nicolay on March 18. "I find my parents as well as ever; my mother better than usual, and full of her old good spirits; my father at 66 with not a gray hair, with ruddy cheek and ravenous appetite of a growing boy. . . . There is little comfort in the country now. The weather is hideous, *i.e.*, what people insanely call 'beautiful, fresh, cold weather.' A cloudless sky, white shining distances, and a thermometer ten degrees below o according to Meinherr Fahrenheit. I have escaped six winters and my good nature has been nipped and frozen in this absurd springtime."

"Poverty everywhere," he added; and he warned

Nicolay, who was still consul in Paris, "You had better not come here till you are kicked out and our crazy friends in the Senate have legislated all the dead-beats not in office into an eternity of bread and butter." Among other possible resources which he and Nicolay had talked over was a biography of Lincoln; but he reports: "Nobody is keen for our book. We will have to write it and publish on our own hook some day, when we can afford."

As the spring wore on, Hay took great pleasure in gardening, in walks, and in working and idling in just sufficient measure so that work and loafing were alternately satisfying. He leased his five-acre apple-orchard to "a quaint and most worthy man, named Smith, a Methodist colporteur who peddles the Gospel with Methodist sauce in the winter and vexes the envious soil in the summer." "Two fine industrious Yankees," the Durfee boys, "have taken the vineyard and the ten-acre block" on College Hill — "thoroughly good fellows with sand in their gizzards." Hay himself spent a good deal of time on the different places, destroying caterpillars, "digging some, planting, pruning." Here follows a confession from which we infer that traces of the New England conscience still clung to him. "I find a singular love for that kind of work in myself. It is the sense of justification it gives me for not doing nothing. If I stay at home I cannot idle or read for amusement, without being haunted by the ceaseless reproach of misspent time. But in the fields, tiresome and monotonous as the work may be — such as shovelling dirt or dropping corn — it frees me utterly from the sense of responsibility for the passing hour. I am doing work, substantial, real work, which will have its result doubtless some day, and so I plod on and watch the sun, glad after all when my day is done and I can ramble home through the magnificent hills and valleys that surround this town."

Nevertheless, in respites from the haunting reproaches, which we may suspect were not very acute, he enjoyed natural beauty without thought of material profit. "I never was so close to nature before since I was a child," he tells his Diary. "I have watched the flowers, like a detective, this spring." And then he goes on in quite the romantic vein, to rhapsodize over "a little patch of wild woodland that is very sweet and solitary — full of fresh woodsy smells and far enough from any farmyards to be utterly still — barring the birds and the grasshoppers — whose racket only makes the solitude more perfect, by proof." Another day he stumbled on a bit "of open turf, thick in blue grass and superbly illuminated with great purple and field pansies that had probably bloomed for years unseen by any eyes, but

the bright, beady ones of orioles and jays and cat-
birds. It was worth the price I paid for the land, to
feel that this exquisite show, so lavishly running to
waste year after year, was mine. I would not pluck
them —the violets and phlox, the windflowers and
bluebells — because I loved them."

In the valley pastures of his neighbors, however,
he picked "redbud hawthorn, apple bloom and plum
blossoms, right and left, making what [he] thought
an equitable return in killing about a thousand ugly
green-black-yellow caterpillars that had raised their
tent on the limb of a splendid crab, all pink and fra-
grant in its May bloom. . . . Then at the risk of my
neck I clambered up the bank by Grover's — where
the curving precipice looks like a ruined amphi-
theatre of the woodland gods that are gone — I got
a handful of columbine, and then came slowly down
to the river and along its pebbly banks home. I can
never get enough of looking at the River. It has its
new fresh beauty every morning and noon; and a
new and unimagined transfiguration every sunset."

So sings the landscapist in words, the Romanticist
whom Nature stirred with genuine though vague
emotions.

But what should he be? As a weaver of prose idyls
he could not hope to keep body and soul together.
A breadwinning occupation must be found; and the

quest for it, in the case of a man like Hay, whose aptitudes were many, offers some of the excitement of a sport. Would his temperament, or would opportunity, triumph in the choice?

Two or three possibilities came to nothing. Munroe, the Paris banker, had suggested that Hay might enter that house; but he now backed out. Of another offer Hay says: "I can't survey the prospect of plunging into this affair without a sort of shuddering horror." He disliked the job of claim agent, in spite of its lucrativeness. The law did not attract him. He could not forget that he had spent four years in Washington as Lincoln's secretary, — a memory which exacted a certain dignity of him.

"I can scarcely say now to myself what my plans are," he records on June 3. "Let me see. Go to Springfield — see some publishers in New York and Boston — write L's book for him — write two lectures, and that will pretty well fill up the summer. If it were only myself that I thought of I would stay here. I will have an income — all things succeeding — of at least 500 [dollars] a year, and I can bring that up a few hundred by writing — and have a more tranquil mind than anywhere else."

Just after he wrote these lines, he learned through the *New York Times* that he was to be appointed Secretary of Legation to act as *Chargé d'Affaires* at

Vienna, the post Motley had quitted in dudgeon. On receiving the official notification, which had been misdirected and was a fortnight late, Hay left Warsaw for New York. Of his journey he records the following: —

"Rode to Carthage in the same seat with Robert Lincoln, a second cousin of the late President. He is forty-one years old, looks much older. The same eyes and hair the President had — the same tall stature and shambling gait, less exaggerated; a rather rough, farmer-looking man. Drinks hard, chews ravenously. He says the family is about run out. 'We are not a very marrying set.' He is dying of consumption, he said very coolly. There was something startling in the resemblance of the straight thicket of hair, and the grey, cavernous eyes framed in black brows and lashes, to the features of the great dead man. He was a pioneer of our country. Knew my father since long years. Brought a load of wheat to Gould & Miller in 1842 with ox teams; got $90 in gold for it. Told me that in 1860 he had talked to 'Abe' about assassination. Abe said: 'I never injured anybody. No one is going to hurt me.' He says he was invited by Abe to go to Washington at the time of the inauguration, but declined, thinking it dangerous — a naïveté of statement I thought would have been impossible out of the West."

Hay sailed on June 29, 1867, from New York on
the *City of Boston* — the steamer which not long
afterwards disappeared in mid-ocean and has never
been heard of since. Ten days later he landed at
Liverpool, and, like most Americans, he lost no time
in going up to London. There he enjoyed during a
brief stay the double pleasure of seeing some of the
celebrities of the time and of visiting Westminster
Abbey and other monuments which had long been
shrines in his imagination. He lunched at 54 Port-
land Place, with Charles Francis Adams, the American Minister, where, he says, "we tore our friends
to pieces a little while. Motley got one or two
slaps that were very unexpected to me. Sumner and
his new wife were brushed up a little." It was to
this marriage that Hay referred in his Paris Diary:
"Col. Ritchie informed me today of Sumner's engagement to Mrs. Sturgis Hooper. He wrote a letter to Mrs. Adams announcing his engagement, but
did not even mention the lady's name. This is em-
inently characteristic. The great point with Sumner is that *he* is to be married. If the lady happens
to get married about the same time, all the better for
her. But this is quite a secondary consideration."

Hay's record of an afternoon spent in the Houses
of Parliament contains some interesting pen-portraits. In the vestibule he met Lord Eliot, "looking

with his blazing head and whiskers as if he "had just come through hell with his hat off. . . . On the Government bench, to the right of the Speaker, the most noticeable man was Disraeli [who was just carrying through his Reform Bill]. He has grown enormously in the public estimation in this session. . . . In the great fight now beginning between Privilege and Democracy in England, the Democrats will have need of all their skill and discretion, for the Aristocracy seem to perceive to a great extent the meaning of the occasion, and they will throw everything away in the fight that does not seem essential. If the Republicans are not distracted by false issues they will conquer at last, by the force of numbers. But they must make a good fight or suffer long delays.

"While we were there, Disraeli, Gladstone, Forster, Newdegate and several others made short conversational talks. I was very much impressed with their directness and simplicity of statement. I think the exclusion of the public, by taking away all temptation to display, has a very fine effect on parliamentary oratory. Nothing could be clearer and finer than Disraeli's and Gladstone's manner of stating their points.

"The members sat with their hats on, taking them off when they rose to speak, and replacing them immediately afterwards. Many had their feet

on the back of the bench in front. Yet on the whole
their demeanor was very attentive and respectful.
They have a very decided way of expressing their
approbation or disapproval of the member speaking.
I admired Newdegate's coolness in holding his own
and talking, unmoved by a general growl of ill-
natured comment, until the Speaker called him to
order."

The debate in the Commons not being specially
interesting, Hay's party crossed to the House of
Lords and took seats on the steps of the Throne.

"The Lord Chancellor was in his seat. In front of
him the Clerks; on either side, on benches, the Peers.
The Government occupying his right; Lord Derby
at their head. Nearest us, on the right, were the
spiritual Lords; the Archbishop of Canterbury, an
elderly and rather infirm-looking man; the Bishop of
Oxford, a fine, portly prelate, whose blue riband
made me think of a prize ox; the Bishop of Bath and
Wells and the Bishop of London.

"On our left sat the Duke of Buccleugh, a stiff dry
Scotchman, with a wen on his forehead. Next him
snored comfortably Viscount Sidney. Then came
Lord Stanhope. Then the Duke of Argyll, small of
stature and red of hair. Moran pointed out to us the
tall, slender, finicky Marquis of Bath, who was
severely nipped by the Cotton Loan; Earl Powis, a

smaller Forrest [1] without the moustache; the Duke of
Richmond, a good-looking silver-haired man; Lord
Stratford de Redcliffe, a rather undersized old gentleman, white-haired, bent, and not in the least the
grand manner that Kinglake [2] fancies; and the Duke
of Buckingham and Chandos, the most remarkable-
looking nobleman I ever saw — who looks in style,
station, dress, way of getting over the ground, face
and feature like a brisk country grocer in New England. Yet he is one of the best bloods that the
English stud can show and is a bright fellow besides,
as his plucky retrieval of his estates, ruined by the
waste of his father, shows. Bourgeois as he looks,
he is as proud as any one of his class, they say. The
Earl of Bradford is a good-looking, youngish man.
Lord Romilly and Lord Cairns, two recent additions
to the law Lords, made short, sensible speeches while
we were there."

That evening, "a good-hearted grain-dealer from
Milwaukee, who has been to Paris for ten days and
comes back bored to death because he could n't tell
a cabman where to drive," took Hay and his companions to Cremorne and the Alhambra; "which
are," Hay writes, "dreary beyond the power of human tongue to describe. Yet they were full of the

---

[1] Edwin Forrest, the American tragedian.
[2] In his "History of the Crimean War."

same class one finds in the Mabille and elsewhere, who have nothing better in God's world to do. . . . We passed down the Haymarket for a quarter of an hour. The streets were full of poor old women and some not so old, painted, bedizened and miserable. . . . It was certainly in London that Pope learned that 'Vice is a monster of such frightful mien,' etc."

Before leaving London, Hay called on Motley, just back from Vienna. "I shall never have any more doubt," Hay records, "as to the long mooted question whether it hurts a man to cut off his head. It hurts like the devil. He received me very coolly and stiffly, not speaking a word in reply to my salutation. He answered in the dryest and briefest way my questions about his family. I asked when he had left Vienna and he began to talk. He grew almost hysterical in his denunciation of the 'disgusting, nasty outrage of his being turned out.' 'His resignation had been forced from him by a trick and then snapped at, to give the place to somebody else.' 'But the crowning insult of all was his recent letter of recall.'

"He evidently thought that the Senate was going to keep him in by rejecting all nominees, and was bitterly disappointed at the turn things had taken. He wanted to stay at Vienna a few years more to make the necessary researches in the archives there for his history of the Thirty Years' War.

"We talked an hour or so. As it is not possible to justify entirely the conduct of the Government in this matter, I did not attempt that, but explained to Motley how I thought he was mistaken in imputing it to any hostility on Seward's part. Seward's utter indifference to attacks and his philosophic calmness under abuse, I think, render him a little indifferent to the sufferings of his sensitive fellow-creatures under the same inflictions. He never dreamed that Motley would take that letter in such dudgeon, though it must be admitted that it was a frightful one for a gentleman to write or to receive."

At a farewell dinner at Mr. Adams's Hay reports that they "talked among other things of the late extraordinary recantation speech of Earl Russell. Adams says Russell has been always, in his way, our friend, Gladstone has not; has been led away by his impulses now and then. Adams thinks Disraeli has forced the present bill on the Tory party, that he has led them the devil's own rigadoon of a dance. If so, I take back all the credit I have given them for shrewdness and sagacity, and transfer it all to Dizzy himself. Then Adams gave a most humorous account of the visit of the Prince of Wales to the

Monitor. They evidently dislike Fox at No. 54. I hardly know why."

Hay went to the Continent by way of Salisbury and Stonehenge. Early in August he reached Vienna, where he established himself in "an apartment of three good rooms, kitchen and servant's room," for which he paid 1500 florins a year. It being summer, society was out of town, so that he had all the more leisure for making himself familiar with the city. His zest for sight-seeing had not worn off, and for him sight-seeing included not only galleries and monuments but the habits and customs of the people.

"The great luxury is music," he writes enthusiastically to Nicolay. "One of the Strauss family leads in the Volksgarten several times a week, admission 40 kreutzer, not 20 cents. Or you can cool your nose on the bars of the enclosure and hear it for nothing —if you are not *Beamter* [an official]. The opera is good — the only ballet I ever saw that was not a bore. *Faust* was superbly given a few nights ago. Mr. Motley has a box and has given me the reversion of it till October, in which I am luxurious. The acting is very fine also in the Hofburg Theatre, the classic — and Offenbach is lord over all in the other show-houses. *Blue Beard*, *Belle Hélène*, and the *Grand Duchess*, have delighted the town for the last fortnight." (September 2, 1867.)

Vienna was forgetting the tragedy of a disastrous war and Paris was hastening towards destruction to the tuneful frivolities of Offenbach — so uncertain is music in registering the moral values of a period.

"The suburbs of this town — the environs rather — " Hay goes on, "are very beautiful. I spend most of my Sundays in the mountains and valleys of this chain of the Tyrols that seems to have been caught and turned into a wild pleasure ground."

At Vienna, Hay came for the first time upon a people still bound by ancient religious superstitions and upon a government which still permitted a large measure of ecclesiastical control in the affairs of the State. He observed with increasing wonder the persistence of medieval ideals. The frequency of Church festivals, encouraged for obvious reasons, stirred in him surprise and amusement. On such occasions, he writes, —

"The whole town shuts up shop and goes to the country. They eat a good dinner, drink a good deal of beer, and smoke many cigars, and the economies of the week vanish in the enjoyment of a day. When they go off on these excursions they are very sensible about it, enjoying themselves in a most hearty and naïve way. They do not seem to need the excitement and amusement that the Parisians crave or demand. They are contented to lie on the

grass and look at the white clouds, to loaf through
the balsamic woods, to live and let the world roll on.
They break very easily into groups of two, and are
not ashamed to let the world into the confidence of
their tender sentiments."

Vienna prided itself, indeed, on being the gay
capital; and to foreigners, the Viennese seemed a
people incapable of emotions deeper than a waltz
could express, or of griefs too poignant for a waltz
to soothe. Only the year before, Austria, beaten by
the terrible Prussians at Sadowa, had lost her leader-
ship; but she was now outwardly cheerful. The war
had forced her to adjust herself to more modern
conditions; and Hay studied, as best he could, the
progress of the Compromise with Hungary and the
various reforms which were eagerly debated in parliament. As his official duties took up little of his
time, he spent his leisure in excursions, or in watch-
ing the folk life in the streets, or at the theatre and
opera. One of his keen pleasures was visiting the
galleries. Already at the Louvre he had begun to
cultivate his taste in paintings and statues, and in
London he "walked through the National Gallery
and saw for the first time Turner. I would go to him
very often if I lived in London," he adds. On his
way to Vienna, he had seen, at Antwerp, some fine
examples of the great Flemings. Now, at the Belve-

dere, he went on to explore the magic world of the fine arts. He sets down his enthusiasm with delightful frankness, not caring whether his riper judgment may repudiate his first impression.

Thus, on going to the Belvedere, the first thing his eyes light upon are "the two sway-backed horses that romp before the palace in an attitude suggesting a sudden attack of *mollities ossium*. A man who has once seen and thoroughly studied the Marly horses at the gates of the Champs Elysées, has his judgment formed and his verdict forestalled for any other horses that have ever been cast or hewn. All the other rampant horses I have ever seen impress me as imperfect imitations, or desperate variations of the incomparable marbles of Couston."

For subtlety, fervor, and characteristic flashes of humor none of his notes on paintings excel the following description of Rubens's portrait of his second wife.

"I found food for my new love of Rubens," he says, "whom I detested in Paris, but to whom I have made reverent recantation since Antwerp. In fact, the picture I was most curious to see was his Helen Fourment, that odd and fantastic, artistic pillorying of a pretty woman's immodest fancy and a husband's proud and sensual love for the disrespectful admiration of all time." . . . [with some difficulty]

"I came before the object of my search. It stood in a good light by a window. . . . I felt as glad as if I had found a lucky stone. So she stood, those centuries ago, before her fond, jolly husband, to whom Art was its own excuse in everything. You can see in the pretty naïve face, with its great blue eyes, full yet of childish wonder, framed in those splendid, crisp locks of gold, the struggle of love and vanity against natural modesty. She snatches up the artist's furred cloak and wraps it round her with a quick, coquettish grace—and all the warring sentiments are appeased. They are as old as Eden, the vanity, the sensualism, the suggestive concealment. And as she stands thus, in that attitude where grace and awkwardness are, as in all real women, so charmingly blended, the fond eye of the Artist husband catches the fleeting loveliness and fixes it forever. The sweet, artless, spoiled child face that we know so well, that walks with Rubens in the garden in the Pinacothek at Munich, that goes sailing up to heaven in the altar-piece at Antwerp, and stands on the *volet* of her husband's stupendous work, *The Descent from the Cross*, is here most exquisitely drawn, and the enamoured artist revels in the red and white and blue and gold of cheeks, lips, hair and eyes. And yet you see that he loves no less the soft, round pink knees and the fat, white feet. You are glad Rubens had such a wife, and very glad he did not marry your sister."

The man who wrote that assuredly lacked neither discernment nor literary skill; yet he still felt himself a novice in art criticism. "I think I shall be friends with the Belvedere," he records after his first visit. "I spent a day there some weeks ago, to get the 'hang of the schoolhouse.' A Western boy, who had never learned his letters, on his first day at school was asked by the schoolmistress if he could read. He replied, with the spirit of Western pluck, he reckoned he could as soon as he got the hang of the schoolhouse."

Equally vivid are Hay's sketches of street scenes in Vienna. Here is one of a religious procession.

"Monks in dozens with shaved heads, the first honest shaved heads I have ever seen, all sorts of ecclesiastical supes with candles, that flickered in the wind and went out. Some lit them conscientiously and shaded them with their hands. Others marched on stolidly, careless of appearances, with shameless black wicks. Six expensive-looking fellows carried a heavily embroidered baldaquin; six more lighted them with gorgeous red lamps. Under the baldaquin walked a very pompous party, who from time to time stopped the procession and made a remark or so in an unknown tongue; upon which the whole pro-

cession and the majority of the bystanders ducked,
beat their breasts and moaned as if in severe indigestion. A smell of incense filled the air, which to
me always has an odor of good company, I do not
know why. I took off my hat with the rest, and was
grateful for the incense and the music. I believe
Austria is the only country on earth where the priests
wear top boots. It gives them a remarkably rakish
and knowing air. They feel their oats more plainly
here than anywhere in the world."

And here is a view of the Viennese Ghetto, swept
away in the modernizing of the old town which was
in process while Hay was writing:—

"As I go in the early morning to take my plunge
and splash in the Danube water in Leopold Stadt,
I walk through the Tiefen Graben, the deep ditch
which marks the site of the ancient moat of the
outer fortress of the city. . . .

"The Tiefen Graben is so far below the average
level of the city that, about half way down its length,
Wipplinger Strasse strides far above it in the air. In
the T. G. you wonder what that suspension bridge is
for, and in Wipplinger Strasse you gaze with amazement at the men and wagons burrowing at the bottom of the ditch. The Tiefen Graben runs into the
Gestade, and out of this dark, foul and utterly ignoble place starts the Talzgries, which runs for a

few hundred paces and ends in the broad, bright, garish sunshine and wide daylight of the Donau Arm.

"Along this unclean street rolls an endless tide of Polish Jews, continually supplied by little rivulets running down from the Judenplatz and the *culs de sac* of that neighborhood, not running, but trickling down the steep, stone bed of the cañons called Fischer Stiege and Marien Stiege and Wachtel Gasse, Quail Alley. These squalid veins and arteries of impoverished and degenerate blood are very fascinating to me. I have never seen a decent person in these alleys or on those slippery stairs. But everywhere stooping, dirty figures in long, patched and oily black gabardines of every conceivable material, the richest the shabbiest usually, because oldest and most used, covering the slouching, creeping form, from the round shoulders to the splay, shuffling feet. A battered soft felt hat crowns the oblique, indolent, crafty face, and, what is most offensive of all, a pair of greasy curls dangle in front of the pendulous ears. This coquetry of hideousness is most nauseous. The old Puritan who wrote in Barebones' time on the 'Unloveliness of love locks' could here have either found full confirmation of his criticism or turned with disgust from his theme.

"What they are all doing is the wonder. They

stand idle and apathetic in the sunshine, or gather
in silent or chatty groups of three or four, take snuff
and blow their aquiline noses in chorus on dubious
brown handkerchiefs. They have utterly revolu-
tionized my ideas of the Hebrew. In America we
always say, 'Rich as a Jew,' because even if a Jew
is poor he is so brisk, so sharp and enterprising that
he is sure to make money eventually. But these
slouching rascals are as idle as they are ugly. It occurred to me that it might be those long coats that
keep them down in life, and that the next generation,
if put early into roundabouts, might be spry fellows.
But the Jesuits moved the world in their long coats.
I suppose the curse of the nation has lit on these
fellows especially.

"All this quarter is subject to them apparently,
for the little, obscure shops in the blind alleys have
Hebrew signs. This was another shock to me. Think
of tallow and onions advertised in a corner grocery
in the sublime and mysterious characters in which
the Tables of the Law were carved. I saw that this
morning."

Such is the Ghetto by daylight. Hay is equally
graphic in describing it by night, when he "walked
again through those blind alleys and swarming
streets. The veil of darkness made the crowd more
easy and confidential. The noise of traffic was over,

but the small hucksters were busy shovelling their green peaches and astringent pears into buckets, or cooping up their melancholy chickens and ducks that seemed heavy-hearted and humiliated that the day had passed and they were not stewed. The talk in the streets was noisier and freer; the dinner and the darkness had loosened these awkward tongues. Porters and charwomen stood in discreet corners and squeezed each others' hard fingers. The same mysterious Hebrew glided by, a little brisker as the night gathered and loafing time was shortened.

"In the Gestade I came across a group of little Goths who had pulled off their trousers and were lashing each other merrily with them. Old women sat dozing on their doorsteps, too tired to rest well; almost always alone. Their men were dead or off to the beer shops. While the women are young, they go with them. But with age comes for them only the brute's drudgery and the brute's repose. Under the shadow of the tall black hulk of Mary-Stairs Church, young women sat in silence with shabby and ignoble-looking men. And overhead, between the high walls of the narrow streets, you could see as clear and dark blue patches of sky, as if you stood on the icy spire of the Matterhorn."

"Began to-day to study the substratum of Viennese life," Hay writes on September 13, 1867; but I find few later allusions to it. "I am mentioned in the *Fremden Blatt* as ' Der Amerikanische Minister Camel-Hey.' That looks deliciously Oriental: I can imagine myself in a burnous and yellow shoes."

He continued all the while his observations of the upper classes. After spending Christmas Eve at Mrs. Lippitt's, he notes: "The young ladies were as pretty as ever and very easy and gay. I never saw better breeding than there is in the Haute Bourgeoisie of Vienna. They talked German to me for the first time, and I was astonished at their wit and the profoundness of their criticism and observation, which I had utterly failed to see in their English. (I think one reason diplomatists are as a general rule so stupid is, that they are so much in the habit of speaking a foreign language.) The whole household praised my German so that I grew ashamed to speak it."

Here and there Hay's Diary shows us glimpses of life at Vienna, and of the theatrical life which was closely bound to it.

"Last night" (December 17), he says, "was the first reception of the Duc de Gramont,[1] and the first night of the new ballet, *Nana Sahib*. The French Embassy was pretty well filled with pretty faces and toilettes. Some of the Hungarian women were

[1] French Ambassador.

strikingly beautiful. . . . The Archduke Wilhelm
was at Gramont's. The ladies took an enormous
interest in him on account of the vow of celibacy
which as Grand Master of the Teutonic Order he
must take. There was also a daughter of Alexander
Dumas, a miraculous conception of ugliness."

Under the date 18 February, 1868, is an account
of a ball at the Palace in honor of the wedding of the
young Grand Duchess of Modena to Prince Louis
of Bavaria.

"In the Diplomatic Circle," Hay writes, "I was
presented to the Emperor [Francis Joseph] by Baron
Beust. His Majesty was especially courteous. He
spoke among other things of the wonderful resources
we had displayed in our recent war and of the sudden
and complete peace that had followed. He spoke of
the difficult position [of the] President and complimented him highly on his 'energy and courageous
consistency.' The ball was given last night in my
opinion to afford the Imperial family and the great
officers of the Empire a valid excuse for absenting
themselves from the ceremonies of the silver wedding of the King of Hanover, which took place at
the same time, with great éclat in the *Kursalon*. . . .
The occasion has been awaited for some time, not
without uneasiness, as it was thought not improb-
able that the dispossessed King might indulge in a

demonstration that would seriously compromise his position with the courts both in Vienna and Berlin. But no one could have imagined that his reckless anger and vanity would lead him so far. He made a speech of the most violent character, in direct contravention of all the recent treaties made with him at such enormous cost by the Government of Prussia, and in defiance of the laws of propriety which should have restrained him as the guest of Austria.

"It is generally considered something more than a coincidence that Mr. de Bismarck yesterday declared that if the Hanoverian intrigues were not speedily discontinued, the severest measures of sequestration would immediately be put in force. It remains to be seen whether, even yet, the King of Prussia can be persuaded from his rigid adherence to the dogma of divine right, to allow justice to be done to an avowed public enemy."

"*April 22.* Post came in and while we were talking artillery began. He could n't keep still, so we went out and saw a neat little review in the Parade Platz. I thought it was the Imperial Baby, but was wrong; for to-day 100 guns thundered the glad tidings to Austria that they had another omnivorous Hapsburg to provide for."

Of one other celebrity, Prince Napoleon, familiarly

known to his contemporaries by his nickname "Plon-Plon," Hay speaks.

"*June 7, 1868.* I went over to the Golden Lamb, Leopoldstadt, about 1 o'clock. I was received, I believe, by Col. Ragon. Count Zichy was in the antechamber with the Colonel. Heckern came in before long. He introduced me and Zichy. We talked a good while till Werther (Prussian) who was with the Prince came out and Zichy went in. Heckern began girding at Werther about the supposed treaties and intrigues he had cooked up with the Prince. Werther, to escape persecution, turned to me and talked impeachment. Zichy made a long stay. Ferri-Pisani came in. At last Zichy emerged and I went in. The Prince received me in a pleasant offhand way and we began at once to talk about America and his visit there. He remembered most of the names now prominent in politics. He spoke of Seward — said he ought to have prevented the President's trip to Chicago. Said he remembered Colfax, a young blackfaced man — President of the Legislative Body — he meant Grow. He spoke of Stanton as a man of great merit and deplored his leaving the War Office, but remembered Schofield and was much pleased with what he saw of him. After a few words about Germany, and the interesting moment in which he visits it, the interview ended by my retiring."

Although the fame of actors and singers is often more fleeting than that of grandees and politicians, the following notes are interesting, if only as registers of John Hay's taste at the time he wrote them.

"*September 11, 1867*. Heard to-night *Minna von Barnhelm* at the Burg. It was well played by Sonnenthal, whom the ladies love because of his good legs; by La Roche, who is said to be a son of Goethe and who really resembles him strikingly; by Meixner and Schöne. Either a majority of the audience understood French, or they were well bred enough to seem to, for in the long scene between Minna and Riccaut de la Marlinière they listened with the same quiet attention which they always give to the play. The women were Bognar and Schneeberger — the former good but gaspy, and the latter first rate. Baumeister was excellent as the Wachtmeister. . . . There is too much talk in the German plays to suit us."

A few days later Hay saw *King Lear* at the Burg Theatre. "A general dead level of respectable acting that was very dreary in effect," is his criticism. "I remembered Forrest's storms and tempests of passion — often overdone, sometimes in bad taste, but always full of wonderful spirit and inexhaustible physical energy; and the careful and somewhat lachrymose style of Wagner suffered very much by comparison. Then Schlegel's text, though very correct and scholarly, is not Shakespeare. There is not a word of Shakespeare that can well be altered now. The blast of his mighty thought, sweeping through his words for three centuries, has attuned them to an immortal and perfect harmony. I was very curious to see Shakespeare in German. It is certainly very fine. But I shall not go often."

Of the nobles, Hay had a poor opinion. "Literature is considered here rather a low business," he says. "If a noble is clever and can write verses, he is very proud of it, but as a gentleman is proud of being able to dance a clog dance or play the banjo well. So they never put their names to their poems, but have a literary name, which is kept rigidly distinct from the one that bears sixteen quarterings. Count Anton Auersperg is Anastasius Grün, Baron Münch-Bellinghausen is Fried Hahn."

A little later he writes: "The Great Princes here speak very bad German — like '*Fiaker*.' They learn in their youth nothing but French, dogs, horses, women. They are embarrassed when they meet with cultivated men, and so avoid 'mixed society.' Together, they are all alike." Hay tells of one eccentric person, Henikstein, who "took me in and showed me his coffin and the skeletons of his friends. One of a woman, '*une bonne amie à moi,*' whom he chucked under the chin and made the bony head wag and grin in the candlelight, and the teeth rattle. A music box played dirges. Hatchments hung all around dated 186–."

A glimpse of the Court is given in this memorandum: "To-day (December 30) Countess Königsegg received for the Empress at the Burg. A small, richly furnished room. Men and ladies in brilliant uniforms, and the richest and most *éclatant* satins, coming and going. The brilliancy of colors was suggestive of ophthalmia. In the evening, drove out to the Augustan, where Prince Hohenlohe was receiving for the Emperor. Along the avenue to the Pavilion, pine-wood torches gave a glaring light. Inside the door of the vestibule was ranged a semicircle of some dozens of splendidly dressed menials, with heads powdered as if by a passing snowstorm, to head off the unwary from improper stairs and force them into the broad way that led in to Hohenlohe. He is a youngish, stiffish, very pleasant-spoken man, baldish on the bump of firmness. Esterhazy was there, with the handsome clothes, gallant bearing and feeble face you would expect from an old youth who has squandered all of his estates that he can."

Hay had few occasions for sending official despatches to the State Department, but he always en-

THE ROVING DIPLOMAT — VIENNA 303

riched them with information and comment which
must have rejoiced Mr. Seward; for it was rare then,
in America, to get authentic news of the Austrian
crises. I quote a single passage from one of the despatches, because, although it is dated February 5,
1868, it is still fresh, and it shows how early Hay
adopted that gospel of Peace which, when he came
to be Secretary of State, he labored to spread
throughout the world.

"The great calamity and danger of Europe to-
day," he writes Secretary Seward, "are these enormous armaments. No honest statesman can say
that he sees in the present attitude of politics the
necessity of war. No great Power is threatened.
There is no menace to peace that could not be immediately dispelled by a firm protest of the peace-
fully disposed majority of nations. There would be,
therefore, no danger to any people, but a vast and
immediate gain to all from a general disarmament.
It need not be simultaneous. It is idle to say that
France fears an invasion from Prussia or Prussia
from France, and an honest understanding among
the Western nations would keep the peace from the
Eastern side.

"Why then is this awful waste of youth and treasure continued? I believe from no other motive than
to sustain the waning prestige of Kings. Armies are

to-day only useful in Europe to overcome the people in peace, or by groundless wars to divert their attention from domestic misrule. With the disappearance of great armies, the welfare of the people would become the only mainspring of national action, and that false and wicked equilibrium by which now the interests of one man weigh as heavily as those of millions of his fellow creatures, would be utterly destroyed."

Hay watched intently the struggle of Austrian Liberals to free themselves from the Clerical control that threatened strangulation.

"The Church is enormously rich," he writes, "and has thus far succeeded in retaining its vast possessions free from the requisitions of the sorely pressed and almost bankrupt government. In Vienna nearly every one of the great religious orders are still in full possession of the vast estates acquired by their predecessors in the Middle Ages. The Schottenhof, a reminiscence of the Scotch Benedictines of the twelfth century, the Molkenhof and others are little cities of themselves. The Liberals, there are a few Liberals here, are very bitter upon this non-producing and all-consuming body."

"It would be disastrous," he says a little later, "if the Church should have the wit to take advantage of this juncture to lay upon themselves a free

tax, and trade the sums thus easily raised against a
re-affirmation of the Concordat.   The existence of
this incubus is now seriously menaced.   It is improb-
able that it can much longer continue to oppress and
crush the life of this nation.   The Church is making
frantic efforts to save it. . . . The toothless old giant
that Bunyan set away out of the active field of fight
two centuries ago, has still wit enough to make the
proudest monarchy of earth hew his wood and draw
his water."

We are not concerned to follow the course of this
conflict between Church and State, in which the
State finally gained a slight advantage; but we can be
amused, as Hay was, at the reactionary party, who,
when there was a popular rejoicing over the passage
of a favorable vote in the House of Peers, "were furious and either silly or malicious enough to telegraph
the Emperor that a revolutionary *émeute* was in
progress.   They scared the Archduchess' mother out
of bed, and Aristocracy in general sat and shivered
in its nightshirt until the crowd, tired with its loyal
jubilee, went home to bed."

Having plenty of leisure Hay went on several
journeys.   He "poked round Poland, lonesomely
enough, but fully compensated by the unusual and
peculiar towns [he] passed through."   He found Warsaw "a very respectable place," with two theaters

and a fair opera. " Cracow was the quaintest and
most entirely satisfactory little town [he] ever saw.
It has only 40,000 inhabitants, but it has a cathedral
and theatre, (where [he] heard a very fair burlesque),
and a regular mediæval Jews' Quarter."

Late in the autumn, he made a flying visit to
Turkey.

The pocketbook in which he jotted down hour by
hour the sights which most impressed him on this
trip shows how keenly and also how independently,
he observed. He does not record the ordinary things,
or give rein to moralizing and emotions. He makes,
rather, a skeleton from which he might afterwards
develop a well-rounded, graphic picture. As usual,
he puts in bits of landscape. Here, for instance, are
glimpses on the Danube.

"Wild and superb scenery to Orsova. Red sand-
stone hills by Greben. The lake. The Pass of Kazan.
Long before we came to it we could see the dense
veil of vapor behind the hills. A sheer granite rock
on the left of the Greben Lake like the Schreckhorn.
As we entered the pass a wild storm of rain and wind
came howling through: the rain whirling like a volley
of bullets. Nature making a last desperate stand.
The cliffs rising higher and higher, till the last one
sprang sheer 2000 feet, its head buried in the tattered
clouds. Just beyond a tranquil collapse. Here is

most plainly seen the remains of Trajan's road. Not only the mortise holes but a portion of the gallery itself hollowed in the rock exists." (November 9, 1867.)

At Constantinople, he wrote in more detail, probably with the purpose of working up his notes into an article. After landing at Galata in the forenoon, and getting quarters at the Hôtel de Byzance on the Pera hill, he and his companions — "An American," named Whittlesey, "and a young Bostonian, a Quincy" — prepare for sight-seeing.

"Dress and go to the Whirling Dervishes. Enter a pleasant walled place. Pass into a light anteroom where you put on overshoes. Go through a door hung with a heavy and thick curtain into a circular room. Green pillars. To the right, Christians: left, Turks. Galleries above. Ladies' gallery — grated, and painted with trees and shrubs, all slanted to Mecca. The Dervishes all standing around the circumference of the circle. The old sheik enters. They bow profoundly. He sits down, kneels, and the praying begins. He mumbles and mutters and in the gallery over the entrance another sings the responses in a nasal twang. The whole body rise and go to the centre of the room and fall on their knees. They heave and sit, rising and kissing the floor in time to the singing. After the prayer is finished they go back to the place around the circumference and the old fellow in the choir sings a long solo. After a moment of silence the orchestra begins a subtle dizzying sound of wind and wood instruments. This continues some time, buzzing, sultry. Then the old sheik rises and starts around the room and the rest follow, all bowing to the mat he has been sitting on. Their costumes are exactly the same in cut, differ in color. The old sheik and his boy are green; the second sheik and his boy are brown. They go around three times. Then the sheik stands still and the whole party range themselves again in the circumference; throw off their cloaks. The music becomes a shriller, louder music of drums and flutes, and the dervishes cross arms over chest, the hands resting on the shoulders, and march by the sheik. As they pass him they begin whirling, at first slowly and then faster, throwing out their arms, very regularly, their dresses widening downwards. Garibaldi and morning (?) dress of young ladies of to-day. Concentric circles. Looking over shoulders. Different types. . . . Turk in the corner, fervent piety. Catholic Turks telling their beads during the performance. Foreigners. . . ."

On another day the party crossed the Bosphorus, visited Scutari, climbed Mount Boulgourlou on stallions, enjoyed the magnificent view, and on their return saw a performance of the Howling Dervishes. Hay describes them almost as minutely as he did the Whirlers.

"The Dervishes enter barefoot this time. Sitting in a circle singing. Sheik praying. As each one entered, kissed his hand. After a while they rise, and begin singing and swaying. This continues an hour. The motion and the time change, becoming always more rapid. The performers form a straight line across the end of the room. Two rows of older fellows sit cross-legged in the middle of the room to keep up the shrill singing. Reel and put on nightcaps. Violent, brutal excitement. The negro, clapping hands, wiping face, growls.

"Green and yellow child among the performers. The sick children. Very heavily clothed. Very much like a negro shout. Instruments of torture about the room. Not now used. Bad fame of the Dervishes. Great influence. Lay brothers. Old sheik of a great family."

Hay and his companions sailed from Constantinople to Trieste by an Austrian Lloyd steamer. As it steered westward Hay "watched the matchless view of the city, cut off by the Golden Horn Promontory. The reason why this view is so famous, he discovers, is that as you look back St. Sophia and the Mosque of Achmet, with their many minarets, are fused into one. Soon Olympus looms up, and "velvet hills." Then, the magic passage through the Ægean, among islands which live in memory as colors — pearl, opal, sapphire, amethyst. At Corfu, Hay went ashore and spent several enchanted hours. "The water," he remarks, "has the same delicate green as the Stamboul, if seen directly, blue, if seen obliquely." He stayed long enough at Trieste to see the city, and to exchange calls with the eccentric American Consul, Alexander Thayer, the biographer of Beethoven. After running into a snow-storm on the Semmering, he reached Vienna in the evening of November 23.

Writing to Nicolay while his impressions were still vivid, he sums them up in a few lines: —

"A magnificent day on the Danube to Orsova, and another to Rustchuck — over the railway all day to Varna — and by breakfast time the next morning we were staring with delight of greenhorns at the unparalleled spectacle that greets you as you sail down the Bosphorus into Constantinople. That closes for me in this world, I verily believe, my sensations of great cities. The last is infinitely finer than anything I ever imagined. I am pretty sure there is nothing that approaches it on earth. We had perfect weather — June at its prettiest in Illinois, for instance — and this staid with us all the time. We passed a day in Asia and climbed Mt. Boulgourlou and saw the gates of the morning. We had great larks, which I have not time to write."

In March, he had a glimpse of Italy, and wished to go up the Nile; but time, and perhaps money fell short; for his salary as *Chargé* at Vienna was not lavish.

By the spring of 1868, Hay began to think of turning homewards. The State Department was slow in appointing a minister. It offered the office to Horace Greeley, who declined, thus depriving the world of a unique sight — the editor of the *Tribune* among the archduchesses of the House of Hapsburg. Finally, Henry M. Watts, a Pennsylvanian, accepted the post, the first article of Pennsylvanian patriotism being, "Thou shalt decline no office." On August 12, 1868, just a year from the date of his arrival in Vienna, Hay resigned.

Some time before he retired, he sent his former chief, John Bigelow, the following letter, which, between its banter and seriousness, serves as a charming bit of autobiography: —

To John Bigelow

April 27, 1868

I had no idea when I came abroad last summer that I should be here so long. I thought they would fix up the vacuum (abhorred of nature and office-seekers) in a few months — so I came for a flyer, principally because I was a little ashamed of having been in Europe nearly two years and having seen nothing. I have had a pleasant year of it. There is very little work to do at the Legation. I have sinned grievously against certain ten-day regulations that I have heard of. I have seen all I care to of Prussia, Poland, Turkey, and Italy. I have drawn my salary with startling punctuality. I have not wearied the home office with much despatches. My sleep is infantine and my appetite wolfish.

I am satisfied with my administration of this 'arduous and delicate post.' I believe that is the regular shriek of the Radical Press in alluding to the Vienna Mission. You and Mr. Adams worked while you were in harness. I am not sure but that a serious man could always find work in either of those two missions. But equally sure am I that no two other American diplomats can catch each other's eyes without mutual guffaws, unless they have a power of facial muscle that would put the Roman augurs to shame. Just let me get into Congress once, and take one shy at the Diplomatic Appropriation Bill.

I am very glad I came. Vienna is worth while for a year. It is curious and instructive to see their people starting off in the awkward walk of political

babyhood. They know what they want, and I believe they will get it. The Aristocracy is furious, and
the Kaiser a little bewildered at every new triumph
of the Democratic and liberal principle. But I don't
think they can stop the machine now — though
they may get their fingers mashed in the cogs. I
don't think the world ever seemed getting ahead so
positively and quietly before. Two years ago —
it was another Europe. England has come abreast
of Bright. Austria is governed by Forty-Eighters.
Bismarck is becoming appalled by the spirit of Freedom that he suckled with the blood of Sadowa.
France still lies in her comatose slumber — but she
talks in her sleep and murmurs the *Marseillaise*.
And God has made her ruler blind drunk, that his
Helot antics may disgust the world with despotism.

If ever, in my green and salad days, I sometimes
vaguely doubted, I am safe now. I am a Republican
till I die. When we get to Heaven, we can try a
Monarchy, perhaps.

CHAPTER XII

THE ROVING DIPLOMAT — SPAIN

AT the end of October, 1868, Hay sailed for the second time into New York Harbor, with a larger fund of experience in his head, but with his purse no richer and his prospects no brighter. During much of his stay in Vienna his health had been bad, a reason for his wishing to come home. Few records remain of the ensuing months. Presumably, he visited Washington, to see whether under the new administration — Grant was elected President in November — he might find employment. Neither then, nor later, was Hay a professed office-seeker. He never had the art of making those in power take his talents at their real worth — much less, at more than their worth, which is the secret of many place-holders. An innate refinement, coupled with shyness, and an abiding personal dignity, kept him from the suppliant's posture. He took it for granted that, as he was sufficiently well known by the leaders at Washington, they would summon him if they wanted him.

Perhaps he was promised another diplomatic billet, in the overturn which, according to happy custom, would begin as soon as the new President was inaugurated. Meanwhile, Hay went to Illinois, saw his relatives, looked after his tenants, and applied himself in earnest to literary work. Lecturing was still, although the prestige of the lyceum was waning, a profitable profession for those who caught the fancy of the public. Hay had long looked upon this as a possible resource and he now tested it. On January 27, 1869, before the Young Men's Christian Association of Buffalo, he delivered a lecture on "The Progress of Democracy in Europe." "Had a fair house — very attentive and good-natured audience," he notes in his Diary. "Was reasonably successful — especially pleased at the absence of trepidation and duration of my voice." Writing to Edmund Clarence Stedman a few days later he adds: "I have tried an experiment since I saw you last. I have faced a large audience and spoken a piece without breaking down. I lectured in Buffalo and in a few Western towns. I will do more of it next winter."

He closes his letter to Stedman with the following hint: "I hope to see you later in the spring. I shall pass through New York on my way to Europe. I left some unravelled threads of occupation over there, and must go over once more — my own master now — and pick them up."

The "unravelled threads" proved to be his appointment as first Secretary of Legation at Madrid. On July 29, being already at his post, he jots down this memorandum: "Drew on Barings for $146.66 for month of transit."

Hay's diplomatic service in Spain fell during a dramatic crisis. The profligate queen, Isabella II, had been expelled. Republicans of various shades were hoping for a republic. Liberal Conservatives worked for a monarchy, which the Liberals among them wished to make constitutional, while the Clericals intrigued to restore the old absolutism in which they throve. Marshal Serrano was provisional regent. Hay came just in time to witness the contest, and so strongly did he sympathize with the Republicans that he must have found it hard to keep up the feint of diplomatic impartiality.

The duties of his office consumed much of his time. The Minister, General Daniel E. Sickles, was one of the typical wastrels who succeeded, partly by rough capacity and partly by truculence, in pushing their way to the front during the Civil War. Dissolute in his personal habits, loose in money matters, and unscrupulous in his methods, he rose to the command of the Third Corps of the Army of the Potomac, and, at the battle of Gettysburg, he stationed his troops, without orders, in a position which brought disaster upon them and threatened the defeat of the Union army. Fortunately for Sickles, he had a leg shot off in the battle — luck which prevented his being court-martialed, and enabled him to pose during half a century as the hero of Gettysburg. No bullet was ever more beneficent to its victim than that which crippled him. At Madrid Hay seems to have found him an unexacting chief.

The Secretary applied himself to learning Spanish; but before he attained fluency in that, his knowledge of French opened many official doors. He watched the political crisis with intense interest. In Paris he had seen the growing restlessness of Liberals under the Imperial despotism; in Vienna, he saw a constitutional monarchy emerge from an autocracy; and now in Madrid he hoped that his ideal, the Republic, would spring into vigorous being.

A group of statesmen, who would have been remarkable in any country, carried on the struggle for ascendancy in Spain. Foremost among them was Castelar, whose reputation as the advocate of Republicanism had crossed the Atlantic. Next, ranked Prim, "a soldier, conspirator, diplomatist, and born ruler; a Cromwell without convictions; a dictator who hides his power; a Warwick, who mars Kings as tranquilly as he makes them"; Serrano, the regent, dignified and conciliatory; Sagasta, still at the halfway stage between politician and statesman; Silvela, Cánovas del Castillo: these were leaders whom Hay studied as eagerly as a zoölogist studies a strange fauna. Something in his temperament — his love of color, perhaps — caused him to understand and enjoy their passionate oratory. For Castelar he had a profound admiration.

Hay seldom missed an important debate. The Cortes, he writes on October 1, 1869, "resumed their session to-day after a vacation of some months. The Diplomatic Body have a little cage holding fifteen. We have three cards and one I stole. The seats all vacant in the hall. The President comes in in solemn procession with the *maceros* and secretaries. The *maceros* dressed out of Froissart. Rivero wears white kids during the whole session. His opening speech. Figueras replies. Figuerola, Orense, and Castelar sitting together on the top bench of the Extreme Left. Figueras, a Western Senator sort of man in build and carriage, with a wonderful aptitude of speech and good knowledge of parliamentary practice. Orense, the noble factor of the play. Rivero scolds the Deputies like a schoolmaster, knocking them over the knuckles without *merci* or *misericordia*. The Government sits on a bench distinguished from the rest by being in blue velvet instead of crimson. Out of 304 Deputies, not more than 100 present. The afternoon sun pouring in through the window facing the West. Lighting up. The *maceros* relieving each other. Not many nobles."

The next day Hay went to see Castelar. "Found him at his own door, coming home with his hands full of documents. Walked up with him — and had a long talk about everything. He speaks French fluently — learned it in exile in Paris, where he supported himself and many others by writing for South American papers. He has an exquisite face — a soft, sweet tenor voice, a winning, and what the Spaniards call *simpatico*, manner.

"He spoke of Napoleon's sickness and of the humiliating spectacle of a great nation looking for its destiny in the *cuvette* of an old man. We talked a good deal of art and Italy. Of Spain he spoke sadly; he seemed to feel that the insurrection in Catalonia was premature and ill-advised. He thought there were evil days coming for the Republicans in Madrid. He said, 'We have just had a hard hour's work to persuade the party of action not to precipitate an insurrection to-night. This would be madness. Madrid is thoroughly monarchical. It is a city of placeholders. The militia is in great majority monarchical. There are 10,000 or 12,000 regular troops here. An insurrection would be smothered in blood. Yet it is hard to keep the fiery young fellows from trying it.'"

Of Castelar's manner as an orator, Hay gives this glowing description: —

"*Oct. 3, Sunday.* The discussion to-day on the Suspension of Guarantees occupied all the afternoon and will be continued to-morrow.

"Castelar was superb. His action is something marvellous. He uses more gesticulation than any orator or actor I have ever heard. His voice is, as I suspected, rather rich and musical than strong, and he uses it so remorselessly that it is apt to suffer in an hour or so. But his matter is finer than his manner. I have never imagined the possibility of such fluency of speech. Never for one instant is the wonderful current of declamation checked by the pauses, the hesitations, the deliberations that mark all Anglo-Saxon debate. His whole speech is delivered with precisely the energy and fluency that Forrest exhibits in the most rapid passages of his most muscular plays; and when you consider that not a word of this is written or prepared, but struck off instantly in the very heat and spasms of utterance, it seems little short of miraculous. The most laborious conning and weighing and filing of the most fastidious rhetorician could not produce phrases of more exquisite harmony, antitheses more sharp and brilliant, metaphors more perfectly fitting — all uttered with a feverish rapidity that makes the despair of stenographers. Then his logic is as faultless as his rhetoric. He never says a foolish or careless word. All history is at his finger's ends. There is no fact too insignificant for his memory — none too stale to do service. They are all presented with such felicity and grace too, that you scarcely see how solid they are."

Again and again Hay returns to enthusiastic praise of Castelar. "His action is as violent as Forrest," he writes Nicolay. "His style is as florid as Gibbon. . . . He never writes a speech. Yet every sentence, even in a running debate, when all the government hounds are yelping at him at once, is as finished and as elegantly balanced as if he had pondered all a rainy Sunday over it. I am afraid he will cease to be the Republican idol before long. He has too much sense and integrity to follow the lead of the Socialist fanatics."

Of three other Spanish orators Hay has sketches, hasty but penetrating.

"Sagasta, Ministro de la Gubernacion, greatly distinguished himself on Monday. He defended the Government, especially himself, with wonderful vigor and malice. He is the hardest hitter in the Cortes. Everybody calls him a scamp, and everybody seems to admire him, nevertheless. He is a sort of Disraeli — lithe, active, full of energy and hate — tormented by the Opposition to the proper point of hot anger,

he made a defensive offensive that enchanted the
Government benches.

"Silvela also made a good speech or two — but
Silvela is rather too good a fellow for this kind of
work. He is very sincere and candid, but lacks the
Devil, which makes Sagasta so audacious and Prim
so cool.

"Prim's speech Tuesday evening after Castelar
had announced the intention of the Republicans to
retire, was a masterpiece. He begged them to re-
consider — he was frank, open, soldierly; he begged
them to stay, and threatened them with severe measures if they went — he was not savage and insulting
like Sagasta — nor phrasy like Silvela; but he was
the perfection of enigma, as always. His speech
was powerful and impressive in its deep simplicity
and greatly affected Castelar and the Republicans.
Castelar answered in the same tone of exquisite
courtesy, rejecting the advice which was coupled
with a threat. The law passed, and the Republican
Deputies left the Chamber."

Even latter-day readers, ignorant of the intri-
cacies of Spanish politics in 1869, cannot fail to enjoy
these portraits of historic figures. What would we
not give to have a similar series, sketched by a foreigner as receptive, keen, and detached as Hay, of the
leaders of the French Assembly eighty years earlier?

The diplomatic business which chiefly concerned the Legation had to do with Porto Rico and with Cuba. The latter island was in insurrection, and President Grant signed a proclamation recognizing the Cubans as belligerents; but Hamilton Fish, his Secretary of State, wisely deferred issuing it. At Madrid, Sickles and Hay would have gone further and had the United States Government interfere in behalf of Cuban independence.

"The amount of talk we have done since we came here is something portentous," Hay writes Nicolay on October 7, 1869.

"I have been always on hand as a medium of communication, and so have seen more of the *gros bonnets* than usually falls to the lot of secretaries. We have a good enough time of it; have done nothing but show our amicable intentions. The Government here is crazy to accept our offered mediation, but does not dare. The cession of Cuba to the Cubans would be a measure too frightfully unpopular for the Government to face in its present uncertain tenure. Still, if it continues to grow stronger, as now seems probable, it may take the bit in its teeth and do something after a while."

Nearly four months later, Hay reports again to Nicolay: —

"I have no news for you. This Legation has absolutely nothing of importance now in its hands. There is a great deal of tiresome routine work which employs the fingers more than the brain, and, by way of keeping the circulation regular, there is dancing enough to keep the feet from rusting. I am getting rather tired of it, and shall begin to plume my wings for flight some time in the spring. I am sorry Sickles has not had a better chance, but nothing was possible with Fish's system of platonic bullying. I am afraid Cuba is gone. This Government wants to sell out but dares not, and has no power to put a stop to the atrocities on the island. The only thing left to our Government is to do nothing and keep its mouth shut; or interfere to stop the horrors in Cuba on the ground of humanity, or the damage resulting to American interests." (January 30, 1870).

Hay kept his Diary without regard to sequence. In the midst of the abstract of the daily happenings, he would insert the draft of a letter to be sent or the copy of one received; or he would outline a poem, or set down maxims and reflections. Here is a page of observations from the Madrid period: —

"Indolent people imagine they would like to be busy. Industrious people know they would enjoy being idle.

"The English servant is a statuesque image of propriety. The French a sympathizing but respectful friend. The Spanish and Italian have the subordination of children. An American revenges himself on fate by insolence.

"Americans in Europe waste time enormously in calculating when the mail will arrive. A mail is like a baby — you can't hurry or retard it by talking about it.

"Politicians like corals build and die: others succeed.

"Mad agitators imagine they lead, as the people come after.

"When Sherman marched to the sea, Bummers were miles in advance. They carry no baggage of character or responsibility and so go fast. Rousseau held a Moses necessary."

John Hay's best chronicle of his life in Spain is contained in his "Castilian Days," in which he combines, in finely balanced proportion, description, information, and personal impressions. In those pages you learn how minutely Hay studied the Spaniards. He takes you to the theater and the bull-fights, to the churches and the palaces and the Prado Gallery; he visits Segovia and Toledo, the Escorial and Alcalà. Along the way, he sketches in characteristic figures, beggars, priests, peasants, nobles. And all the while he pours out his lively comment.

He wrote these papers during the first months of 1870; and though the range of his knowledge and the deep relief and variety of his background prove that he carefully prepared himself by reading Spanish history and literature, he never rouses in you the suspicion of having crammed for the occasion. Whatever notes he made for the preparation of his "Castilian Days" he probably destroyed: for they have not come to light. His Diary also contains only the account of his early meeting with the Spanish statesmen, most of which I have quoted above. Very few letters remain. Yet in spite of this gap, the book itself is the best memorial of his stay in Spain.

On May 1, 1870, Hay presented his resignation to General Sickles, regretting that "pecuniary circumstances" compelled him to retire. This reason entered into his decision, and perhaps if he had had independent means he might have continued in the service; but a desire to return to the more stirring life of America, coupled with the conviction that he had completed his training in Europe, chiefly influenced him.

He did not quit Madrid until summer. A final letter, written on June 30, contains a bit of autobiographic retrospect, and notes of an excursion to Toledo, which he took in company with congenial old friends from Washington.

To Miss Harriet K. Loring

I have a curious year to look back upon — more
entirely out of the world than any since I came into
it. . . . I went with Mrs. and Miss Hooper and Miss
S. to Toledo, and had a few halcyon days, favored
by fate, weather, and other accessories, in that delicious old town. I have rarely had such larks, — the
ladies went crazy sketching adorable doorways, and
I sat by, on the shady side, and chaffed the picturesque beggars grouped around in the rags of the
period. I felt the coil of cares slipping away from
me, and leaving me young and appreciative again
as when

> " I roamed a young Westerner, o'er the green bluff,
>   And climbed thy steep summit, oh, Warsaw, of mud."

For the first time since I can remember I have
been busy this year, and it does not suit my complexion. There is a good deal to do in the Legation,
and I have imposed a good deal of work upon myself
beside, having gotten interested in Spanish history.
I have a veritable workshop for the fellows who know
things. I cannot conceive how a man like Mr. Motley should have preferred England, with its pitiful
annoyances, to Austria with its quiet and its archives.
I should like to read about twenty years. The first
ten would be necessary to reach the proper point of

humility, and the last one might hope to gain something substantial.

"I am glad I committed the folly of coming," he confides to Nicolay. "I have seen a great deal and learned something. I speak the language — well enough to be understood, but not well enough to be taken for a Spaniard — *à Dieu ne plaise*."

Before he bade good-bye to Spain, Hay had the disappointment of seeing the Republican cause there founder, and the Spanish Cortes looking Europe over for a candidate to the Bourbon throne; and before he took steamer for home, the Prussians were already engaged in a war which, though he little suspected it, was to result not only in the checking of Republican ideals, but in the revival of Authority and Privilege, thinly veiled under modern conditions and entrenched behind the magnificently organized military despotism of Germany.

CHAPTER XIII

JOURNALISM

WHEN John Hay landed at the New York dock on a September morning in 1870, he was already thirty-two years old, carrying in his memory a treasure of experiences which few could match, but counting little, very little money in his purse or in the bank. His travels had made him what from early boyhood he had longed to be, a citizen of the world; equally at home in London or in Paris, in Vienna or in Madrid. To make a living was now, as it had been since 1865, his first concern: because the American community still regarded bread-winning as the normal condition of every man, whether the bread he won were plain and crusty, or accompanied by those luxuries which are the necessaries of the rich.

Hay knew himself too well to suppose that he could ever succeed as a money-maker. His talents, rare and sparkling and delightful, procured for him the friendships and intimacies which wealth cannot buy; but these commodities were not listed in Wall Street. By instinct an artist, he could not be satisfied with the Bohemian life in which poor painters, writers, poets, sculptors and journalists forgot their poverty. He mixed with them, but he was never wholly of them; for a strand of fastidiousness ran through his nature, and Bohemia would not be Bohemia if it were fastidious. Dignity, too, characterized Hay from his youth; and while he might be jovial among his chosen cronies, he was constitutionally shy, and never would permit liberties to be taken with him. "No matter how intimate you were," his best friend told me, "or how merry the occasion, nobody ever slapped John Hay on the back."

He came home in 1870 expecting to go to Warsaw for a while, and then, unless something better turned up, to seek an editorial position on a newspaper. Possibly, he might support himself by lecturing. But journalism, the refuge of whoever can hold a pen, seemed to him the most promising make-shift, especially as he had already, during one of the intervals between his European trips, served as an editor of the *Chicago Journal*.

Going uptown after landing — the custom-house inspector had no quarrel with him — Hay called on some of his friends. Toward evening, he fell in with Whitelaw Reid, and they dined together at the Union League Club. Then, as the story runs, Hay accompanied Reid to the *Tribune* office, for a last chat before taking the midnight train for the West.

On his table Reid found the freshest despatches, some of which would serve as texts for editorial comment. One, containing important news from Europe, Reid handed to Hay, asking him what should be said about it. Hay volunteered to deal with it himself, sat down at a table, and, in very quick time, he gave Reid a leader which overjoyed him. The next day, when Horace Greeley saw it, he said: "I have read a million editorials, and this is the best of them all."

Such is the legend — unverifiable in its minutest details, but undoubtedly true in its substance — of John Hay's joining the staff of the *New York Tribune:* for it is almost needless to say that, with Horace Greeley and Whitelaw Reid both so enthusiastic over his maiden effort, they urged him to stay in New York and serve the great newspaper.

The invitation attracted Hay, but before accepting it he wished to see his family in Illinois. He was also, apparently, considering the possibility of joining a Chicago newspaper. On his way out he wrote this letter: —

To Whitelaw Reid

CHICAGO, ILLINOIS,
Sep. 29, 1870.

MY DEAR MR. REID:

I leave here in a day or two for Warsaw, Illinois, where I shall spend a few weeks with my family. I shall then probably go on to New York, and shall not fail to call upon you.

I thank you most cordially for your kind and satisfactory letter.

The *Republican* was hopelessly water-logged, and the present transfer is a *sauve qui peut* of the owners.

If you should by accident have anything to say to me before I see you, my address is always Care Charles E. Hay, Springfield, Illinois.

Nicolay desires me to convey his kind remembrances to you.

Thence Hay journeyed to his old home, where he took up again the simple, unpretentious life with as much relish as if he were not a licensed cosmopolite.

To J. G. Nicolay

WARSAW, ILLINOIS,
October 13, 1870.

I have just received the enclosed from W. It is a model of holy and unselfish anger against foul and infamous outrage. I have written him a letter of cordial sympathy and you will doubtless do the same. The article he refers to, I wrote after you left Chicago, for the *N. Y. Tribune.* I have not seen it.

I flitted on Tuesday after shipping my charming wards. I found Warsaw with a broad grin on its face at the lovely grape crop. My father made 1200 gallons of good wine, and even my shy little vineyard made its *début* with 240.

I wish you could have been here and eaten grapes with me during the past week. They are of a most exquisite flavor and sweeter than I have ever seen them anywhere in the world. Especially the much abused Catawba, which people were thinking of ploughing up, has nobly asserted itself and produced a superb vintage. We are now through, and ready for the frost when it comes.

The weather is lovely. The great river is wrapped at daybreak in a morning gown of fog, but soon brightens up, and the light has a regular spree on the many-colored foliage of the hills and the islands.

I am doing nothing and find it easy to take. I walk a great deal and eat for several. I have gained two pounds in weight the first week.

I have a very cordial letter from Howells saying he thinks my decision the best one; that the publication in the *Magazine* will not hurt the book, but will be a positive advantage to it. So my mind is at rest on that score.

On his return to New York, Hay accepted Whitelaw Reid's invitation to the *Tribune*. His accession came at a turning-point in the career of that journal.

Greeley still kept his post of editor-in-chief, but the work of editing was done by a staff composed chiefly of "Greeley's young men," the most remarkable group of editorial writers which any American newspaper had seen. Few of them were over forty; two or three were under thirty;[1] all had known the stimulus of the Civil War; all spoke the language of 1870, which made that of 1860 seem obsolete. Whitelaw Reid virtually managed the paper, although Greeley still shaped its general policy. The venerable George Ripley conducted the department of literary criticism; Hassard was musical critic; Bayard Taylor wrote on anything which touched his miscellaneous interest; Bromley had already approved himself an all-round journalist of high rank, and William Winter had begun his unparalleled career as dramatic critic; Smalley, having achieved notoriety as a war correspondent in the Rebellion and at the battle of Sadowa, was organizing the *Tribune's* news bureau in London. Of them all, Greeley declared Hay was the most brilliant. We do not hear that the veteran and the newcomer ever discussed their meeting at the Niagara Conference; if they did, Greeley bore no grudge.

[1] The veterans were George Ripley, literary editor, born in 1802; Charles T. Congdon, born in 1821, and Bayard Taylor, born in 1825. The birth dates of the others were Noah Brooks, 1830; Isaac H. Bromley, 1833; George W. Smalley, 1833; J. R. G. Hassard and William Winter, 1836; Whitelaw Reid, 1837; John Hay, 1838; Montgomery Schuyler, 1843.

To identify Hay's editorial contributions to the *Tribune* during the four years and more of his service on its staff would not be very fruitful, even were it possible. Although the paper had ceased to be Greeley's personal organ, editorial writers followed, of course, the general views of the manager, but the public seldom recognized the author of this or that article. The editorial "we" leveled alike the brilliant and the commonplace. If anonymity dimmed the fame of the individual, it also lessened his responsibility.

And yet among his fellows the special correspondent or the editor enjoyed his full measure of glory. This was true of Hay, whose reputation seems to have been won almost immediately in the sanctums of New York.

The following letter, written soon after he had buckled on his harness, describes his work: —

To J. G. Nicolay

NEW YORK TRIBUNE,
December 12, 1870.

I have delayed writing for a few days, knowing you had seen Reid, and that he had told you I was alive. I am living at the Astor House, which is now run on the European plan, and gives me a room on rather reasonable terms. I am working daily on the *Tribune*, writing editorials, or, as it is here technically called, *brevier.* I get salary enough to pay my board and washing.

I cannot regard it as a successful experiment as yet, though Reid and the rest seem satisfied. I do not find myself up to the work of writing so much every day on a given theme. But the *Tribune* force is sufficient to allow a good deal of subdivision, and so far I have written just what I please. . . .

Reid talks of sending me to Washington — not as reporter, but as a sort of heavy-swell correspondent; whereat I rather reluct. I do not like to blame and I mortally hate to praise. Which somewhat narrows a letter-writer's field.

Leaving Hay's entry into authorship for the next chapter, I quote the most pithy of the letters which pertain to his work on the *Tribune*.

To Whitelaw Reid

NEW YORK TRIBUNE,
Monday, 1870.

I have read all I could find for three or four years,[1] and don't believe I can do much worse. But why do you talk of columns and halves? — the foregoing ones have not averaged a half. However, I will go

---

[1] Files of the *New York Tribune*, which Hay had gone through in order to familiarize himself with its methods and its treatment of recent history.

to-night — see with what eyes are left me, and write till the time of stereotypers comes and the voice of the devil is heard in the hall.

I am so seedy that I will go home for a nap, and come out this evening so fresh that a daisy would look *blasée* beside me.

Dios le guarde a V. muchos años.

On October 8, 1871, the Widow O'Leary's cow kicked over a kerosene lamp and started the conflagration which nearly destroyed Chicago. As soon as the magnitude of the fire was understood, distant newspapers hurried their correspondents to the spot, to report it. Hay went for the *New York Tribune.* The next two letters describe the difficulties that he encountered.

To Whitelaw Reid

CHICAGO, 12 Oct. 1871.
Thursday evening.

I arrived here this morning 38 hours from New York, and found Keenan [1] at the telegraph office. He got here last night and prepared a despatch which they would not send. Stager said if he sent for anybody he would for his friend Bennett of the *Herald* (who has had two men on the ground since Tuesday),

[1] Henry F. Keenan, then on the *Tribune* staff: author of *Trajan, The Money-Makers,* etc.

but he would not do it, for them, nor for us, nor any-body. We worried them until morning, and Smith of the Associated Press at last consented to send clandestinely 1000 words if we would restrict our-selves to that. I wrote a despatch with which Keenan has gone to the office. I think I will send no more letters by telegraph. We will telegraph what seems desirable for a day or two, and write letters to go by mail.

P.S. Keenan has just returned. Stager is inex-orable — would only let my letter go to the Asso-ciated Press, — refused to let the *Herald's* go even that way, — says they are several thousand messages behind, and will permit no special despatches to go at present; — eight wires are broken.

I will go on writing. I will decide to-morrow if there is anything requiring heroic treatment. If so, Mr. Keenan will go to Detroit (the stations nearer are under Stager's control), and telegraph. Other-wise you must rely on the Associated Press for news —unless the restriction is let up—and upon us for letters.

To Whitelaw Reid

[CHICAGO, 15 Oct. 1871.] Sunday.

This ends my labors for the present. I send a des-patch to-day, and Keenan makes up the news for it.

To-night, if I can get away, I will go to Springfield. If anything of sufficient interest transpires there to-morrow, I will send it. Tuesday, to Warsaw for a day or two, and then New York again.

I have done as well as I could. I have a clean conscience. Your condemnation will not gall my withers. I have given the Great Moral Organ [1] 16 hours a day ever since I arrived.

I think it due to Keenan to say he has done all anybody could do. His failure to get off a despatch on the night he arrived was inevitable. Since that he has been ahead. Friday he managed admirably and had the wires nearly the whole evening. He made a favorable impression in the telegraph and newspaper offices. The *Herald* had five men who went off to New York in relays and got up their despatches on the way. I don't think that is worth while. Keenan will stay a few days and then report for relief to you.

Journalism makes insatiate demands upon its votaries; it often has slight scruples as to propriety; but the following letter shows that it did not quite succeed in turning John Hay into a society reporter.

[1] The *Tribune* had been nicknamed the "Great Moral Organ," and its staff accepted that title.

To Whitelaw Reid

[WASHINGTON, December, 1870.]

Here is a sketchy letter with nothing in it — which you can use or kill.

I have had no chance for any decent work. I wrote no account of the wedding[1] because the family assumed to be dead agin it — Mrs. Sprague[2] having spoken with some severity of Howard J. Q. for having taken notes. I do not do these things, but would have gushed if you had especially wished it. I gave Mr. White the points the night before. I found Mrs. S. had accepted for me invitations for Friday and Saturday, so that instead of being with you Saturday night, I shall not report until Monday morning.

So many people have spoken of you and sent greetings that my paper would not hold their names. The Chief Justice[3] and the ladies were sorry not to see you. He said the Great Moral Organ had improved enormously under your management and was now easily at the head of the dailies. Spofford[4] also spoke of the excellence of the paper.

In a street car the other night I met Zach Chandler.[5] He says Greeley is all right — he hopes that

[1] The wedding of Miss Chase to Mr. William Hoyt.
[2] Mrs. Kate Chase Sprague was Miss Chase's sister.
[3] S. P. Chase.
[4] Ainsworth R. Spofford, Librarian of Congress.
[5] Zachary Chandler, United States Senator from Michigan.

you are all right. He knows I am all right (interrogatively). He says the *Tribune* must support the Administration and not get switched off. Asks if it will do any good for him to go up to New York and talk to you, and H. G. I said, 'No! write! Your name and vigorous style would have as much effect as your personal presence.'

I am between Celery and Cherubs. I dine with Sumner Sunday.

I will take your orders when I get back as to whether I shall write an R. article or do up P. The statue is worse than I expected.

The *Tribune* used the versatile Hay in many ways. His first-hand acquaintance with European public men, and with politics abroad, made him the special warder of foreign topics. He not only read the Continental journals, but also secured the collaboration of such celebrities as Castelar, whose articles he translated and of the French novelist, Arsène Houssaye, who was then in high vogue.

To Whitelaw Reid

[NEW YORK, 11 March, 1875.]

Here is a letter of Houssaye's which ought to be printed as soon as there is room; not *must* but *desirable*.

He sent a column or two of puffs of his ball.[1] I think what I have put together at the end of this letter would be well enough. The rest your *Nuevo Mundo* might like, and I have put it back in the envelope.

Enclosed is a private note to you which I have translated. He wants some money.

I have another in my pocket and must take an early day to translate it.

The projector of the *Chicago Inter-Ocean* is the subject of the next note, brief but not lacking a characteristic touch.

To Whitelaw Reid

Feb. 16, 1872.

J. Young Scammon of Chicago was here this morning, and said he might call again during the day. If he comes, give him welcome. You know who he is — one of the salt. He is starting a new paper in Chicago, and wants advice. He has wads of money — more than he will have when his paper is a year older. He is coming with me to the Century to-morrow night.

The Presidential year 1872 saw a political upheaval which, if it had been led by a man of command-

[1] Houssaye had recently given a luxurious ball which served Paris as a three-days' wonder.

ing influence, might have hastened the end of the evil methods of Reconstruction: but Horace Greeley, the Democratic candidate who opposed President Grant, was neither a sound political thinker, nor a magnetic political standard-bearer. On being nominated by the Democrats at Baltimore for President, he withdrew from the *Tribune*, which Reid, however, kept steadfastly loyal to him. The Liberal Republicans, or bolters, who hoped to work a purge, found themselves dished when the Democrats both stole their platform and chose the impossible Greeley to defend it. During that summer, Hay took a trip West, and reported on the situation to Reid.

To Whitelaw Reid

SPRINGFIELD, ILL.,
August 1, 1872.

I got here last night with a horrible cold. Start tomorrow for Warsaw. I spent a day at Saratoga, and there, just before the train started, Henry Richmond told me in strict confidence of the tribulation of the Democratic party in their hunt for a governor [of New York State]. Kernan is a candidate, and he thinks that his being a Catholic and an Irishman may be a disadvantage in view of the fact that Hoffman is to be ruled off by this element. He thinks that Church is the best man, and that Church will run, if there is a strong appeal made to him. It would be a great personal sacrifice, for Church is a poor man and needs his salary as Judge. But he thinks, if he were asked on behalf of Mr. Greeley, he would yield and run. This, at his request, I told him I would communicate to you. Think of it, and do what you may think expedient.

I met at Cleveland none but Grant men, who of course all assured me that there was no Liberal movement in the State. I think myself there is not much.

In this State it is very different. A large proportion of the best men in the State — not only prominent men, but captains of tens in the counties — are heartily enlisted in the work. The organization is rapidly getting into shape. The German vote is astonishingly strong and united. In this city it is almost unanimous. There is a good Liberal Republican vote in most of the counties, which is estimated at ten per cent of the entire Grant vote. I think this rather sanguine. But there is a pretty bad Democratic bolt in some districts. In Pike, 150 Democrats have signed a manifesto against Greeley. In Winnebago there is some discontent. But there will be an excellent fight made. If we carry Pennsylvania and Indiana the prospects here will be vastly increased.

My little Brother is President of the First Ward Club in Springfield, and my Uncle is President of the

General Grant organization. Alas! Alas! for life is thorny and youth is vain.

To Whitelaw Reid

... I have been at home three days recovering from my cold, and am now pretty well. The weather is hot, but my appetite wholesome. I go to bed at $9\frac{1}{2}$, and sleep like a bear. I shall come back prepared to introduce this somnolent tendency into the columns of the *Tribune*.

The good work is going on beautifully here. The Liberals comprise some of the very best men in the country and the bulk of the Germans and Democrats. They seem hurt when I intimate a doubt of their carrying the State. They feel sure of it, and have the figures to show for their faith. It all depends upon the solidness of the Democratic vote. The Liberals and Democrats will reduce the Republican majority of 50,000 to nothing at all. If the Democrats vote solid, or even lose less than 5 per cent, the State is safe for Greeley. Every Democrat I have seen says they will not lose two per cent and considers even that a liberal estimate.

Carry the news to Hiram! [1]

We are all still in the dark about North Carolina,

[1] Hiram Barney.

but expect to know definitely to-morrow. But at all events it is a great success for Greeley.[1] I suppose that even at Long Branch [2] there is some recognition of nasty weather ahead.

Some of these days you must come out here with me. You are growing such a swell that nothing short of palaces and houris will content you. But I think you might like a day or two among our bluffs and vineyards, and my father and mother and sister already regard you as a personal friend.

My sister (who is a Greeley man of great energy) has just sailed into the room announcing definitely our victory in N.C.

Carry the news to Hiram.

I will go to tea.

The Lord continue his liking for you.

To Whitelaw Reid

WARSAW, ILLINOIS,
November 27, 1872.

I have just received your letter of the 21st and am of course greatly concerned at the news it con-

---

[1] The country still believed that North Carolina had been carried by the Liberals as first announced, and most of those actively connected with the management of the campaign continued to believe that they had actually carried the State. They subsequently claimed that this fraud, as they considered it, changed the drift, which up to that time had been strongly in favor of Greeley.

[2] President Grant's summer residence.

tains.[1] I had seen a paragraph of the sort in the papers here, but had imagined it a malicious exaggeration. It is a most serious matter for all of us. Unless he soon recovers, there will be infinite trouble. . . .

I had a mixed sort of journey. I was snowed up on the Erie Road and spent Sunday in Cleveland. Arrived in Chicago Monday, the most terribly cold day I remember. The weather and the Epizoo,[2] everybody warned me, would destroy my audience, but had a very fine one and very amiable. I spent a day in Springfield. *En passant*, Scammon talked *Inter-Ocean* to me, but I bited not. Since I came home, five days of the loveliest weather I ever saw. I lectured last night gratis for our Free Library, and the whole population turned out. I start back next week — lecture at Cleveland on the 5th December, and expect to be in New York on the 9th or 10th. My Young Christian talk is preying on my mind, but I am getting along with it. It will be the dullest and heaviest of all. I have no vivacity left — not a vivacity to my back. I shall never recover my tone until St. Paul [3] goes to 70. There is some wonderful bedevilment going on with it evidently, — what,

---

[1] Shortly after the election Horace Greeley broke down, physically and mentally. He died on November 29.

[2] The epizoöty was prevalent through a large part of the country at that time.

[3] Chicago, Milwaukee and St. Paul Railway stock.

I can't imagine. If J. brings me out, I will take care of yours and J.'s. If I am swamped, I can go through bankruptcy, and that is said to be an edifying experience.

I will be in Springfield next week, and will try to see Harlan [1] and Palmer.[2] My uncle was elected to the Legislature after declining to run and refusing the nomination. Cullom [3] will be speaker, and wants to be Senator. But at present there seems no prospect of beating Oglesby. Logan [4] and Oglesby![5] *Par nobile!*

I sleep and eat very well. I really need a month or two of idleness. But I can't stay any longer. Please tell Mr. Nicholson to send my mail up to Dec. 4 to the Kennard House, Cleveland. Retain all after that.

The next letter to Reid from which I quote was written in the mayor's office, Springfield, Illinois, on

[1] James Harlan (1820–99), United States Senator from Iowa, 1855–65, 1867–73.

[2] General John M. Palmer (1817–1900), Governor of Illinois, 1868; Liberal Republican candidate in 1872; United States Senator, 1891–97.

[3] Shelby M. Cullom (1829–1913); member of Congress, 1865–71; Governor of Illinois, 1877–83; Senator, 1883–1913.

[4] General John A. Logan (1826–86), member of Congress from Illinois, 1859–62, 1867–71; Senator, 1871–77, 1879–86; unsuccessful Republican candidate for Vice-President in 1884.

[5] Richard J. Oglesby (1824–99), United States Senator, 1873–79; thrice Governor of Illinois.

September 3, 1873, his brother, Charles E. Hay, being the mayor.

Thus far have I marched without accident. I was to have gone in to Warsaw to-day, but my brother was trying some firemen for bathing a YELLOW dog in kerosene and then setting him on fire. I am happy to state they no longer belong to the Fire Department.

I thought I was going to have cool weather, but to-day it is tropical. The cholera has burst out again with great fury in the Southern part of the State, but *M. le Maire* says he has pared its claws here. He hauled up several of the richest and oldest citizens here for not policing their property — including his own grave and reverend uncle. It did not amuse them.

If you can find a minute in the intervals of the mad delight of house-hunting, please tell me how things are. . . .

By the way, I met at Barlow's two of the most interesting people I have ever seen in my life; Laurence Oliphant[1] and his wife, who was a L'Estrange. It is a combination I have never seen before, the highest knowledge of society and the world, combined with a mystic and passionate philanthropy. He

[1] Laurence Oliphant (1829–88), journalist, war correspondent, novelist, member of Parliament, who, with his mother and wife, fell under the baleful spell of Thomas L. Harris, a "prophet."

talked to me in a way that indicated he would like to write occasionally for the *Tribune*. I think it might be worth while to ask him. He is the author of that brilliant book "Piccadilly," and was for a long time Paris correspondent of the *London Times*. He knows everybody and everything. Dick Taylor was there, and said he wanted to meet you. Dana[1] was there, but I don't recall his saying anything of the kind.

Not long after this, Hay became engaged.

On August 14, 1873, he writes to Whitelaw Reid: "I made a toilsome journey to Sharon last Saturday and came back Monday. Next Saturday I am going to Saratoga, and will return Saturday night or Sunday morning. I am getting completely bunged up by my travels — have got a good, honest catarrh which will last a week or two longer. But I am sustained and soothed. . . . I wish I could see you in the same predicament. The fact of being in love, and seeing a good woman in love also, is a wonderfully awakening thing. I would not have died before this happened for a great deal of coin. Get well, and then get engaged. Time flies."

Hay lost no time in letting his old friend Nicolay into the secret.

[1] Charles A. Dana, editor of the *New York Sun*.

To J. G. Nicolay

August 27, 1873.

I ought not to leave you to learn from strangers that I am engaged to be married to Miss Clara Stone, of Cleveland, Ohio. I do not know when it will be. There will be an internecine war before Mrs. Stone consents to give up her daughter — wherein I sympathize with her. Before many centuries I shall win. She is a very estimable young person — large, handsome and good. I never found life worth while before.

Miss Stone was the daughter of Amasa and Julia Gleason Stone. Her father, a prosperous financier of Cleveland, became a chief benefactor of Western Reserve University in that city.[1] Hay and Miss Stone were married there on February 4, 1874.

"I am going to be married," he wrote E. M. Stanton on January 8, 1874. "If you want to see the last of me, be at Mr. Stone's, 113 Euclid Avenue, Cleveland, Ohio, on the evening of the 4th of February, and I will show you a lovely woman[2] in a white dress and a man in a black coat, who is now and always

Yours faithfully."

[1] He founded Adelbert College in memory of his son, Adelbert Stone, who was drowned while an undergraduate at Yale College.

[2] "Her name for this month only is Miss Clara L. Stone." (Written as a foot-note by Hay.)

For more than a year after their marriage, the Hays lived in New York and he continued his relations with the *Tribune*. Mr. Stone, however, whose health was infirm, wished to have them near him in Cleveland; and when Hay's own health was impaired, by night work on the *Tribune*, his abandonment of journalism followed.

CLARA STONE HAY

CHAPTER XIV

AUTHORSHIP

JOHN HAY may be said to have grown up with a pen in his hand. Endowed with an unusually delicate suggestibility, he imitated, like other youths, — without being aware of it, — the writers, principally the poets, who delighted him. But besides this endowment, he possessed an authentic talent of self-expression, and the desire to use it. In those earlier poems of his, we see reflections of Poe, of Byron, of Shelley, and of others. Always facile, and equally at his ease in prose and in verse, he turned off occasional pieces, one of which, "Carrier's Address to the Patrons of the *Daily Illinois State Journal*, Springfield, January 1, 1861," has been preserved. Seldom can the newspaper carriers of any town have presented to their patrons so remarkable an effusion. It glows with patriotism: it greets liberty, at home and abroad; it salutes Italy, recently emancipated, in a stanza like this: —

> How long! how still Italia slept,
>   While hireling hordes above her reigned,
> How sad the tears that freedom wept
>   To see her holiest shrines profaned.

Into the midnight of her dreams
  There stole a whisper faint and far,
And flushed them with a light that gleams
  On lands beneath the Western star!
And as the tender morning broke
  In glory on the Tuscan sea,
The sleeper murmured, as she woke,
  "THE STATE THAT WILLS IT, SHALL BE FREE."

And Hay prophesies, as very few of his elders would have dared to do then: —

Though sullen fate and traitor rage
  A few brief days the fight prolong —
Our LINCOLN's name shall light the age,
  In history's scroll and poet's song!

Among Hay's papers is a copy of *Harper's Weekly* for October 19, 1861, in which appears a story, "Red, White, and Blue." This also may be by him, for it has his exuberance and his clarity; but it is unsigned. During the war, and afterwards on his diplomatic travels, he often relieved his emotions in a poem. Several of these are sprinkled through his notebooks, the handwriting being almost illegible from the jolting of the train. That he sowed these in some of the magazines and papers of the time is possible, but I have been unable to trace any of them in print. To the *Atlantic Monthly* of December, 1869, he sent a paper on "The Mormon Prophet's Tragedy," a spirited account of the attack on Joseph Smith, and his shooting in Carthage jail by a Christian mob, on April 27, 1844. Some of the participators in that crime lived in Warsaw, — Nauvoo, the Mormon settlement, was only fifteen miles to the north, — and as Hay was then five years and a half old, he may have remembered something of the excitement which filled the entire country.

He brought back from Madrid his bundle of Spanish sketches, and a portfolio of fugitive poems. The former he had no difficulty in placing with James R. Osgood and Company — a feather in the young writer's cap; for that firm were the successors of Ticknor and Fields, the publishers of the chief American authors of the century. A happy accident hurried his poems into print.

To the *Overland Monthly* for September, 1870, Bret Harte contributed "Plain Language from Truthful James," in which he introduced the Heathen Chinee to an international audience. The following month, during Hay's visit to his family in Warsaw, he is said to have written two poems, "Little Breeches" and "Jim Bludso," in the supposed dialect of the unshorn Westerners. Some one reports that he was with Hay in the hotel overlooking the river at Keokuk when he dashed off "Jim Bludso." There have been other statements and counter-statements, and much speculation: but it is safer to accept Hay's own account, which appears below. Even the suggestion that the "Heathen Chinee" started him in this vein of dialect verse, needs confirmation; because that amazingly clever satire is not in dialect, nor is it imbued with the sentimental spirit peculiar to Hay's "ballads."

Whatever its origin may have been, Hay printed "Little Breeches" in the miscellaneous columns of the *Weekly Tribune*, on December 2, 1870, signed only by his initials.[1] It had an instant success, comparable to that of the "Heathen Chinee" itself. Its popularity soon led him to put forth "Jim Bludso," and then a third, "Banty Tim," which *Harper's Weekly* published. Later he added three more to the series.

In letters to friends, Hay tells of his dash into literature. To Nicolay, he writes on December 12, 1870: —

That ridiculous rhyme, "Little Breeches," of mine has had a ridiculous run. It has been published in nearly the whole country press from here to the Rocky Mountains. As my initials are not known and they generally get worn off on the second print, I have not been disgraced by it.

I met G. at breakfast this morning, who called me

[1] To the *Daily Tribune* of December 6 he contributed "The Surrender of Spain," one of the most stirring of his serious poems.

Nicolay and was very cordial. That reminds me
of Madrid, where we were all called Sickles by the
Señoritas for a week or two. . . .

Have you seen the first [1] of my "Castilian Days"
which, by a Hibernicism of Fields, is a night? He
seems greatly pleased with the stuff I have given
him, and proposes to make a book of it next year. I
went on there and spent a day or two very pleasantly
among the *geistreich* of Cambridge and the Hub.[2]

To W. D. Howells

TRIBUNE OFFICE, December 29, 1870.

I thank you cordially for your delicious book.[3]
I had a copy before and can now indulge in the luxury of giving it away. You are my delight and my
despair. Where the demon did you find that impos-
sibly happy way of saying everything? It is a thing
that the rest of us blunder on, once in a while, but
you never miss. It is no trick or fashion, and so we
will never tire of it till we tire of living. You see the
critics all notice this, and not knowing what else to
say, they say Hawthorne and Irving, etc. . . .

I am plodding along, doing rather better than I
expected. Have you ever seen a piece of dialect I

---

[1] "A Field Night in the Cortes."
[2] Other parts of this letter are printed in Chapter XIII, pp. 335, 336.
[3] *Their Wedding Journey.*

wrote, — "Little Breeches"? It has had an appalling run. It is published every day in hundreds of papers. Two political papers in the West have issued illustrated editions of it. I mention this to show what a ravenous market there is for anything of the sort. I can't do it — but you could. That Western novel of yours must not be much longer delayed.

When I said I can't, it was not measly but true. I wrote another one, and Reid says it is very bad — in which I agree, — so it is not to be published and I will do no more songs. . . .

To J. G. Nicolay

March, 1871.

. . . They send you the February *Atlantic*. The March number has nothing from me, and therefore it won't pay to buy it. The April number has a first-rate article on Spanish holidays by a youth to fortune and to fame unknown. Item. The March *Lippincott*, which has a Warsaw story into it.[1]

I am rubbing along, doing my day's work daily — not entirely satisfied with myself but drawing my pay *regular*. The correct press and the unsuccessful critics pound me black and blue, but I eat my diurnal

---

[1] "The Blood Seedling," interesting because it displays in its treatment that unconscious conflict between realistic substance and a somewhat romantic spirit which was more marked in *The Breadwinners*.

hash with a good appetite, and get more than is right for everything I do. I have just sold a third dialect poem to *Harper's Weekly* for $50 to be published with a picture. It is called "Banty Tim" and touches the contraband. Have you seen "Jim Bludso"? I send you a copy. It has been more widely liked and denounced than "Little Breech."

Horrible power of drink! Last night I met —— at the *Tribune* door — you know him, the wittiest journalist of our time. He was covered with mud and plastering. Had been rolling in the gutter — was crying like a sick child — said they had kicked him out of the last place he was in, — begged me for twenty cents, and sobbed with joy when I gave him fifty. Some night he will die in the street. You and I have kept drinking company all our lives, and yet have never felt for an instant the claws of temptation. Let us thank God!

To W. D. Howells

NEW YORK TRIBUNE,
December 24, 1871.

I am badly frightened about that article. I will do it to-morrow or next day if possible; but I am awfully worritted with many things, and need twenty-five hours a day.

Here is the paragraph of editorial to which you

refer. I am delighted with the success of your book,
and was sure of it, though the delay of the second
edition is infamous and shows little faith. I met an
angry man this morning who went to Dutton's for
the "Wedding Journey" and not finding it, had to
buy "Castilian Days."

Mr. Howells, who was then managing the *Atlantic
Monthly*, — although James T. Fields held the nominal editorship for a while longer, — joyfully accepted
the Spanish papers, and advised printing some of
them in the magazine before Osgood brought them
out as a book. Five [1] appeared thus in serial form,
between January and July, 1871; then they were
all issued in the autumn under the title "Castilian
Days."   Almost simultaneously, the same house
published "Pike County Ballads and Other Pieces."

To his friend, Albert Rhodes,[2] Hay wrote on
June 19, 1871: —

"I am the creature of accident. I am not to blame
for the absurd vogue of my doggerel. If you want
to read something to purge your soul, some good,

---

[1] January *Atlantic:* "A Field-Night in the Spanish Cortes";
February: "Spanish Living and Dying"; April: "Red-Letter Days";
May: "The Cradle and Grave of Cervantes"; July: "Tauromachy."

[2] Born in Pittsburg, Pa., in 1840; United States Consul at Jerusalem; later, at Rotterdam, Rouen, and Elberfeld; contributed to
Scribner's and other magazines. Published, *Jerusalem As It Is*, 1865;
and *The French at Home*, 1875.

honest, hard, horse-sense, read my 'Castilian Days'
— when they come out, which will be next fall."

Hay did not simulate modesty. Being human, he
could not fail to enjoy the reputation which his ballads brought him; but that he did not overestimate
them appears from his reply to Richard Henry Stod-
dard, the poet and literary worker, who wished to in-
clude some of them in a compilation he was making:—

To R. H. Stoddard

THE TRIBUNE, October 5, 1871.

I hope you will not suspect me of affectation when
I tell you I don't want to go into Griswold's book.
I am no poet, — I make no claim whatever that way.
There is hardly one educated man in my acquaintance but has written as much verse as I. By an unlucky accident I put a quaint story into rhyme and
gave it to Reid, and the people who would n't read
you or Tennyson to save your lives, read this, and
guffawed over it and — *me voilà* a poet! Then Osgood came and tempted me, and the mischief was
done.

Now, if I keep quiet a year or two, all that will be
forgotten and will be as if it never was. I do not want
the memory of it preserved in standard books which
will go into libraries.

There is nothing I respect so much as the name of

a poet. If I had done anything like your work or
Stedman's, I would be indifferently conceited over
it. But I have never written a rhyme which deserved to be printed, — still less to be gathered up
and kept as specimens of literature. I can do some
things as well as most men of my weight, but poems
are not of them. Let me up, and pass on to the next
man in H.!

I also read with infinite delight Harte's savage
article on Miller.[1] I don't agree with it. I think the
wild cuss is a poet. But Harte did sling his scalpel
in a most stylish way. I believe I would have enjoyed it if I had been the subject. . . .

Hay's "Castilian Days" contains many of the best
pages he ever wrote — best, that is, in style. After
nearly fifty years the book stands unapproached in
English as a panorama of Spanish life and history,
of Spanish legends and superstitions and landscape.
Hay comes, an outlander from the New World, into
that ancient Iberian country, where many centuries
have petrified customs and beliefs, and the Past
almost blots out the Present. Hay views all with
keen eyes. His thirst for observing is unquenchable.

---

[1] Cincinnatus Heine Miller (1841–1913), who, as "Joaquin" Miller, had just published the *Songs of the Sierras*. Miller affected the
flannel shirt and cowhide boots of a son of Nature and was fêted in
London.

He can make you see things as he saw them — fixing, in the vivid sentence which remains, the play of light and shade, the flash of a momentary street scene, or the fleeting impression. He furnishes information, but not in the guide-book way; and as he never writes merely to instruct you, he is rarely dull. Perhaps a Spaniard would not accept Hay's judgments — what native ever accepts a foreigner's criticism of his own people? — but he could not fail to acknowledge the young American's general sympathy, or his enthusiasm for the undisputed noble monuments of Spain.

Those who accuse him of writing as a Protestant or as a Puritan, when he lays bare the bigotry and ignorance and lack of any religion which reveals itself in righteous conduct, misjudge him. His condemnation is unsectarian, — the verdict that a normal ethical nature, regardless of creed, would pronounce at the sight of degradation due to the long rule of Jesuits, and friars, and to the Inquisition, which survived, in a milder form, down almost to the time when Hay knew Spain. But that is only one feature of the book. The lasting impression it leaves is of variety, clear-sightedness, and candor; together with Hay's zest in observing and his exhilaration in narrating.

Among pen-pictures of travel produced by Americans, we may reckon only Mr. Howells's "Venetian Life" as a rival of "Castilian Days"; but Hay by his higher actuality surpasses that delightful minor masterpiece. Howells, the more practised and smoother writer, breathes through his pages a quiet almost wistful atmosphere which accords perfectly with his theme. But Hay employs a manner of treatment which suits his Spanish subjects not less admirably: for in Spain there is often no atmosphere, no mediating haze, only an air so translucent that you feel that you can touch the distant mountains, and there is no compromise between dazzling sunshine and cypress-dark shadow. Scarcely less praiseworthy is the balance which he keeps between vivid description and not less lively impression, between information and interpretation. The later literary landscapists — Lafcadio Hearn and Mr. Percival Lowell in Japan, and Mr. Henry James, for instance — tend rather to impressionism; so much so, indeed, that in some of Mr. James's sketches the objective fact seems only a text or stimulus to release in him a flood of subjective emotions and of reflections not always pertinent.

But, comparisons aside, "Castilian Days" holds its place in American literature. No book in its field is more exactly what it purports to be, and few display an ampler range of qualities — wit, irony, enthusiasm, shrewdness, honesty, indignation, romance, charm. Free alike from the reserves and the cynicism of maturity, it speaks the perennially alluring language of youth. Having won favor while running in the *Atlantic Monthly*, it at once received a more than friendly recognition on its publication as a book. A score of years later when, having passed through many printings, a revised edition was called for, Hay wisely decided to let the papers stand as he originally wrote them, in the first half of 1870.

"I have never gone back to Spain," he says, in a brief, model preface, "and I have arrived at an age when I begin to doubt if I have any castles there requiring my attention. I have therefore nothing to add to this little book. Reading it again after the lapse of many years, I find much that might be advantageously modified or omitted. But as its merits, if it had any, are merely those of youth, so also are its faults, and they are immanent and structural; they cannot be amended without tearing the book to pieces. . . .

"I must leave what I wrote in the midst of the stirring scenes of the interregnum between the secular monarchy and the short-lived Republic — whose advent I foresaw, but whose sudden fall was veiled from my sanguine vision — without defense or apology, claiming only that it was written in good faith, from a heart filled with passionate convictions and an ardent love and devotion to what is best in Spain. I recorded what I saw, and my eyes were better then than now. I trust I have not too often spoken amiss of a people whose art, whose literature, whose language, and whose character compelled my highest admiration, and with whom I enjoyed friendships which are among the dearest recollections of my life." [1]

In 1893, the Spanish Princess Eulalia came over to represent Spain at the World's Fair in Chicago. Hay sends Mr. Adams this amusing note on meeting her at dinner.

Her Royal Highness CLEVELAND, June 9, 1893.

I dined with H.R.H. Eulalia at the R.W.; with a heart overflowing with kindness, R. introduced me to all the Castilians and Bourbons as the author of a book about Spain which they really ought to read, etc., — unconscious, the good R., that my unhappy little volume treats the august family of Spain as a set of *pas grandes choses* from Wayback, who have no place outside of penal and reformatory institutions. Still, if they can stand the Hymn of Riego at the British Embassy, they can stand an abusive book they have never heard of.

[1] Preface to revised edition, 1890.

In Hay's Diary, for November 1, 1904, there is an interesting entry in regard to "Castilian Days." The Presidential campaign, it should be recalled, was then drawing to a close.

"We had a brief cabinet meeting. I was somewhat chaffed on account of the story in the papers that the Irish had demanded of Cortelyou [1] my expulsion from the Cabinet, and that he had replied that he could not promise that, but assured them that a Catholic Irishman should be appointed First Assistant Secretary of State. They are evidently after me. I found on my desk to-day a pamphlet carefully printed, consisting wholly of extracts from 'Castilian Days,' showing that twenty-five years ago I had whacked with the freedom and irresponsibility of youth the Spanish Catholic Church from Torquemada to Padre Claret."

A book which is made a campaign document a generation after it was written is still alive; and this book will still live, not because sectaries, religious or political, once found in it stuff for controversy, but because it appeals to intelligent readers.

John Hay's poems fall into three classes. First, and most famous, are the "Pike County Ballads" —

[1] George B. Cortelyou, private secretary to Presidents McKinley and Roosevelt; subsequently, Secretary of Commerce and Labor, Postmaster-General, and Secretary of the Treasury.

named from the Pike County where he spent much of his boyhood. There are six of these. "Little Breeches" and "Jim Bludso" rolled out spontaneously; the others seem rather the product of the impulse, common in artists, to follow up a happy stroke by repeating it with variations. In the complete edition of Hay's "Poems," put forth in 1890, "Golyer" and "The Pledge at Spunky Point" have been added. They are good, and if the first two had not, in a way, exhausted the possibilities of their type, we should probably think more highly of them.

For one of the reasons why dialect poems capture the public is their novelty. Commonplaces which, if written in commonplace grammatical English, could bore us, seem strange, and therefore rare, when they come dressed in dialect, which serves to attract attention, just as the foreign costume does on the Italian, or Russian, or Japanese peasant. This is, of course, not all. A peasant may carry a precious load on his back, and the dialect poem likewise may be the vehicle of a very important message.

The best example of this in modern English literature we find in Lowell's "Biglow Papers," where the Yankee conscience expresses itself with characteristic irony and with surpassing wit, on questions of fundamental significance. In adopting the language of the country folk, Lowell was able to score his points more effectively than if he had written them in polished academic diction: for we still have an instinctive belief that the old farmers, or village characters, speaking their racy vernacular, must be as honest as they are unsophisticated, and represent, somehow, the simple, ultimate ideals of the country. As Lowell uses them they are the Yankee equivalent of the Greek chorus, except that, instead of mellow wit, the Greek old men abound in moral platitudes.

After Lowell the two Americans whose dialect poems have attained a popular vogue almost equal to his are Bret Harte and John Hay: nevertheless, they are not in his class. For neither the California 'Forty-niners nor the Mississippi roustabouts and rowdies were involved in any epochal issues such as Hosea Biglow knew he was adjudicating. The heroism of Jim Bludso, however, is as genuine as that of Horatius Cocles, and Hay's skill consists in causing persons of all sorts to feel the genuineness of it. The dialect helps, because it introduces us without delay to the actors, the situation and the catastrophe; but the story itself becomes so pressing that we almost forget the dialect in our eagerness to learn the end. That is as it should be: bad grammar and slang cannot long hide absence of ideas. In one of the later ballads, "The Pledge at Spunky Point," however, we

are conscious that Hay lays stress on dialect for its
own sake; as for example, in this stanza: —

> But Chris'mas scooped the Sheriff,
>   The egg-nogs gethered him in;
> And Shelby's boy Leviticus
>   Was, New Year's, tight as sin;
> And along in March the Golyers
>   Got so drunk that a fresh-biled owl
> Would 'a' looked 'long-side o' them two young men,
>   Like a sober temperance fowl.

Here the obvious effort of the writer is to collect
dialect phrases; in " Jim Bludso " and "Little Breeches," on the other hand, he rightly put the story first.

But besides the novelty of dress, and the intrinsic
interest of the story, the moral sentiments pro-
claimed in these two ballads undoubtedly account in
large measure for their hold on the masses. In long-
settled communities, having their accepted laws and
creeds, their customs and special proprieties, it comes
to be tacitly assumed that virtues and vices follow the
line of social cleavage; but in a pioneer social medium,
like that which Hay describes, men are what they
are. Hypocrisy, dissembling, and all the subtler
forms of pretending to be what you are not, in order
to stand well with the conventional system, are comparatively ineffectual. How can you conform, where
all is in flux? The pioneer sees that good and bad do
not follow creed: that it is not going to church, or say-

ing prayers, or listening to sermons that counts. He scouts at original sin, although, if you asked him why, he would probably say, "because he has seen virtues cropping out unexpectedly in the most unlikely persons." And then, deep down in the human heart lie the desire for equality and the conviction that most souls are "saved." Theological distinctions are a late product of human speculation. The rough-and-tumble frontiersman, deprived of every opportunity to "be good" in the traditional, church-going way, may, by a single act of heroism, exemplify the noblest ideals that are preached in any pulpit.

The moral of this attitude of admiration for the valiant, unselfish deed and of unconcern for the professed doctrine, Hay put plainly in the most famous of all his stanzas, that which concludes the ballad of "Jim Bludso": —

> He were n't no saint, — but at jedgment
> I'd run my chance with Jim,
> 'Longside of some pious gentlemen
> That would n't shook hands with him.
> He seen his duty, a dead-sure thing, —
> And went for it thar and then;
> And Christ ain't a going to be too hard
> On a man that died for men.[1]

Over

---

[1] After Whitelaw Reid died in 1913, *Cleveland Town Topics* printed an interview which Mr. W. R. Coates had with him in 1910. Mr. Reid said: "I was responsible for the last lines in 'Jim Bludso,' although I did not write them. Hay brought in the poem, having finished it on the train. I told him it would n't do, that there must be something

His summing up of "Little Breeches" is only a variation on this gospel — the gospel which the founder of Christianity preached, "By their fruits ye shall know them": —

> And I think that saving a little child,
>   And fotching him to his own,
> Is a derned sight better business
>   Than loafing around The Throne.

In regard to the much-debated origin of "Little Breeches" the following note, from Hay to J. T. Fields seems to me to be conclusive, unless it can be proved that the "bit of Western talk" to which he refers was not the "ballad" in question.

To James T. Fields

NEW YORK, Dec. 7, 1870.

Have you seen a bit of Western talk I wrote one morning in Boston and published when I got here? It has had a surprising circulation. The whole Western press has copied it, clear through to the Pacific. It is too flimsy for criticism of course, but the little touch of humanity in it has covered its sins.

besides the recital of an heroic act, some thought drawn from it that was vital and would live. He immediately sat down and added another stanza, closing with: —

> "'Christ ain't going to be too hard
>   On a man who died for men.'

In that same way, I am responsible for the last stanza of 'Little Breeches.'"

As this note is dated only five days after the publication of the ballad in the *Weekly Tribune*, and as Hay was visiting the "*geistreich*" Bostonians at the time, the presumption is overwhelming that "Little Breeches" was born, not in his natural habitat on the prairie, but in Boston or Cambridge.

In time Hay came to loathe the mention of the poem which made him famous, as much as General Sherman loathed the sound of "Marching through Georgia." Everybody quoted it to him: wherever he went among strangers he was introduced as its author; the parodies on it were numerous. He used to say that the rattle of it dinned in his ears through life like a tin can tied to a dog's tail. When he republished his poems, he put "Jim Bludso" first in its place.

To E. C. Stedman, who wrote to consult him in regard to selections for "An American Anthology," Hay replied: "I do not want to interfere with your editorial conscience, but would like timidly to suggest that you do not use 'Little Br——' in your *recueil*. You would pardon the cheeky request if you knew how odious the very name of that hopeless fluke is to yours faithfully."

The first English edition, printed in 1871, was entitled "Little Breeches," and the *London Athenæum* commented on it in the tone of condescension then typical of the English in their estimate of American publications.

"It cannot be denied," said the *Athenæum*, "that there is a quaint vigour in Mr. Hay's manner of telling these anecdotes, but there is nothing in the ballads to warrant the praise bestowed upon them by the American press." [1]

Nevertheless, following their habit of insisting that the outlandish or uncouth was essentially American, the English took up the "Pike County Ballads," and when Hay went to London as Ambassador he heard his lines on many British lips.

His mature feeling toward the two poems he expressed in this letter to one of his former colleagues on the *Tribune*:—

To Joseph B. Bishop [2]

WASHINGTON, D.C., January 11, 1889.

. . . I thank you very much for your kind letter and the enclosures, which I would not otherwise have seen. I thoroughly appreciate a good word spoken for "Jim," who is a friend of mine. I shudder and hide in the cellar only when the boy with the small Knickerbockers [3] is mentioned.

---

[1] *Athenæum*, no. 2291.

[2] Mr. J. B. Bishop was on the staff of the *Tribune* from 1870 to 1883; then he went to the *Evening Post*, 1883–1900.

[3] Referring to "Jim Bludso" and "Little Breeches."

A curious thing happened during that summer when we were holding up the Republican party by the tail.

On the first appearance of J. B., Mark Twain wrote to me, saying that I was all wrong making him an engineer, — that only a pilot could have done what I represented him as doing. This troubled me somewhat, though I thought I was right. During the summer of '87, a cotton broker of New Orleans, a son of my J. B. (whose name was Oliver Fairchild, by the way) came to see me at the *Tribune* Office, and absolutely confirmed my story, saying that his father was engineer of the *Fashion*, and died in just that way. But the case was of course uncommon — the pilot usually does the work — and Jim Givens comes again to discredit me.

I am afraid this is ominous of my fate, — to be right as a historian and wrong as an artist.

To a later correspondent Hay sent this final statement about the original "Jim Bludso."

To M. H. Slater, Colorado

WASHINGTON, February 13th, 1905.

I think your idea of the mistake arises from there being two Fairchilds in Hancock County. I knew Oliver Fairchild very well, that is as a child and as a man grown who was generally on his boat and rarely at home. His son, Henry W. Fairchild, of New Orleans, was a schoolmate of mine. When I said I got the story from him, I merely meant that I got the details of the burning of the steamer *Fashion* and the death of his father from him. There is no mistake in the name.

We need not examine the rest of the Poems in detail. The volume contains a group of "Wanderlieder" inspired by a special occasion, or by scenery, or by legends and tales which captivated him. Best among them is "Sunrise in the Place de la Concorde,"[1] which passes very naturally from a sketch, delicate yet distinct, of the actual Place, to an imaginative review of the intermittent pomps and tragedies and heroisms which it had witnessed.

"The Sphinx of the Tuileries" is a fine example of political invective which is saved from being a diatribe by its righteous indignation. Napoleon III, he says, —

is a Sphinx indeed.

For the Sphinx with breast of woman
   And face so debonair,
Had the sleek false paws of a lion
   That could furtively seize and tear.

[1] See Chapter IX., pp. 226, 228.

> So far to the shoulders, — but if you took
> The Beast in reverse you would find
> The ignoble form of a craven cur
> Was all that lay behind.

The closing lines lift the subject from the denunciation of a base individual to the affirmation of unyielding faith: —

> The people will come to their own at last, —
> God is not mocked forever.

In "Boudoir Prophecies" Hay plays sarcastically with the changed fortunes of Queen Isabella and Empress Eugénie — a piece apparently slight, yet having barbs which hook it into the memory. "A Triumph of Order," reminiscent of the horrors of the Paris Commune, is a bit of realism as unqualified as one of Manet's drawings. And yet, in the midst of almost photographic closeness to life, Hay interjects a stanza with this unusual figure: —

> For the joy of killing had lost its zest
> In the glut of those awful days,
> And Death writhed, gorged like a greedy snake,
> From the Arch to Père-la-Chaise.

If we turn to some of Hay's narrative poems, we shall see in them the predominance of the spirit of Romanticism as contrasted with Realism. (These labels are, in truth, somewhat vague, and they smack of literary cant; but they will serve our purpose here.) For Hay, like many another artist of his generation, was possessed by the two conflicting tendencies. Happily, in him there was no struggle, far less quarrel, between them: and so he was saved from the effort of deliberately choosing, as well as from the conscious partisanship, which troubled some of his contemporaries. When a subject kindled him, he wrote his poem on it, in whatever metre, style, or method he best could, never inquiring whether he was obeying the tenets of Realism or Romanticism. Therein, at least, he followed the practice of the world's men of genius instead of that of the world's doctrinaires.

The Poems faithfully represent John Hay's nature, not less than his gifts, in that they display versatility, manifold interests, a quick perception, responsive emotions, irony without malice, and an aptitude for the unexpected turn of phrase. The variety of his metres is remarkable. His ear was musical, although not always correct. Perhaps his lapses came from rapid composition, rather than from any real deficiency in his metrical sense; for he often seems to improvise, rather than to work over and polish his verses. To improvisation belongs the charm of freshness, which Hay's poems seldom lack: its danger lies in its uneven texture. At his best, Hay delighted in flowing metres and well-matched, sonorous rhymes. Sometimes, especially in his earlier verses, we catch a musical sweep which might be thought Swinburnian were it not that the poem antedated Swinburne's first volume. He did not need to go in search of images, because they swarmed upon him unsought.

If Hay's general poems enjoyed less repute than they deserved, it was because they came at a time when the verse-reading public was engrossed in the finicalities of metrical forms — in the forgotten masterpieces of the Cherry-Stone Carvers, and the finds of the seekers after banal subjects and bizarre rhythms. Since their day has long since passed, it may be that now Hay's poetry, which springs from his genuine nature and not from a mere fad or fashion, will appeal to the grand-children of those who first read it.

I hesitate to assign subjective significance even to those poems which appear, on the surface, to be personal confessions. The real artist is a very elusive creature, who, by virtue of the intuition which makes him an artist, glides like Proteus into so many shapes that the critic may mistake the imaginary creation for the creator himself. Still, in such a poem as "Lagrimas" Hay seems to give vent to a personal mood, or, if not that, to a mood which waylays men of his temperament when they discover, poignantly,

that the momentum of youth has slackened and that
the things which they had taken for granted would
last them through life, were the perquisites of youth
alone, and with youth have vanished.

LAGRIMAS

God send me tears!
Loose the fierce band that binds my tired brain,
Give me the melting heart of other years,
And let me weep again!

Before me pass
The shapes of things inexorably true.
Gone is the sparkle of transforming dew
From every blade of grass.

In life's high noon
Aimless I stand, my promised task undone,
And raise my hot eyes to the angry sun
That will go down too soon.

Turned into gall
Are the sweet joys of childhood's sunny reign;
And memory is a torture, love a chain
That binds my life in thrall.

And childhood's pain
Could to me now the purest rapture yield;
I pray for tears as in his parching field
The husbandman for rain.

We pray in vain!
The sullen sky flings down its blaze of brass;
The joys of life all scorched and withering pass;
I shall not weep again.

There, indisputably, is a sincere poem, welling up from a heart which knew that passion and suffering are two aspects of the same experience.

As if to round out his poetical expression, Hay wrote a cluster of epigrams, from which I cite half-a-dozen examples. Some of them have the tang of worldly-wisdom before it has soured into cynicism.

2
There are three species of creatures who when they seem
coming are going,
When they seem going they come: Diplomates, women, and
crabs.

3
Pleasures too hastily tasted grow sweeter in fond recollection,
As the pomegranate plucked green ripens far over the sea.

5
What is a first love worth, except to prepare for a second?
What does the second love bring? Only regret for the first.

10
Maidens! why should you worry in choosing whom you shall
marry?
Choose whom you may, you will find you have got somebody
else.

11
Unto each man comes a day when his favorite sins all forsake
him,
And he complacently thinks he has forsaken his sins.

13
Who would succeed in the world should be wise in the use of
his pronouns.
Utter the You twenty times, where you once utter the I.

17

Try not to beat back the current, yet be not drowned in its
　　waters;
Speak with the speech of the world, think with the thoughts
　　of the few.

18

Make all good men your well-wishers, and then, in the years'
　　steady sifting,
Some of them turn into friends. Friends are the sunshine of
　　life.

Thus when Christmas, 1871, greeted John Hay,
he enjoyed the distinction of being the author of two
volumes of poetry and prose, either of which made
him a citizen of the republic of letters. Fortune,
whose favorite he always was, welcomed him with
both hands.

CHAPTER XV

FRIENDSHIPS

"FRIENDS are the sunshine of life." That might well be John Hay's motto, the maxim which, had he been one of the Seven Sages, he would have bequeathed to posterity. His genius for friendship showed itself early in childhood and never failed him to his dying day. His associates delighted in him because of his playful wit, the richness and variety of his conversation, his deep-rooted kindliness, his frankness, — a quality which does not always make for friendship, — and his sympathy. They did not think of him as the successful author or the brilliant editor; and later, when he walked on the highest levels of public life, he still remained for them — not Hay the Ambassador, not Hay the Secretary of State, but Hay the friend.

As it is by these intimate contacts rather than by external events, which often seem so casual as to be almost negligible, that we can best come to know him during his middle decades, I shall quote freely from his letters to his associates.

Above other American letter-writers, he had spontaneity — that quality without which a letter can hardly escape being artificial, if not insincere. The notes which Hay dashed off on the spur of the moment reflect his passing mood; they tell news of his work and of family plans; they give his opinion of the book he is reading or of persons; they sparkle with the wit which comes to him as he writes; they are delightfully indiscreet. If his purpose is to send information, he states it, but without pedantry. So his best letters have that charm of unpremeditation which belongs to the best talk; and, in this respect at least, they come nearer than any others to Byron's, which are the best in English.

During his bachelor life in New York, Hay made many acquaintances outside of the circle of his *Tribune* associates. We hear, at one time, of a small coterie, composed of Whitelaw Reid, Dr. Richard H. Derby, and half a dozen other men, with their wives and sisters, where these existed; and this club, which met informally at the houses of its members to dine or sup, was a shrine of comradeship. By chance, a memento from it has come to me, which, though scarcely more than a bagatelle, is perhaps worth preserving; not so much because it displays Hay's sprightliness as because, through his jesting, we may discern his seriousness.

Those were the days of Mental Photograph Albums, and on February 25, 1873, Hay made this

portrait of himself for the album belonging to Miss
Lucy Derby.[1]

1. Your favorite color?	Tri*color*.
2. Flower?	Buckwheat.
3. Tree?	Industry.
4 Object in Nature?	School girls.
5. Hour in the Day?	The Shepherd's Hour.
6. Season?	Currie-powder.
7. Perfume?	The odor of sanctity.
8. Gem?	Jem Brady.* — *prize fighter*
9. Style of Beauty?	The accessible.
10. Names, Male and Female?	Jack and Jill.
11. Painters?	Fresh air and sunshine.
12. Musicians?	Infants (aetat. 6 mos.)
13. Pieces of Sculpture?	The Sphinx.
14. Poets?	The unpublished.
15. Poetesses?	The Nine — (none since).
16. Prose Authors?	Lindley Murray.
17. Character in Romance?	George Washington.
18. Character in History?	Susan B. Anthony.
19. Book to take up for an hour?	"Jonathan Wild."
20. What Book (not religious) would you part with last?	Dante — (because there is no temptation to waste time in reading it).
21. What epoch would you choose to have lived in?	The Twentieth Century.
22. Where would you like to live?	Everywhere.
23. What is your favorite amusement?	Worrying the wicked.
24. What is your favorite occupation?	Sleep.
25. What trait of character do you most admire in man?	Luck.
26. In woman?	Pluck.
27. What trait do you most detest in each?	Undue prosperity.
28. If not yourself, who would you rather be?	Her second husband.
29. What is your idea of happiness?	A bad character and a good digestion.
30. Of misery?	Life.

* A prize-fighter.

[1] Now Mrs. S. Richard Fuller, to whom I am indebted for this
find.

31. What is your *bête noire?* — A pen.
32. What is your dream? — Tiflis.
33. What is your favorite game? — "Woodcock's Little Game."
34. What do you believe to be your distinguishing characteristics? — Sweetness and light.
35. If married, what do you believe to be the distinguishing characteristic of your better-half? — Self-sacrifice.
36. What is the sublimest passion of which human nature is capable? — Waltzing.
37. What are the sweetest words in the world? — "It's early yet." (*Bleib ä Bisserl*).
38. What are the saddest words? — Too late.
39. What is your aim in life? — The Universal Commune.
40. What is your motto? — Love your neighbor, but be careful of your neighborhood.

After Hay's marriage, he and his wife lived for a year in New York, and then removed to Cleveland, Ohio, where they made their home for nearly ten years. During that time they were frequently absent, and on one occasion they spent two seasons in Washington. Still, Cleveland was home to them. Mr. Stone built a house for his daughter on Euclid Avenue. Hay opened an office, his theoretical duties being, it appears, to assist Mr. Stone in managing large financial interests; his main business, however, — the work which, in spite of many interruptions, gave continuity to his energy during this period and later, — was his collaboration with Nicolay on the Life of Lincoln. I shall return to this biography later, merely begging the reader to bear in mind that it lay in the background of Hay's thoughts, whether he mentioned it or not, through all the years covered by the following letters.

If we except Mrs. Whitman and Miss Perry, the encouragers of his college poetic dreams, Mr. Howells was probably the first literary figure with whom he became acquainted. Although only a year and a half older than Hay, Mr. Howells commenced as author in 1860, when with John J. Piatt, he printed his first volume," Poems of Two Friends." This Hay read in Springfield, and on his journey East, he stopped over at Columbus in order to greet and congratulate the unknown young poet — an indication of his enthusiasm. But Howells happened to be away, and it was not until a little while later, when Hay was in the White House, that they met.[1] Thenceforth, strong friendship bound them together; and Hay was one of the earliest and loyalest of the novelist's admirers.

A note to one of his European correspondents gives a glimpse of his early married life.

To Albert Rhodes

NEW YORK, January 28, 1875.

I was right glad to hear from you and to learn you thought of coming back to us. You have evidently

---

[1] Hay must also have known of Howells through his campaign *Life of Abraham Lincoln*, published in 1860.

had a good time, and I suppose you are now coming back, to let loose a brilliant book upon the university world. Come, and have the success you have so well merited.

I am leading a quiet life and shall be glad to have you *égayer* it somewhat with your French airs and graces. We are established for a year at 11 East-Forty-Second Street (wide street, you know, near 5th Avenue) in a pleasant house, and there is always something in the larder (I don't know what a larder is, but it is euphonious) wherewith to barricade your bowel against the wolf. . . .

To Whitelaw Reid

NEW YORK, April 29, 1875.

I can't walk, stand or sit — but by special grace I am still able to lie on my stomach. If you can think of a subject you would like to have treated from that point of view, send it over, and I will worry it.

Yours in Job-like dejection.

In the late spring of 1875 the Hays went to Cleveland, where they lived at 514 Euclid Avenue until their new house was ready. The following year, serious trouble with his eyes caused him to forego writing for several months. He seems to have suffered from what later oculists diagnose as eye-strain,

JOHN HAY AT THE TIME OF HIS MARRIAGE IN 1874

which caused head-aches, nervous dyspepsia, and depression. Prolonged rest benefited him; but the distressing symptoms recurred at intervals all his days.

Into the life of Cleveland he entered with his customary adaptability. Mr. Stone's position was a point of vantage in making Hay acquainted with the magnates of the city. His own interests introduced him to the political leaders, many of whom had known him in Washington days or through the *Tribune*.

Whatever social life Cleveland offered, the young couple had access to; and Hay had not been there long before he organized a dining-club composed of eight or ten men of various occupations, and at its dinners one heard the best that Cleveland had to give. Hay himself, according to the testimony of the most distinguished of their survivors, was the best after-dinner talker of them all.

To Albert Rhodes

514 EUCLID AVENUE
CLEVELAND, OHIO, July 9, 1875.

Many thanks for your recollection. But Mrs. Hay saw your book at a store in this city and made *cadeau* of it to me. I have not read it yet, for Madam has been devouring it herself and occasionally reads a page aloud to me, which justifies my long-standing opinion of your sparkling style and observant eye. Please accept our thanks for the pleasure the book has given us, as much as if we had got it for nothing.

I have been a little of everywhere since I saw you. First I went to Boston; then to Illinois, where I passed ten days at my father's and met all my brethren who are still alive.

To Whitelaw Reid

CLEVELAND, OHIO, June 3, 1875.

Yesterday morning, after we had been here an hour or so, the corner of the new house was laid, and ever since my ears have been full of the muffled click of the chisels of some half hundred workmen on the soft yellow stone. Mr. Stone is much better than I had expected to find him. He is lame, and walks with a crutch, but otherwise he is much better than he was in New York. Of course he is far from well, but I feel as if there was a good chance for a steady recovery now. This removes a heavy weight from my mind.

We have had as yet no talk about our business plans. That will be postponed until after my return from Warsaw. If he is then decidedly better, we can come to some conclusion in regard to the winter.

I have felt a dozen times yesterday and to-day a sort of blind impulse to go down to Printing House

Square and write some brevier. The moment the obligation was removed, the desire to write began to be born again.

I hope you have endorsed the Ohio platform of the Republicans. It is almost perfect, and I suppose Hayes [1] to be a good sort of man. The Democrats have made so bad a use of their success in this State that there ought to be a show for Hayes this time.

To Whitelaw Reid

34 PUBLIC SQUARE, CLEVELAND,
July 19, 1875.

I merely put that address there for the sake of grandeur, to let you know that we have at last got into an office and have carpeted it and set up desks and bought some note-paper and a waste-basket, and are now ready to skin the pensive Buckeye with neatness and dispatch.

. . . Don't think of sending me the Thiers autograph. I would have it prettily framed, if I were you. It is a very nice thing for your children. It is the thanks of the French Republic, *voyez-vous!*

. . . I never saw so many pretty girls as there are in Cleveland. Hurry along!

The *Tribune* is marvellously full and good. I can't

---

[1] R. B. Hayes, nominated by the Republicans for Governor of Ohio, was elected in October.

read it all nowadays, but I struggle through as much as I can stand. It is a far bigger paper than I thought when I was there in the kitchen helping to cook it. Only don't waste your nervous system altogether. Save Hassard and some of the rest, and you can keep it as good as it is for a lifetime.

Scattered through Hay's letters to Whitelaw Reid are references to the growing family. This, for example, is his unusual form of announcing the birth of the elder daughter, Helen: —

"DEAR REID: It is painful, but I must tell you. My wife says, when you come to the house, that you have got to hold the baby."

In another letter to Reid, on quite different matters, we light upon this amusing parenthesis: —

"(Mrs. Stone gave me to-day a portrait of herself with my wife (*ætat.* five months) sitting in her lap. It is the image of my infant to-day, which I hope disposes forever of the foul and widely-circulated calumny that the baby looks like me.)"

And here is probably his earliest description of his son Adelbert: —

"My *Tribune* commenced coming the day after I telegraphed. I suppose it may have gone wrong a day or two on account of there being no street number on the address, but it is all right now, and with a boy and a *Tribune* in the house we are sufficiently furnished to feel comfortable. The young man's name is Adelbert Stone Hay, — no Jr. in mine, if you please, though I fought off the name single-handed against great odds. He is a fine little man-child, ugly and strong, lean and big-boned, with a boundless capacity for sleeping and eating, and as yet no music in him. Long may he fight it out on that line.

"There is nothing in which a bachelor's ignorance shines out so flagrantly as in his feeble-minded conviction that babies look alike. There is no family-likeness even, between my two. My little girl, who was quite ugly at first, has become very pretty. I do not think the boy ever will, from present appearances, but he looks already like a railroad maker and statesman. Mrs. Hay, the Lord be thank't, is very well. The babies take none of her health or good looks away from her."

In 1883 Hay writes from Cannes to Albert Rhodes:

"The children are all well and gay. The baby is three years old to-day and there are rumors of great doings in the nursery. A cake with three candles and an orgie with *sirop*.

"I too have a letter from P. His glory is not satisfying to his soul. He seems disconsolate. Where, my brethren, is happiness? In the dictionary."

Hay watched the *Tribune* with a former editor's special interest, and, being free from the drudgery of its routine, he often expressed regret for the pleasant hours past. "I wish I could drop in on you for an hour or so," he writes Reid. "When I am in New York I hardly ever go to anything — but now it makes one homesick to read the ads in the *Tribune*." (June 5, 1875.)

To W. D. Howells

536 Euclid Avenue, Cleveland, O.,
February 20, 1877.

I send a few lines of vituperation for the Contributors' Club [1] as your wisdom may ordain.

I hear you are to write a "No Name" [2] story, but I do not believe a word of it. Your name is too valuable to veil. If you do, let me know, in strict confidence. I cannot afford to read the "No Name" books. I fear I might plunge into some such ditch of M. and water as D. Your comedy [3] is delicious. My wife reads it to me.

The last *Atlantic* has come, and we think that no magazine has a right to two things as good as you and James at once. Is not "The American" aston-

---

[1] A department of the *Atlantic Monthly*.

[2] The Boston publishing house of Roberts Brothers brought out a series of anonymous novels under this general title.

[3] *A Counterfeit Presentment.*

ishing, even to us who always believed in him? Of
course not "æsthetically attractive" — but — well!
well! let us be patient! Such things have always
been.

In the spring of 1878 Hay's health was so seriously
impaired that the doctor told him he must lie off all
summer. As Mrs. Hay could not accompany him, he
suggested to Nicolay to join him on a tour of recrea-
tion.

To J. G. Nicolay

Room 1, Cushing's Block, Cleveland, O.
April 6, 1878.

. . . [The doctor] suggests — see how great minds
jump together — what you did — Colorado. Only
you suggested *taking* me. *Eh bien!* Can you go? If
you can't, I am rather inclined to Switzerland instead.

If you can go, let me know, and when you can get
off. It won't cost you much — all the extras I will
stand, and you will come back to Washington so fat
they will charge you double.

Let me know at once.

I think I shall go to Philadelphia about May 1st
and consult Weir Mitchell before starting. So that
all definite plans can be postponed till then.

To *Whitelaw Reid*

514 Euclid Avenue, Cleveland, O.
July 5, 1878.

. . . I wish you could ever have as lazy time as I
had for ten days at Warsaw, — though I suppose
you could not have endured it. We were all together
without our wives, and spent every precious minute
of the time in loafing and remembering our childhood.
I got acquainted with my brother Leonard over
again, and liked him better than ever. If I had not
been too lazy to take down his talk, it would have
been all good copy, about life on the frontier. But
as I was going to say, I wish you would take care of
yourself in some way. It is getting to be a mania with
me, . . . and I made myself a nuisance at Springfield by croaking at Charles Hay,[1] who works nearly
twenty hours a day. I am grieved and ashamed to
see that the *Tribune* is as good and better without
me. Why can't you make up your mind to let it go
a little while on the momentum you have given it!
It is a tremendous paper. I see it more plainly than
ever when I am away. Every one I meet says the
same thing; it has fairly conquered criticism. If you
would now learn to sleep and eat like a Christian,
it would be all the better for you and your congrega-
tion. . . .

[1] John's younger brother.

Nicolay being unable to take the European trip, Hay invited his brother Leonard, and the two renewed their youth while traveling in England and on the Continent. John's memorandum book contains brief notes which show that he was not too worn out for sight-seeing. As usual, he listed the paintings and monuments which particularly attracted him. At Amsterdam the "towers are out of perpendicular. Read Zola, *Une Page d'Amour*. Black and bitter as gall."

At the station of Ehrenbreitstein Hay saw the Empress Eugénie: "bowed," is his laconic note; with what recollections on his part of their meeting thirteen years before, may be imagined. The brothers spent some time at Schlangenbad, where John took the baths and was assured by Dr. Bauman, who looked him over, that "there was nothing serious." At Schwalbach, Dr. Carl Genth examined his eyes and " saw no organic trouble whatever."

One other item reads: —

"Weight of J. H. July 26, 1878. Kilo 66, gr. 500; German pounds, 133; English pounds, 146½. Weight of L.H. Kilo 71, gr. 500; German pounds, 143; English pounds, 157¼."

In September the brothers came home.

To Whitelaw Reid

CLEVELAND, July 27, 1878.

... I don't see any good reason why we should not set December 7 as the Saturday night on which we shall beguile Howells down to New York, and I will come too. Only you are not to have any spread on that evening, for we shall want to go to the Century.

Howells's play, produced here Friday, is a translation of that pathetic Spanish tragedy, Yorick,[1] which you and I saw some years ago at the Fifth Avenue. Howells has greatly improved it. It is a beautiful tragedy now and Barrett[2] played it magnificently — but it is too sombre and heart-breaking to have much money in it.

I have not congratulated you on your great coup.[3] It is the biggest piece of intelligent journalism, as distinguished from mere enterprise, that has been done in the country. The leader-writing about it has been as good as the cipher-work, — can't say better, for obvious reasons.

I have not thanked you either for taking me to

---

[1] By Estébanez, whose play in Spanish is *Un Nuevo Mundo*.

[2] Lawrence Barrett (1838–91), actor who, during his last years, starred with Edwin Booth.

[3] Deciphering the Florida despatches which were held by Republicans to prove the corrupt practices of the Democrats.

Teaneck, that Sunday. I never had really talked with Walter Phelps [1] before, and I should not have felt like leaving the world without meeting so original and lovable a character. He is charming — mind and heart both, — one of the fellows that ought to live forever to help sweeten a brackish world.

To the playwright himself, Hay sent not only congratulations on *Yorick's Love*, but this fragment of dramatic criticism.

To W. D. Howells

CLEVELAND, O., October 28, 1878.

I went home last night moved and shaken to the core by your play, [2] and I woke up this morning with that vague sense of calamity with which a sorrow of the night before tinges the morning. I hardly know how to begin my report to you. If the theatre was merely a temple of art and poetry I could congratulate you on a great and glorious triumph. I am sure I never saw Barrett play as well, with such sustaining agony of expression. I went in to see him after the second Act, and he was haggard as a ghost and drenched with perspiration, but he showed no di-

[1] William Walter Phelps (1839–94) whose home was at Teaneck, near Englewood, New Jersey; he was a Congressman, 1873–75; Minister to Austria, 1881–82; and minister to Germany, 1889–93.

[2] *Yorick's Love.*

minution of energy in the last Act. The play throughout had a terrible clutch upon the feelings of the
audience, in spite of the young man who played
Edmund, who overdid his part and left the audience
behind him with no inclination to catch up. In all
Barrett's scenes the attention was painfully intense,
only interrupted by quick and electrical storms of
applause.

The audience was like your other one last year,
an *Atlantic Monthly* crowd which crammed every
inch of space. They appreciated the good acting
and the good writing as well. The exquisite versifi-
cation in the second Act, for instance, was remarked
upon by a dozen people about me, who, I should
have thought, would not care for such things. It
was a great tragedy, nobly played, in short; and it
had last night an honest and legitimate success. The
success was yours, too, for it was a very different
play from the one I saw at the Fifth Avenue Theatre some years ago, improved almost beyond recognition. It was the best written play I have heard for
a long time.

Now shall I go on with the hateful candor of a
friend, and tell you the further impression it made on
me? I do not believe that, as the play stands, it will
ever have great runs, or make you much money. The
plot is so simple, the story so sombre and heart-

breaking, that after the play becomes known, few people will go to see it except those who enjoy the very best things in writing and acting. It is too concentrated, too intense. The five people in it are in such a profound agony that an ordinary audience would grow nervous. They must laugh once in a while, and if you do not give them the chance to do it legitimately, they will do it in the wrong places. I do not know how the Greeks managed with their awful simplicity and work, but Shakespeare had to throw in what I dare not call padding.

Perhaps I am croaking in vain, after all. The play is magnificent. I wonder how any contemporary Spaniard could have done it. Your part of the work, it seems to me, is faultless, and Barrett's is unquestionably the stoutest piece of work I ever saw him do. (You made an improvement in keeping Shakespeare behind the flies. He was almost grotesque in the original.) The applause was of the sharpest and most spontaneous kind and the people were roused and moved in a very uncommon way. Perhaps I am morbid and cannot look at the prosperous side of things, but I think you will prefer to have me say what I think, even if I am wrong. I am sure I never left a theatre feeling such a sense of tragedy as last night, except when I walked out of the Academy of Music one afternoon and felt that I ought to go and tell the police that Salvini had smothered his wife and killed himself.[1]

Turning to brighter things, Mrs. Hay and I are just starting across the ocean with Miss Blood,[2] with the assurance of a happy voyage. The first number is delightful. It gives the pleasure we feel at the first note of Wilhelmj's fiddle; we know he can keep on doing it as long as he likes.

To J. G. Nicolay

CLEVELAND, O., January 11, 1879.

I think Colorado must be the thing after all. I went to Europe in May, had the quietest summer of my life. Spent a month or so in England, loafing in city and country; did not go to a single dinner-party or opera; then loafed through Holland and Belgium; up the Rhine to Schlangenbad, where we stayed a month; then a little of Northern Italy and Switzerland; then the [Paris] Exposition and Scotland, and a week's sleepy rest at Windermere, and home. In all this I was more quiet than I would have been in Cleveland. After I got back I imagined I felt better for a month or so, but the other day I had the most ridiculous attack I have ever had — thought I was

---

[1] Tommaso Salvini first acted *Othello* in New York at the Academy of Music in the autumn of 1873.

[2] A character in *The Lady of the Aroostook*.

dead for half an hour. The doctor said it was nothing at all serious — simply the effect of the cold. But I feel rickety yet.

I have been trying my best to get to work again, with very indifferent success. But I feel to-day as if I might make some headway for a while. I will write you later and tell you how I get on. Perhaps I can come to see you later in the season, but I can't say certainly yet. I won't come unless I can bring at least, say, 33,000 words.

In the autumn of 1879 William M. Evarts, the Secretary of State under President Hayes, succeeded, after much urging, in persuading Hay to be Assistant Secretary — a post which he filled until the installation of Garfield's Administration.

To Albert Rhodes

DEPARTMENT OF STATE,
WASHINGTON, June 8, 1880.

I received your letter of the 22nd and the "Vie Moderne" at the same time. I thank you very much for sending it to me. I have always been greatly interested in Flaubert's work and am glad to know something of the man. I have read, I believe, all his works except the "Éducation Sentimentale," which I see you call in your admirable letter to the *Tribune* "the weakling of his brain" — so perhaps I have not lost much in missing that.

I am always glad to hear from you. I have no news to tell you except that I have two daughters and a son — all healthy and happy — and that I have only one aspiration in life and that is two — to get out of office and to stop having headache.

To Whitelaw Reid

DEPARTMENT OF STATE,
WASHINGTON, February 11, 1881.

MY DEAR WHITELAW REID:—

My heart is full of your happiness.[1] I give you a thousand congratulations. The best thing has happened to you that could happen. You will be at peace the rest of your life so far as the greatest of all questions is concerned. You will have a good wife — good through and through — and I can tell you what that amounts to.

I need not tell you how I have desired and hoped for this. I have rarely met a young lady whom I liked so much at first sight as Miss Mills; and Mrs. Hay sanctioned my judgment of her noble qualities by some feminine judicial process which does not require long acquaintance. . . .

---

[1] Mr. Reid had announced his engagement to Miss Elizabeth Mills.

The proposition on your last page takes my breath away. I suppose I shall decline it finally, but I shall take pleasure in thinking it over for a while. It is a great temptation.

I had a letter to you lying sealed on the table when this momentous missive was handed to me. But I tore it up — it was all about politics, new cabinets, and myself, and such small deer, not worthy of your present frame of mind.

Well! God bless you and yours, now and always!

The proposition which took Hay's breath away was that he should act as editor-in-chief of the *Tribune* while Reid spent his honeymoon in Europe. This was, in truth, a final token of the value which Reid set on his judgment. Hay's literary ability nobody questioned; but judgment and tact are the compass and rudder without which a newspaper can never make port, and Reid plainly trusted in him for both.

Hay accepted the offer, partly to assist his friend, and partly because he liked to try his hand at new and formidable undertakings. The Reids were married on April 26, 1881; and for six months Hay sat in the editorial chair which Horace Greeley had occupied.

To Albert Rhodes

CLEVELAND, O., February 19, 1882.

Many thanks for sending "Serge Panine." I should have written to ask for it, if it had not come. I am just now *alité* by an attack of diphtheria which will soon be over, I am told; and then we shall attack "M. Panine."

I have read all the stories in Halévy's volume and find them delicious. I suppose he is Jew by religion as well as by blood; otherwise his irreverence would never be so light and dainty.

To W. D. Howells

CLEVELAND, March 26, 1882.

Your letter had a powerful effect on Mrs. Hay and me. Our minds were in solution and your letter precipitated them in an eye-twinkle. We had been intending to go to Europe, but thereafter all was vague; — now we shall go to Florence. What larks! We shall sail in the White Star steamer of July 15; if you took the same it would be — butter upon sausage, as Josh Billings once said in an inspired moment. I have been working hard, and laying up great store of MS. I shall go down to Washington next week and talk with Nicolay and then be free, for a vacation of respectable size.

... I never promised myself that much of a spree in my life. I feel a little superstitious about it now — as if it were too good for the likes of me. But to escape the envy of the Gods I will take a lot of historical notes in my trunk, ostensibly to write a few chapters, but really to ballast me, and lower my spirits with the thought of duty unperformed.

... I am still not well, and the doctor tells me not to be worried if I take a month more to get well in.

> Man nennt das grösste Glück auf Erden
> Gesund zu sein;
> Sein grösseres ist gesund zu werden.

When I see you I will tell you what I think of it.

In 1882 the Hays went to Europe and passed the winter. Europe on the East, and the Rocky Mountains on the West — where Hay found simple quarters at Manitou Springs, or Colorado Springs — became henceforth his chosen resorts for recuperation; and as the children grew old enough to travel, they went too. To the many acquaintances whom Hay had already made in England, he added new ones at each visit, and some of these ripened into friends. The bonds thus formed proved later precious in ways he never dreamed of.

To E. C. Stedman

CLEVELAND, O., June 28, 1882.

Mrs. Hay has put a heavy load on me — in charging me to ask you to write some verses in her book. I know, better than most of the profane, what a *corvée* this is. But I begin myself to wish to see the book completed, and you are too important a victim to escape. You will see how worthy the company is of you: — Emerson, Longfellow, and others. Don't damn me too much, — say about half what I deserve.

To complete your kindness and fill up the measure of my imprudence — would you mind giving me a letter to Swinburne? I will not crowd upon him, but if ever I come in his way, I would like to be indebted to you for an introduction to him. . . . We sail from New York July 15.

To W. D. Howells

ACTON PARK, WREXHAM.
September 18, 1882.

Did you learn what Alma Tadema would ask, say, for one of those pretty little pictures of his, the one with two figures in it? If it were not too monstrous I think I would get Mr. Stone to buy it. Do not take the trouble to ask anybody about it if you have not heard. I want also to impress upon your mind that if you ever make another bargain with an English publisher, you must talk guineas, not dollars, nor pounds. He will accept your numerals just as quick in guineas, and you will gain some six dollars in a hundred by it. It is the custom among artists and men of letters, so do not lower the standard.

Saturday last we drove from this lovely place (a seventeenth century house in which the vile Judge Jeffreys was born, now the seat of a family of baronets the most amiable conceivable) to Hawarden Castle, the residence of the Prime Minister. We were disappointed in not seeing the Grand Old Man, who was detained in London by a cabinet council; but Mrs. Gladstone was at home and very gracious. I say all this merely as an introduction to the weighty fact that I saw on the drawing-room table a much-thumbed copy of "A Foregone Conclusion," and the Prime Ministress authorized and requested me to say to you how much she liked it. We went to-day to visit Chirk Castle, a grand old pile of the date of the thirteenth century, still in perfect preservation and always continuously inhabited since it was built. It was a royal appanage until Elizabeth's time, who sold it to the family who now live in it. This is the first thing of the sort I have ever seen except Warwick, and this is in many respects far finer. . . .

To W. D. Howells

. . . After I wrote you in Paris I saw some doctors who told me without collusion that if I would stay in Paris forty days and take douche baths I would be well. They were both great swells and the coincidence of their views rather struck me. I remembered also that it took exactly the same time in Noah's day, to cure the world of most of its infirmities by the same method; and so, like an ass, I gave up, or rather, postponed, my trip to the South, and went through my douches, with, of course, no result whatever. I went back to my doctors and reported. One said: "Better stop your douches! go to Cannes and amuse yourself! You will soon be all right. Forty francs! thank you! good-bye!"

The other said: "*Eh bien!* instead of six weeks, take three months of douches. Take them in Cannes, if you like, or in Nice"; and with that he gave me an entire change of drugs; — "Forty francs! thank you, *bon voyage!*" There was nothing Noachian about three months, so I came away determined to do nothing he told me. . . .

P.S. After shutting my letter I looked at the Christmas *Harper's*, and found, *naturellement*, that your farce [1] was the pearl of the collection. It made me laugh audibly which is *mucho decir*. I would give money to see it on the stage. There is a little woman at the Vaudeville who played in *Tête de Linotte*, who would be the best Mrs. Roberts on earth. But it would be impossible here, as a French sleeping-car is a sad parody on our glorious institution. It has no sociableness, no promiscuity, no chance for love or war.

By the way, how James is catching it for his "Point of View"! [2] In vain I say to the Howling Patriot: "The point of view is clearly and avowedly the point of view of a corrupted mother and daughter, spoiled by Europe; of a filthy, immoral Frenchman; of a dull, well-meaning Englishman!" But they respond: "Miss Sturdy is James himself"; and as she says children are uproarious in America, and women's voices are higher than their manners, there is forgiveness for the writer. The worst thing in our time about American taste is the way it treats James. I believe he would not be read in America at all if it were not for his European vogue. If he lived in Cambridge he could write what he likes, but because he finds London more agreeable, he is the prey of all the patriotisms. Of all vices I hold patriotism the worst when it meddles with matters of taste.

[1] *The Sleeping Car.*
[2] *The Portrait of a Lady* was published that year.

To J. G. Nicolay

PARIS, March 8, 1883.

... I have been so inert and lifeless since I came over here that I have not written a letter except on the stimulus of receiving one. I have never been so idle in my life. It was of set purpose, and I think it has been wholesome.

To give you in a word our itinerary: — We arrived in England the end of last July; spent a few weeks in London, and then went north; saw Lincoln, York, Edinburgh, and Aberdeen; then went to visit a Baronet in the Highlands named Sir John Clark, passed a delightful week with him, then went to the shore of the Northern Ocean at Inverness. Thence down the Caledonian Canal to Oban, Staffa, and Iona. Then back to Hastings, where we had left the children during all these philanderings. We went up to London again after that; went to North Wales to visit another Baronet and M.P., Sir Robert Cunliffe. At his house we met the Judge Advocate-General in Gladstone's Government, Mr. Osborn-Morgan, M.P., who invited us to visit him, which we did, and passed a pleasant day or two in an Inigo Jones house in the mountains of Wales. Then we went on a regular debauch of English cathedrals: — Hereford, Worcester, Gloster, Wells, and Salisbury; and after that, we broke for Hastings again; and after a week of rest by the summer sea we gathered up the whole caboodle and went over to Paris.

I was still rather miserable and at last went to two doctors, W. B., an American Egyptian, and the famous C., the same day. They both advised the same thing, douche baths, tonics, and bromides. I followed their prescriptions pretty faithfully, off and on, until now. In December we went to Cannes with the children, and that has been our home all the winter, — and a delicious place it is, — eternal June with an air loaded with orange blossoms. We made our little tour through Provence: — Nîmes, Arles, Aigues-Mortes, Pont du Gard, — and a longer trip to Florence and Siena, where we met Howells.

I am, I think, considerably better, though I have given up all hopes of being twenty-one again.

We sail for home on the 10th of May in the *Germanic*, and I hope to get to work immediately, or as soon as practicable after that. I saw the Comte de Paris at Cannes and he asked me to give you his Royal compliments.

Thanks for the scrap. King did not write "Democracy," nor did I.

In the next two letters, addressed to Mr. Stone, Hay wrote to interest his correspondent; for the father-in-law was both sick in body and apprehensive in mind, at the signs of encroaching anarchy.

To Amasa Stone

PARIS, March 11, 1883.

DEAR MR. STONE: —

There is a feeling of deep distrust and anxiety in the public mind. A demonstration took place day before yesterday on the Esplanade des Invalides which might easily have become very serious. A few bakers' shops were pillaged and a crazy creature named "Louise Michel" tried to get the mob to march to the Élysées Palace, but the cuirassiers came on the ground and dispersed them. Another riot was feared for to-day, and the streets are full of soldiers riding in every direction. Commerce is in a great state of prostration. The laborers have had the mischief put into their heads by trade-unions, etc., and the consequence is that cheap merchandise is coming in from Germany and underselling the French on their own ground. Then the politicians in the Assembly are so eager for their individual advancement that no government lasts more than a few weeks and a painful impression of uncertainty has thus grown up throughout France.

. . . [Helen] has learned a good deal in the past year. She reads very well and has begun to write and knows a good deal of French. Del is half a head taller than she and is getting along pretty well in his studies also. They are all lively, but have caught little colds in this harsh and damp air. Paris is a poor place to live in.

LONDON, May 2, 1883.

... I have been reading the life of Carlyle, and the other day I walked down to the little house where he lived and died and near which his statue now stands in bronze. At your age he suffered precisely as you do, deep, nervous depression, persistent indigestion and loss of sleep — a general disaster and irritation of the entire nervous system. His misery seems to have been of the keenest character. Yet he lived to be eighty-six years of age, and the last twenty-five years of his life were comparatively healthy and free from pain. I met the other day at dinner an old gentleman named H., eighty-two years old. He told me that between sixty and sixty-five his digestion seemed hopelessly impaired. He could eat and drink nothing and slept very little. Now he dines out every night and is the gayest of the company wherever he is. I rely on your strong constitution, your sober and moral life, the reserve of vitality you have about you, to wear out all your present troubles and to bring you to a healthy and happy condition again. You have so much to live for, to enjoy the results of the good you have done and to continue your career of usefulness and honor.

Yours affectionately.

To Henry James

CLEVELAND, August 11, 1883.

MY DEAR JAMES: —

When I was in Florence, Larkin Mead [1] made for me a very admirable bronze medallion of Howells, and I write now to beg that if you find yourself soon in Florence again you will let him have a shy at your head also for me. I have written to him about it. It will give you almost no annoyance at all, as he works with great swiftness in such things, and if he succeeds with you as well as he did with Howells, the portrait will do you no discredit and will be a great ornament to my house.

I am nearly through my year's hard work, and am to start in a day or two with Nicolay to the Rocky Mountains for a few weeks' idleness.

I greatly enjoyed your Daudet in the *Century*, though demurring a little at your undue generosity. Your palinode was excessive, I thought. He *is* a "great little writer." The "Evangéliste" is dreary,

---

[1] Larkin Goldsmith Mead, born in 1835, American sculptor; brother-in-law of W. D. Howells.

the work of a genius smitten with locomotor ataxia; (if I had known that word was so long, I should never have begun upon it). There is no coördination in it. Besides, a man who is such an idiot morally can never sit down at meat with Shakespeare and you fellows. . . .

To W. D. Howells

IN THE CLOUDS, ROCKY MOUNTAINS,
COLORADO, September 9, 1883.

. . . Nicolay and I are in camp in a most beautiful and rugged eyrie 9000 feet high, sometimes called Crystal Park, not far from Manitou Springs, which is our P.O. address. If you were here, — but some day you will come. — I am looking about for a place to build a hut, which I hope you will share with me. The bigness of the beauty of the place is something I am not able to describe and shall not try. I came away from Cleveland pretty wretched and am already a good deal better. I will come earlier next year and stay longer. I expect to be here at least a fortnight more. . . .

Having seen some of Hay's friendships during the first ten years of his married life, and having learned to know him better, we may now turn to the beginnings of his political career.

CHAPTER XVI

POLITICS

DURING the half-century following the Civil War, American development refutes the common saying that war is good for a people because, in calling out their courage and requiring of them fortitude and self-sacrifice not less than valor, it puts them to the test of ultimate reality. In truth, however, though there have been wars through all the ages, none has ever yet cured the most intimate social diseases, but on the contrary, war causes these to flourish and it raises up other evils of its own.

The two benefits which resulted from the American Civil War were the abolition of slavery and the preservation of the geographical union of the United States. Among the evils it bequeathed were sectionalism, a diminished respect of the citizen for the State, the commutation of patriotism into pensions, the preferment of soldiers to civil offices for which they were unfit, the centralization of the national governmental power, and the unbridling of national extravagance.

Perhaps we should count as a third benefit the swiftness with which, in 1865, the Union and the

Southern armies dissolved. Yesterday, a million soldiers hot from battle; to-day, as if transformed by a magician's wand, a million farmers, clerks, merchants, laborers, operatives — busy again at their peaceful tasks. No military despotism; no truculence of Pretorian Guards; no Prussian war lord and his underlings compelling a nation to worship Moloch as the highest God. In the noblest qualities of a soldier, the Americans had never been surpassed; and yet they testified in disbanding that they knew that peace, not war, is the normal state, the ideal, of civilized society. Small wonder that their muster-out roused the admiration of the world!

But in subtler ways the Civil War harmed American Democracy. It filled every civic office — from president to hog-reeve — with ex-soldiers. Five presidents — Grant, Hayes, Garfield, Harrison, and McKinley — came into the White House, directly or indirectly, because of their military record. The corruption of an institution begins when those who pilot it are chosen for qualities contrary, if not foreign, to its purpose. So, too, the desperate need of money to finance the war led to the adoption of a high tariff, which stimulated unhealthy production: and when the war was over, the beneficiaries of the tariff — like the fever-patient who, on his recovery, finds the morphine habit fixed upon him — demanded

higher protection and still higher. The Republican
Party already ominously strong because of its prestige
in the Civil War, made Protection the cornerstone
of its creed; and it veiled the fact that it was the
capitalists' party by claiming to protect American
labor; yet it revealed its true spirit in encouraging
unrestricted immigration, in order to supply capitalists with the cheapest labor.

The captains of industry, the manufacturers and
mine-owners and promoters, controlled the Government in so far as they caused it to fix the tariff rates
they themselves dictated — a denial of that principle of equality which is the sheet anchor of Democracy. They were numbered by thousands, or at most
by tens of thousands. The multitudes who beset
the Government for favor and support through the
pension system reached a million or more. Dignity,
self-respect, honesty itself, succumbed to the temptation of the pension-mongers. Frauds were so frequent that the Pension Bureau ceased to allow the
rolls of its beneficiaries to be inspected — the most
shameless official conniving at robbery this country
has known.

With the pensioners as with the capitalists the
primal harm was not the shocking waste of public
money but the debasement of civic ideals. The four
thousand million dollars poured out to the veterans

created a vast body of Americans who regard the National Treasury as fair prey for every rapacity. The conception that each citizen should defend public money from theft or waste even more scrupulously than he would a private trust, was dismissed as an iridescent dream. Another stab to Democracy, which cannot function perfectly unless every member is honest.

The influx of millions of foreigners raised further impediments. The aliens came mostly from countries where they had had little or no experience in self-government. They brought with them their tribal, their racial, their religious, and their international feuds. And as they transplanted to America the creeds of discontent and revolution which had long kept Europe alarmed, the word "proletariat" became naturalized here much sooner than many who bore it. They thrust the debate of the social revolution prematurely on the United States, and having never passed through the experience of constitutional methods, they saw no alternative to the Despotism from which they had fled except the Socialism or the Anarchism to which they would blindly leap.

On the surface, the half-century seemed prosperously given up to money-making. Expansion was bound to come, but the artificial stimulus caused its rate and its extent to be unhealthily exorbitant. To watch a nation grow opulent is not necessarily more edifying than to watch the aurification of the individual plutocrat — and what that is the Greeks typified once for all in Midas. This process went on, however, just as surely in Europe as in the United States. Some countries, like Germany, combined the materializing pursuit of wealth with the brutalizing pursuit of militarism. All had their scorn of the vulgar American dollar, and all encouraged their parasitic nobles to marry the daughters of American millionaires, and Kings and Kaisers prudently invested in American securities. Great is cant.

These were some of the principles, unfavorable if not actively injurious, among which American Democracy had to maintain itself as best it could. In an industrial age, the government is inevitably controlled by the masters of industrialism. So the Republican Party, which was in power at the end of the Civil War, became by a quite natural metamorphosis the capitalists' organ.

Like millions of his contemporaries John Hay continued to be a Republican, not because that party fostered plutocracy in granting special privileges to capital, but because, first of all, it *had* saved the Union, it *had* put down slavery. In his youth, it kindled his conscience. He had seen Lincoln guide

its councils and direct its mighty forces to preserve
Democracy on earth; his own associates had been
chiefly Republicans. His instinct was, to suspect that
the seeds of slavery and rebellion still lurked in the
Democratic Party, although he did not question that
individual Democrats were loyal and high-minded
and just. That constitutional country cannot fail
to suffer in which one party claims that it alone is
patriotic. Such was the case in the United States
for two decades after the Civil War.

Hay was keen enough to see that thick-and-thin
partisanship appears illogical, not to say absurd, to
the eyes of pure reason; he repudiated without demur
this or that corrupt politician or party act: but he
held that an institution must be judged by its essentials and not by its details, especially where these
are unworthy. If, like most of us, he could not always escape from the fallacy of his zeal, yet he was
so genuinely open-minded that the dominant friendship of his life was with one who looked with pitying
irony upon political and other orthodoxies and those
who professed them.

Except when Hay voted for Tilden for Governor
of New York, his practice seems to have been consistently loyal. Republicanism, the creed of his youth,
became the habit of his prime. It changed its principles; it drifted out of the old into the new; but it

still harped on the glories of its origin, and it was never so insistent on posing as Abraham Lincoln's party as when it put forth doctrines most opposed to those which he stood for.

Toward the end of the century, the Republican Party was avowedly the capitalists' party; and as such, because capital is timorous and wary and solicitous of self, it became the stronghold of conservatism. Thereby it drew to itself, not merely the rich, but many others whom the dread of a social upheaval turned into conservatives. In this aspect, too, it attracted Hay, an unwavering lover of liberty — but of liberty with order. He believed that the hope of the country, perhaps even of Western civilization, so far as this is based on property, depended upon maintaining the Republican Party as a breakwater against the rising tide of social revolution.

But enough of general outlines of his political creed and its background. Let us examine now his attitude in special cases. Generalities give us only theories about life; particulars are life itself.

During his career on the *Tribune*, Hay's knowledge of New York State politics, not less than his wide acquaintance with public men, led to his being called upon more and more for political editorials. He favored the Liberal movement of 1872, up to the time when the Democrats appropriated it and forced Greeley upon the unnatural combination. Then he supported Grant, and, in the succeeding four years, his Republicanism was unshaken, although he could not fail to detest the revelations of corruption in high places which scandalized the country.

When the Greenback craze, the joint product of half-baked vagarists and professional demagogues, swept through the country, Hay saw clearly that, as this was not a party delusion, but a national menace, it was for the "honest money" men in both parties to unite and strangle it. His correspondence with Reid grows hot.

To Whitelaw Reid

CLEVELAND, OHIO,
24 September, 1875.

. . . I am in a profound disgust about the campaign here. These bellowing, howling hounds expect to carry the State, and I have not heard of any Democrats who will bolt. I had a talk with Mr. P. the other day. He is for Allen,[1] although he has kept quiet; if Allen is elected, he (Mr. P.) would be in favor of the repeal of the Resumption Law. The *Herald* here is an inflation paper. The *Leader* is as straight as a string — copies the *Tribune* every day.

[1] William Allen, Governor of Ohio, 1874-76.

I do not see that you are called upon to modify your attitude in the least in New York. Bigelow [1] is sure to be elected by a big majority, and the whole ticket. You can say this, and not weep over it, without saying anything against Fred Seward.[2] There have never been two tickets so absolutely irreproachable put before the voters of the State, and the platforms are about as good as they could be made.

Think of this State — with half the Republicans and all the Democrats inflationists at heart, and carrying on a campaign on the bald issue whether the nation shall be a liar and a thief or not.

I don't like the job you propose to me of skinning that skunk.

CLEVELAND, O., October 1, 1875.

. . . I think there is no trouble about the position of the *Tribune*. From now until election-day here, October 12, you can hold your present attitude. If Allen is elected, as I fear, it will then be advisable to make no bones about Pennsylvania, but say distinctly that there is not a ghost of a chance for Hartranft,[3] at the same time keeping up a hot fight against the inflation Democrats. There is really no

[1] John Bigelow, Democratic Secretary of State in New York, 1875-77.
[2] Republican nominee for Secretary of State in New York.
[3] John F. Hartranft, Governor of Pennsylvania, 1873-77.

Democratic or Republican Party left, and a man can
with perfect consistency favor the one in one State,
and the other in another. In case of the success of the
Bill Allen crowd, the thing to work for is to strengthen
the Tilden wing as much as possible, either to give
them the control of the party, or to break up the
party into the two natural fractions of honest men
and thieves. The Republicans would then either follow suit or coalesce with the hard-money Democrats.

The bad sign here, and I suppose everywhere, is
that the inflationists are loud and bold, and the
hard-money men, Democrats and $\left\{ \begin{array}{l} \text{Republicans} \\ \text{Inflationists} \end{array} \right\}$
alike, are evasive and cowardly.

The election of 1876 was the first turning-point
since the end of the war. Hay sympathized with the
widespread demand for purification; but he thought
that this could be trusted to the Republicans rather
than to the Democrats and Independents; and he
therefore voted for Hayes, who had made a good
governor of Ohio, and not for Tilden, who had given
his measure as a reformer by cleansing the Tammany-
ized politics of New York.

In the spring of that year, before the party con-
ventions had nominated, Hay wrote enthusiastically
to Reid: —

"If anybody wants a better pair of candidates than Tilden and Blaine, the two most prominent politicians of the two parties, he must wait till he gets to heaven — and finds an absolute monarchy. Better men than these are not given to Republics." (April 21, 1876.)

Blaine was set aside by the Republicans, because of charges that he had used his position as Speaker to enrich himself. The proofs against him were his own letters; and although then and later he tried to explain away sentences which to posterity can have only one meaning, he never compassed his frantic desire to be President. In spite of proofs, however, many of his adherents refused to believe him guilty. Hay too was among the loyal; but in the campaign he gave his allegiance to Hayes, whom the Republicans chose in Blaine's stead.

He writes from Cleveland to Reid, on November 13, 1876: —

"I believe I won't say anything about election. I think the *Tribune* has nothing to regret except a few digs at Uncle Sam [Tilden] which were not quite fair, and your article on Wells, David A. Which — well — hold on — let bygones be buried with the decomposed past!

"Give my love to Taylor and Bromley, and tell them to sling a column and a half or so, in memory

of one who wishes he was back at his desk — *Quid
rides?*"

In a letter to Mr. Howells, who had written a campaign biography of the Republican candidate, Hay
speaks without reserve. His mention of Civil Service Reform reminds us of the beginnings of a movement for political purification of which David A.
Wells, referred to in the preceding extract, was one
of the bravest promoters. The "herd of wild asses'
colts" were Republicans, hungry for office, a fact to
which Hay's Republicanism did not blind him.

To W. D. Howells

CLEVELAND, O., February 20, 1877.

I thank you for my share of the "Life of Hayes."
It cheered and comforted me a good deal. The Governor's conduct for the last year has been a complete
confirmation of all you said. I liked Tilden very
much, — voted for him for Governor,— the only
Democratic vote I ever cast. I did not vote for
Greeley; but I never allowed myself to expect as
much from any man as I feel forced now to hold from
Hayes. We are in a bad way. That herd of wild
asses' colts in Washington, braying and kicking up
their heels, is an unsatisfactory result of a hundred
years of Democracy. Of course I do not expect from
Mr. Hayes a reform of the Civil Service. It is too

much for any man to accomplish. Human nature
and free suffrage are against it. But he can and will,
I feel sure, chasten the outrageous indecency of the
present system as much as any one could. . . .

To Whitelaw Reid

CLEVELAND, November 26, 1877.

. . . I do not envy your feelings when you see
who the successor of S. will be. I have carefully
considered your objections to him. You evidently
don't believe the shoddy or gun-stories, — no more
than I do. But you are agin him because he gives
good dinners, and sometimes invites Democrats.
This and the other infamy, that Mrs. S. once gave
some private theatricals and reserved a few seats for
the Diplomatic Corps, cooked his goose. Now this
fixes you also. I have had good dinners at your
house — there were Democrats present, — all the
seats were reserved!! Good-bye, sweet prince, you
can never be a foreign minister!

On the other hand, the *Tribune* can feel cocky
no-end over Platt and Conkling,[1] and thank heaven
that the unclean things have never had its good
word. How Nemesis has been sloshing around during the last year or two! Only she will be off duty
when Butler [2] takes his seat in the Senate.

[1] T. C. Platt and Roscoe Conkling, New York politicians.
[2] Matthew C. Butler, of South Carolina.

Hay's regard for President Hayes deepened as he
watched that conscientious chief magistrate — too
often set down as mediocre, but conscience in high
public station is never mediocre — strive to give the
country a worthy administration. He himself was
becoming the confidant of some of the leaders of the
party, and as his acquaintance was equally extensive
in both Ohio and New York, the two States which
carried more politics *per capita* than any others, he
enjoyed the best opportunity for observing what was
going on behind the scenes. His frequent visits to
Illinois extended his political knowledge to the third
pivotal State.

During the campaign of 1879 he spoke several
times in behalf of the Republican candidates.
Speech-making, even when he had his manuscript
before him, was always an ordeal. In composing, he
alternated between buoyancy and depression: first,
the hot fit, when ideas flamed into his mind; then, the
cold fit, when he read over what he had written and
the words seemed gray and bleak and cold. He suffered by anticipation the misery of stage-fright. But
once on the platform, although nervous to the end,
he rarely failed to win his audience. This success
came always as a surprise to him, and he used to
chronicle it in his notes to his friends, not out of conceit, but as a bit of unexpected news which might

surprise them too. "Luckily," he once said, "the shakes go to my knees and not to my voice."

To Whitelaw Reid

CLEVELAND, O., August 20, 1879.

TO THE EDITOR OF THE TRIBUNE: —

Into whose hands these lines may fall, greeting:

If it is Mr. Reid, hail! and welcome back to civilization!

If it is Lloyd or Nicholson, or some other d—d literary feller —

I wish you would help our Shermanizing a little by sticking into your able and leading pages somewhere the ¶ between the red lines.

I made this speech last night in the strongest Democratic ward of Cleveland to an audience nearly half Democrats, and there was nothing but approval manifested.

Yours in humble expectation,

HAY,

Reformed *Tribune* Man.

August 25, 1879.

. . . As you never read anything but proofs, perhaps the form in which this oration is printed may induce you to cast your eye over it. I am going to say it to a big crowd at North Solon day after to-morrow — *the* Pioneers' Reunion, — all others are spurious.

We are having a red hot canvass, — our side especially; I am invited to make four speeches this week, and am not on any Committee's list either. I shall try it a little — slowly and gently at first, and find out whether I can. I don't call it making a speech unless a fellow can bore his audience heartily and thoroughly for an hour, without having written a word of it beforehand — like William Allen and sich.

October 6, 1879.

. . . I am making a speech nearly every night. Here is my last, made on the Square Saturday night to 5000 people, by the Brush light. Tell Mr. Phelps he bullied me into it last spring.

October 15, 1879.

. . . I left the house early last night, and spent the evening at the Globe Theatre, hearing the returns [of the Ohio election]. . . .

Is n't it a frightful thing to think of, that half the people of Ohio vote so wickedly and blindly in favor of inflation and ruin, not to speak of nullification and other things? With all our tremendous work this summer, we have only a majority of two per cent. On such an issue we ought to have had a hundred thousand. But I suppose the Democratic Party is our Evil — our virtue is developed by fighting it.

The next extract is interesting.

To Whitelaw Reid

November 3, 1879.

. . . Mr. Evarts has written me a most urgent and kind letter — but I have declined the place.

It now looks as if I could get the nomination for Congress, and I find, to my amazement, that I don't want it. This discovery strikes me dumb.

Mr. Evarts, then Secretary of State, had, in fact, invited Hay to become Assistant Secretary. The offer was unexpected, the position attractive, but Hay decided that he ought to decline.

To William M. Evarts

506 Euclid Avenue, Cleveland, O.,
October 28, 1879.

Dear Mr. Evarts: —

I have your letter of the 24th and I cannot express the sentiments of gratification with which I have read it. To be offered the privilege of succeeding Mr. Seward [1] as Assistant Secretary of State is an

---

[1] Frederick W. Seward, son of Lincoln's Secretary of State.

honor as far beyond my ambition as it is beyond my merits, and the generous courtesy with which you urge my acceptance of it, doubles the value of the offer. It is therefore with the greatest reluctance and with positive pain that I bring myself to say that I cannot assume the duties of this position which would otherwise be to me the most agreeable in the gift of the Government. Interests which I cannot disregard, make it impossible for me to be away from Cleveland this winter.

I hope you will permit me to say that the keenest regret I feel in declining this position, is for the loss of the pleasure and benefit which I should derive from daily association with yourself.

Begging that you will convey to the President my profound appreciation of the honor he and you have conferred upon me, and my sincere regret that it is impossible for me to avail myself of it,

I remain, my dear Mr. Evarts,

Faithfully yours,

JOHN HAY.

Mr. Evarts, however, was not to be gainsaid. Reinforcing his own urgence with that of Whitelaw Reid and of other friends, he soon had the pleasure of seeing Hay installed next door to himself in the State Department. There is little to record of Hay's

specific work as Assistant Secretary, and the diplomatic questions then up do not concern us here.
He performed his duties satisfactorily to Mr. Evarts,
for whom he kept through life an affectionate admiration. It was diamond cut diamond when they
had a friendly interchange of wit.[1]

In Hay's development the main thing to notice is
that the year and a half he spent in the State Department taught him the routine of that office, familiar-
ized him with the methods of diplomacy, and introduced him to new groups, native and foreign.

At the same time with Mr. Evarts's invitation
came the suggestion from Hay's friends in Cleveland
that he should enter Congress. No doubt he had
cherished that idea; but being both temperamentally
shy and too dignified to pound his way into any office, he hesitated.

"The Congress matter," he wrote Reid on October
21, 1879, "is not so simple as my high-toned friends
think. All Euclid Avenue[2] says with one accord that
I am the man, but E. A., with all its millions and its
tone, does not influence a single primary, and there
are four or five other candidates, who are all more

[1] I am assured that it was Hay and not Evarts who replied, when
an English visitor at Mount Vernon asked, "Really, now, George
Washington could not have thrown a dollar across the Potomac,
could he?" "Why not? He threw a sovereign across the Atlantic."
I have no means of verifying this.
[2] The fashionable street of Cleveland.

or less strong with the 'boys.' I have not yet made up my mind whether to try for it or not."

When it appeared, however, that the Republican managers favored him he consented to enter the lists. The district in question was so solidly Republican that a nomination meant an election. According to the simple system prevailing there, — and still in happy operation elsewhere, — for providing a docile people with mayors, governors, judges, and congressmen, the candidate needed only to pay to the party managers the price they demanded, and they relieved him of further anxiety. After election, while they divided and spent the spoils, he did his patriotic duty, care-free, in the office which they delivered to him.

The assessment levied on Hay was, apparently, twenty thousand dollars, an amount which he could not pay himself and which, if he had had it, he might have felt scruples against paying: for the transaction, no matter who acquiesces in it, comes down to the bald purchase of office. So the committee visited Mr. Stone, and after congratulating him on the shining honor about to grace his son-in-law, they hinted to him that nothing remained to close the bargain except a check.

"Not a dollar shall you have of me" — or words to that effect, put even more emphatically — was the old gentleman's uncompromising reply. Perhaps the shrewd millionaire suspected that the whole affair was a ruse for tapping his barrel rather than for honoring his son-in-law. In any case he could not be moved, and no other friends or political admirers came forward. The project simmered through the winter; then the managers discovered that Hay was unavailable, and he withdrew.

To Whitelaw Reid

WASHINGTON, March 31, 1880.

I ought to let you know as soon as any one else that I have definitely resolved not to run for Congress. I do not want it, and at last know that I do not.

I think I could be nominated, and the nearness of the prospect set me to thinking of it harder than ever, — with this result. I have written to my friends to put an end to the matter.

We must regret that he was deprived of experience in Congress, the only field in his apprenticeship as a statesman in which he lacked first-hand training. A few years' service in the lower House, or a single term as Senator, would not only have rounded out his otherwise extraordinary equipment, but would have given him the understanding which comes only

from fellowship with the very men who were later to
sit in judgment on his statecraft. Journalism teaches
its practitioner policies, party methods and interests,
and the ways of individual politicians; but the commanding editor is, properly, a critic. Between the
critic and the doer a gulf, wide and rarely bridged,
is set. So, too, the ambassador or the cabinet officer, far from sympathizing with the Congressman's
point of view, is unavoidably, from his position, in
danger of misjudging it. The executive branch regards the legislative as meddlesome if not actually
antagonistic. To his detriment, therefore, was Hay
shut out from legislative training.

If he felt chagrin at being dropped, he soon got
over it, as this letter to Mr. Howells testifies.

To W. D. Howells

WASHINGTON, D.C., May 24, 1880.

Thanks for M.'s letter, which I return. His idea
is as judicious as it is daring. A club which would
hold him and you and me, and then reach out for
H. etc., — and still keep modest, — staggers and
fatigues the faculty of wonder. I wish he and you
would come down here and hold the first meeting of
three at my house.

I feel what the French call a deaf rage when I think
of your having spent a week in Washington, and

my not having seen Mrs. Howells at all, and you
only a minute. If I were a saint, it would be enough
for me to know that you had a pleasant visit yourselves; but I cannot help feeling like the Dutchman
who, when he was in the calaboose and heard from
a later arrival of an uproarious spree the night before
when hogsheads of lager were drunk and two men
killed, — sighed with soft regret — "And I was not
dere."

I did not get the chance I wanted to avow my sin
and ask absolution. I have positively and definitely
given up Congress, and I shall hold no more office
after next March. I think there is no such Apples-
of-Sodom fruit in the world, and I am out, finally,
as soon as I can get away. I would give a pot of money
to get out to-day, — nothing but my personal regard
for Mr. Evarts keeps me through the administration. Yet this is the pleasantest place in the government, and I like and respect the principal people in
office, — which makes an *a fortiori* case against anything else. . . .

The contest between Garfield and Hancock in
1880 should have been fought on the issue of Protection, but the Democrats resorted to strategic re-
treats which landed them far in the rear. Hay of
course supported General Garfield, and how great

a value the candidate set upon his advice is plain in the following letters: —

To General James A. Garfield

1400 MASSACHUSETTS AVE., WASHINGTON,
Oct. 18, 1880.

DEAR GENERAL GARFIELD: —

I did not come down on you while I was at Cleveland, simply because I felt that the truest service I could render would be to stay away — but as it will not take a minute of your time to read this note, I write it to offer my congratulations from the bottom of my heart. I believe that you will carry every Northern State and will go into the Presidency with the most magnificent moral backing any one has had in our time. I know you will feel no selfish gratification in this, but your opportunities for good will be incalculable. Great things are to happen under your administration. It would be an impertinence for me to intrude upon the high subjects that must now be occupying your mind. But even at the risk of seeming presumptuous I will rid myself of this word which has positively haunted me for a week. Beware of your own generosity! On the 2d of November, *you* ("not Launcelot nor another") are to be made our President. I believe it is to be an administration full of glory and benefit to the country — and it will

be glorious and fruitful just in the proportion that it
is your own. You do not need the whispered admoni-
tion of the ancient monarchs, "Remember thou art
mortal." It will pay you to keep a cheap friend to
drone continually in your ear, "It was *you* who were
nominated at Chicago and elected by the people."

Soon after his election, General Garfield proposed
making Hay his private secretary and assigning to
the post a greater distinction than it had had, so
that he would have ranked with members of the
Cabinet. Having deputed Whitelaw Reid to sound
him, and having had no answer, General Garfield
wrote direct. To this letter Hay replied: —

To General Garfield

1400 MASSACHUSETTS AVE.,
Christmas Day, 1880.

I received several days ago from Whitelaw Reid
an intimation of what you were thinking of for me,
and I immediately wrote to him expressing my deep
sense of the honor done me by such a thought, and
the sincere regret I felt that it was not in my power
to take the place. I agree with you in regarding the
position as one of the greatest importance and shall
always be proud that you thought of me in connection with it.

Although my letter to Reid was confidential, I thought he would communicate to you the purport of it, but I infer from yours of the 20th that he has not done so.

I have carried your letter in my pocket and the contents of it in my head and my heart, for several days, with the most earnest desire to catch myself in such a state of mind that I might write and tell you I would undertake the important and honorable duty you offer me. But I cannot delay my answer any longer, and so must say how sorry I am that I cannot see the way clear to doing, it. If I could share your own view of my fitness for the place I should be inclined to sacrifice all other considerations and go to work. But I am not.

To do a thing well a man must take some pleasure in it, and while the prospect of spending a year or so in intimate relations with you and Mrs. Garfield offers a temptation which is almost more than I can resist, the other half of the work, the contact with the greed and selfishness of office-seekers and bulldozing Congressmen, is unspeakably repulsive to me. It caused me last spring to refuse, definitely and forever, to run for Congress. It has poisoned all of the pleasure I should otherwise have derived from a conscientious and not unsuccessful discharge of my duties in the State Department. The constant contact with envy, meanness, ignorance, and the swinish selfishness which ignorance breeds, needs a stronger heart and a more obedient nervous system than I can boast. I am not going back on Democracy. It is a good thing — the hope and salvation of the world. I mean simply that I am not fit for public office. You will find some one, I am sure, who can do these things much better than I could, and will take pleasure in them as well.

All through the heats of last summer I looked forward to the 4th of March as the day of my deliverance. I promised my family, I promised Mr. Stone, who at considerable inconvenience has taken care of my affairs, that I would come home at that time — and although I know that he would acquiesce cheerfully in anything I should do, I should feel some remorse in breaking up the family arrangements for the coming summer. I do not know that I have much hope of ever improving my health, but the doctors give me the usual futile assurances that I will be better out of Washington in the summer time.

I did not mean to make a long letter of this, but the signal honor you have done me in selecting me for the place of the Government nearest yourself, has deeply touched me and I could not acknowledge it by a simple refusal. I felt that I ought to tell you some of my reasons for declining, although they are of a sort that a man of your firm and even character may think trivial and not entirely creditable to me.

There is work for all of us during the next four years, and though you are to have the great rôle, all men of good-will can help more or less. I shall do my share in Cleveland, and now that I am cured of my momentary error about going to Congress, I can do better work than I have ever done before. I shall have a good deal of leisure and shall always be at your service for anything — "except these bonds."

Mrs. Hay sends her regards to Mrs. Garfield. I have of course talked fully with her. She saw both sides of the question, but resolutely refused to assist me in the decision.

Sincerely and gratefully yours.

Evidently General Garfield continued to urge: for Hay soon sent this second letter: —

WASHINGTON, D.C., December 31, 1880.

DEAR GENERAL: —

I have given strict and earnest thought to the matter of your offer all this week, but I cannot see any reason to change my mind. Every word I have heard was in favor of accepting, at first, but in every case, — Reid, Mr. Sherman, Mr. Stone and my wife, agreed with me in the end. Even Nichol — that

Justus et tenax propositi vir — gave up the fight this morning after a campaign of as faithful work as I ever saw. I have myself been on the affirmative side in all my wishes and desires — but the reason, I feel sure, is on the other. I *know* I should not be the help to you which you have thought, but I should be, in the White House, the source of many embarrassments and complications.

I deeply regret that I am compelled to decline this most agreeable and honorable service. I wish I could make you see that I do it in your interests more than in my own. I have had to resist constantly the temptation offered by the pleasures and enjoyments which such a position promises. But regretting all this as I do, I know that my decision is right.

There are many things in which no man can serve you. There are paths which you must traverse absolutely alone. The solitude which seems to you a penalty of your high office, you will find a blessing which can only be gained by wrestling. The footpad, the cut-purse, and the sycophant will always be ready to crowd their company on you. You will find reserve only among honest men.

I wish I could save you one moment of annoyance or perplexity but it is hardly possible that anyone can do that. It is a comfort to know you go into the Presidency with the best equipment possible.

Besides the qualities which are personal to you, you know more of the past and present of government, more history and more politics, than any man since the younger Adams, and you are free from his peculiar infirmities of temper, which so narrowed and distorted his views. "One thing thou lackest yet"; and that is a slight ossification of the heart. I woefully fear you will try too hard to make everybody happy — an office which is outside of your constitutional powers. Confine your efforts in that direction to Mrs. Garfield and the children. As for other matters, do as you think right, and it will be right nine times in ten and not far wrong the tenth time, though the heathen rage and the people imagine a vain thing.

Mrs. Hay joins me in wishing all good things for you and Mrs. Garfield.

Faithfully yours.

The President-elect ran into foreboding squalls in attempting to form his Cabinet. The penalty which a party long in the ascendant must pay is discord: and the Republicans were now split into several factions which either professed mutually conflicting principles or rallied to the standards of rival leaders. Blaine and Conkling captained the two largest divisions of the party; but several of the States — New York, Pennsylvania, and Ohio, to

name no more — boasted their local heads, as proud
and as grasping as chieftains of Scottish clans. It
was Garfield's business to endeavor to harmonize
the dissidents: but harmony could mean only the
preference of one faction to the other; and as he had
been elected by the forces which united to defeat
Grant's nomination for a third term, — the forces
led by Blaine, — he unavoidably promoted Blaine,
and, in order to requite the Independents who had
contributed to his victory, he appointed two of them
— Wayne MacVeagh and Thomas L. James — to
his Cabinet.

Stung at being passed by, Conkling and his faction
swore vengeance, which they believed they were
strong enough to carry out. Garfield, the good-
natured, still sought to temporize, in the hope of
making everybody happy; and besides the sullen
"Stalwarts," he had to appease the usual party war-
horses — privateers in quest of any office, who were
braying lustily for fodder.

To President-Elect Garfield

1400 MASSACHUSETTS AVE.,
February 20, 1881.

DEAR GENERAL: —

The rumors of the last day or two have been very
disturbing — but I have no doubt that we will have
"clear or clearing weather" next week.

I write because you told me to — not because
I think you need this continual buzzing. I suppose
no man in America saw more clearly than you did
the prodigious importance of the omens in the Philadelphia and Pittsburg elections. The Ring is broken;
it can still nominate, but it cannot possibly elect.
The course you hinted at will satisfy every exigency
in Pennsylvania. Illinois and the great "Stalwart"
influence of the Northwest is already as good as secured, I imagine. Your enemy is only threatening
in one direction, and only threatening there so long
as his hostility is masked.

It is again reported from Ohio that Foster [1] is to
go into the Cabinet or abroad. I think all the most
judicious men in the State would regret either course.
This restlessness of our leading men is a great evil.
It seems impossible for a leading Republican ever
to stay where he is put, or to go into private life. I
speak only as an Ohio Republican, without any
wishes for myself or any other man, desiring only
the success of your administration, when I say it
seems to me impossible that any Ohio man should
now go into your Cabinet — unless you should think
it necessary after all to retain Sherman.[2] And you
know what that would be.

[1] Charles Foster, an Ohio politician; later Governor of the State.
[2] Senator John Sherman.

Every other consideration is unimportant compared with the advantage of having a Cabinet of good men. That recommends itself. Factions and localities are of infinitely little moment compared with that single consideration.

But I am wasting your time with platitudes. You are walking with your "head in a cloud of poisonous flies," and we cannot resist the temptation of taking a flick at them now and then.

Our hearts, our hopes are all with you. We are eager to see you here, and the administration launched.

Yours with respect and affection.

John Hay went from the State Department to the editor's office of the *New York Tribune*. Under any circumstances to plunge into such work would have been formidable; for Hay the task was doubly hard because he took it up at the time when the Republican tempest broke. Conkling resigned his United States Senatorship in rage because Garfield ignored his candidates. His colleague — Thomas C. Platt, then a political cipher — nicknamed "Me Too" Platt for his apery — followed suit. But, contrary to Conkling's expectations, the sun rose as usual the next morning, the Government at Washington pursued its diurnal routine, and even in New York

State there were few who lost either sleep or appetite over the theatrical resignations.

The open warfare between the factions laid an additional burden of responsibility on Editor Hay. He could not be sure that he was running the *Tribune* in each crisis as Whitelaw Reid would have done, and therefore he wisely concluded to run it as seemed best to himself. By common consent the editorial page was never more vigorous. Somebody with a taste for epigrams said: "The rule of the paper under Reid was that of whips, while with Hay it was that of scorpions." Assuredly, Hay did not spare the enemies of the Administration, and among his many talents that of invective was not the least. The members of the editorial staff found him strict in requiring punctuality and in judging the quality of their work, but always friendly and reasonable. An eminent journalist wrote of him after his death, that "he was like father, brother, philosopher, guide, and friend, all in one."

To Whitelaw Reid

New York Tribune
New York, May 26, 1881.

So you are married one month from to-day and I am Editor of the *Tribune ad interim* the same length of time. I hope your experience has been less

stormy and more amusing than mine. What a time
we have had! [1] I do not regret it in the least — as a
fight like this has been a godsend in what would
otherwise have been a dull season. I think we have
got on very well — behind none of them in news and
out of sight in editorial. I will not indulge in proph-
ecy with half a dozen cables between us, but to speak
of certainties, Roscoe [Conkling] is finished. That
Olympian brow will never again garner up the thousands of yore. Of course we shall have a bad state
of things for a while and shall almost certainly lose
the State next fall. But that will be after your return,
and I can charge it to *my* leaving the *Tribune*.

The whole thing has been a freak of insanity on
the part of a man who has lost sight of his true relations with the rest of the world. It was the logical
result of the personality of Conkling and the work-
ings of the Boss system.

Schurz [2] begins his editorial work on the *Post*
to-day with a long, serious leader on civil service
reform.

Miss R. is, I think, looking better than when you
left. She plays the banjo and piano — rides and
receives visits and seems very gay and happy.

[1] The fight over the appointment of a Collector of the Port of
New York.
[2] E. L. Godkin, Carl Schurz, and Horace White were joint editors of the *New York Evening Post*.

So far nothing has happened over here to disturb your equanimity or cloud your honeymoon. Enjoy yourself as much as possible. I think we can keep the ship off the rocks.

To Whitelaw Reid

NEW YORK TRIBUNE, N.Y.
June 29, 1881.

... I think there is nothing over here which need trouble you. The *Tribune* seems to suit everybody but the ungodly. Hugh Hastings goes for me every day in eight or ten places, but as it amuses him, and I have adopted my great patent remedy of not reading him, I only know it from Bishop and Miss Hutchinson, who come in to console me when he is unusually violent, — and so I do not object to it. The *Chicago Tribune* had a lot of filthy little digs at both you and me, till I frankly asked Joe Medill to put a stop to it, which he did. It was the volunteer malignity of some "funny man" who wanted a "shining mark." That is to me one of the most curious things in our journalism — the way a man who has never seen you and knows nothing about you, will take a furious antipathy to you and blackguard you for months together, without letting up.

On July 2, President Garfield was shot by the half-crazy Guiteau. Throughout the summer he hung between life and death. Outwardly, there was more moderation in the virulence of the political quarrelers; but they knew that at the President's death the flames would burst out afresh.

To Whitelaw Reid

NEW YORK TRIBUNE, N.Y.
September 14, 1881.

I am glad to hear from you once in a while, and the long intervals only serve to convince me that you are having too good a time to bother about writing letters. Enjoy every moment of the time, for it will never come back again, and though you are, I trust, to have many long years of married happiness, you will never have the first year over again. Mrs. Hay and I are very anxious to go to Europe next year, but we hardly dare promise ourselves that we will go, because of the three small people whom we cannot leave behind, and to take whom will be a constant source of anxiety.

I am getting on so far toward the end of my interim-ity that I am comparatively easy about the rest of it. I do not see that I have made any serious mistakes. Thurlow Weed paid me the high compliment the other day of saying that he was a little afraid at first I would not know the State well enough, but that he had long ago forgotten that I was not a New

Yorker. Of course the credit of it is mostly due to the staff — but I have paid great attention and killed a good deal of matter which might have been embarrassing. I have as far as possible steered clear of rows without making the paper seem feeble. If it had been my paper I would have taken the hide off two or three blackguards — but I did n't want to commit you to new quarrels. If Garfield lives, I think you will find the paper in excellent position, when you return, to give it any direction you see fit. That has been my special object for the last half of my time.

President Garfield died on September 19. When the Reids returned in October, Hay retired from the *Tribune*.

That the friend and adviser of presidents, the intimate of cabinet ministers and party managers, whose fitness no one denied, should be habitually shut out from public service excites our wonder. When Mr. Evarts sought the most competent Assistant Secretary of State he could think of, he asked John Hay. When the editor of the chief Republican newspaper in the United States sought a substitute for himself, he chose John Hay. Why was no permanent office opened to him?

The hints given in this chapter should help us to a clue. Hay's own remark, in a letter to Whitelaw

Reid, who had been offered and had declined the Berlin mission, will further enlighten us. Apparently, when Reid declined, Hay was "mentioned" for the place.

"I thank you for what you said of me, but — don't grin at this! — Mr. Evarts was right about it. I have not the political standing necessary for the place — neither had Taylor.[1] I tried to say a word to Taylor about it when he was here, but he was deaf to any such considerations. Now you may believe it or not, but I would not accept the mission to Berlin if it were offered to me. I know I am not up to it in many respects. At the same time I am free to say I would like a second-class mission uncommonly well. I think White's[2] appointment an excellent one, though I imagine you don't agree with me on that." (March 30, 1879.)

Hay turned now in earnest to the "Life of Lincoln," on which, as on a giant obelisk, he and Nicolay had been hewing at intervals for a long time past.

[1] Bayard Taylor, appointed Minister to Germany in 1877; died the next year.

[2] Andrew D. White, just appointed Minister to Germany.

END OF VOLUME I

DATE DUE

NOV 1 2 '73			
GAYLORD			PRINTED IN U.S.A.